Also by Marcus Katz and Tali Goodwin

Around the Tarot in 78 Days
Learning Lenormand
Easy Lenormand
Tarot Face to Face
Secrets of the Waite Smith Tarot

Marcus Katz

Marcus Katz is an author and teacher of the Western Esoteric Initiatory System (WEIS). As the Co-Director of the Tarosophy Tarot Association, the world's largest Tarot organisation, he has studied and taught tarot for thirty-five years and has delivered more than ten thousand face-to-face readings. His first book, *Tarosophy*, has been called a "major contribution" to tarot tradition by leading teachers. Marcus is also co-creator of ARKARTIA, an interactive online world for tarot studies and experience.

Tali Goodwin

Tali Goodwin is an author, researcher and Co-Director of the Tarosophy Tarot Association. She has created innovative teaching books such as *Tarot Flip* and *Tarot Life*. Her research and 'Cards of Antiquity' campaign brought Lenormand decks to a new popularity, whilst also uncovering A. E. Waite's second tarot images, held secret for over a century. Her work on the life of Pamela Colman Smith, published as *Secrets of the Waite-Smith Tarot*, revealed new insights into the Waite-Smith Tarot and previously unpublished photographs of Pamela Colman Smith.

To Write to the Authors

If you wish to contact the authors or would like more information about this book, please write to the authors in care of Llewellyn Worldwide Ltd. and we will forward your request. The authors and publisher appreciate hearing from you and learning of your enjoyment of this book and how it has helped you. Llewellyn Worldwide Ltd. cannot guarantee that every letter written to the authors can be answered, but all will be forwarded. Please write to:

Marcus Katz and Tali Goodwin
℅ Llewellyn Worldwide
2143 Wooddale Drive
Woodbury, MN 55125-2989

Please enclose a self-addressed stamped envelope for reply,
or $1.00 to cover costs. If outside the USA, enclose
an international postal reply coupon.

MARCUS KATZ & TALI GOODWIN

Enhance Your Modern Readings with the Wisdom of the Past

TAROT
TIME TRAVELLER

Llewellyn Publications
Woodbury, Minnesota

FIRST EDITION
First Printing, 2017

Book design by Bob Gaul
Cover design by Kevin R. Brown
Cover illustration by Autumns Goddess Design/Jena DellaGrottaglia
Editing by Laura Graves
Interior art: For illustration and photo credits, see Art Credit List. (page 361)

Llewellyn Publications is a registered trademark of Llewellyn Worldwide Ltd.

Library of Congress Cataloging-in-Publication Data
Names: Katz, Marcus, author.
Title: Tarot time traveller: enhance your modern readings with the wisdom of
    the past / by Marcus Katz & Tali Goodwin.
Description: First Edition. | Woodbury: Llewellyn Worldwide, Ltd., 2017. |
    Includes bibliographical references.
Identifiers: LCCN 2017039063 (print) | LCCN 2017033314 (ebook) | ISBN
    9780738753393 (ebook) | ISBN 9780738751344 (alk. paper)
Subjects: LCSH: Tarot.
Classification: LCC BF1879.T2 (print) | LCC BF1879.T2 K3853 2017 (ebook) |
    DDC 133.3/2424—dc23
LC record available at https://lccn.loc.gov/2017039063

Llewellyn Worldwide Ltd. does not participate in, endorse, or have any authority or responsibility concerning private business transactions between our authors and the public.

All mail addressed to the author is forwarded, but the publisher cannot, unless specifically instructed by the author, give out an address or phone number.

Any Internet references contained in this work are current at publication time, but the publisher cannot guarantee that a specific location will continue to be maintained. Please refer to the publisher's website for links to authors' websites and other sources.

Llewellyn Publications
A Division of Llewellyn Worldwide Ltd.
2143 Wooddale Drive
Woodbury, MN 55125-2989
www.llewellyn.com

Printed in the United States of America

Contents

Acknowledgments and Permissions

We would like to thank our team of social media moderators: Cath, Charlotte, Derek, Jason B., Jason C., Jenna, Lonnie, Shay, and Steph, who manned the walls of our Facebook group, *Tarot Professionals,* an heroic task that allowed us the time to create this book.

Where practical, we have made all best efforts to trace copyright ownership. If there is any copyright claim not within our knowledge on images used, we welcome contact through our publishers.

Dedications

To Charlotte Louise

To C., C.C., B.C. & Mr. B.E. (Who Guard the Quarters)
To H.B. & H.M. (Constant Companions)
To S.H. (Our new Branch Manager)
To All Those Who Stand Outside Their Time.

In Memory of Rufus Oakapple, brave and curious enough to return.

And as ever, and above all, this book is spiritually dedicated to
Antistita Astri Argentei
The Priestess of the Silver Star
She whose light leads the way to the *Arcanum Arcanorum*, the Secret of Secrets
Vos Vos Vos Vos Vos
V.V.V.V.V.

Introduction

But he planned to make as it were a moving likeness of eternity; and, at the same time that he set in order the Heaven, he made, of eternity that abides in unity, an ever-flowing likeness moving according to number—that to which we have given the name Time.

—Plato, *Timaeus*

You are about to take a journey through time with nothing more than a playing-card deck, a tarot deck, and perhaps a Lenormand deck in your hands with the tarot time traveller to guide you.

On this journey, you will learn how to read the future as you pick up pieces of the puzzle from the greatest tarot teachers throughout history. The tarot time traveller will escort you in a series of ventures to discover many of the eras of tarot and their mysteries.

You will set off to the very beginnings of cartomantic (card-reading) development and learn different ways to read a normal deck of playing cards. You can also time-hop if you wish and choose your own journey of discovery by exploring the time zones that call to you. You might like to start in the present day and work backwards, or go straight away to the swinging sixties and learn how to read from the rebels of the time, or head to the late Victorian establishment figures who influenced modern tarot.

We hope you will enjoy the experience of learning the whole history of the cards in your hands as much as you learn all the special methods included in this book.

If you are an absolute beginner, you'll have a complete course in tarot rooted in elements of a very real tarot tradition. As an existing expert, you can use this book to fill in the gaps of eras you may not have already explored in depth.

Much historical research has gone into this book and there are many unique exercises, so you will also find some fantastic reading lists and decks to explore at the end of each era.[1] You will find each era brought to life with a vignette that opens each chapter and several sections.

We will begin our adventure by surveying the time map of tarot and packing our temporal travel bag with suitable card meanings and emergency methods in case we run into any trouble on our voyage.

Ironically, we do not have enough time to visit absolutely every temporal nexus of playing-card-reading, Lenormand, and tarot development in this book about and for tarot time travellers. In the journey ahead, we will take you to points of interest for the casual reader, tarot scholar, new tarot reader, and the enthusiastic professional. We can only briefly point the way to other avenues such as Kipper cards or the fascinating history and use of the Minchiate, Grand Etteilla, Marseille Tarot, and other decks of antiquity.

Consider our time machine is following *cartomancy* (fortune-telling by playing cards), Lenormand, and tarot like a skipping-stone across the lake of time, where we will look at the biggest splashes and what makes the most ripples. As an example, let us look at the publishing history of the *Book of Thoth*, Aleister Crowley's guide to his beautiful and enigmatic tarot deck. This gives us a rough idea of when there was enough general interest in tarot as a subject for such a book to be published; the big splashes are 1944, 1969, and 1974, and then editions until the eleventh printing in 1985.

We will only be making time-stops at a selection of points in the tarot timeline. Buckle yourselves in, keep your hands away from the edges, and enjoy the ride.

And who knows, perhaps this may not be the only tarot time travel manual to be provided in the coming years; when you work across time, the possibilities are endless and the decks of antiquity call for our further consideration.

We will start from the moment when cards first took their fortune-telling meanings, but really our story starts at the dawn of time. In the beginning of time there was a dream—a dream that became real. In the early dawn and from that darkness of time, we awoke. The

---

1   See www.tarottimetraveller.com for a regularly updated list of addendum and convenient reading list.

world around us took on shape and semblance. In time, one thing began to correspond to another. On cave walls, we first learnt the language of symbols. The symbols then began to dwell in our dreams. As the eons passed, we learnt to create the symbols on stone, bark, papyrus, and upon paper, and the symbols continued to correspond to both our dreams and our reality.

There came a time of a great renaissance and seventy-eight sets of symbols were placed together as an infinitely mutable book of dream and reality. A book with loose pages, free to tell any story in any language for all time. It would forever be able to tell dream and reality of past, present, and future. It is the book called tarot.

As we completed this book and reviewed it again from this beginning, we realised that this is a book about *meaning*—the intention or significance of the images of tarot. Whilst we may read them as a language with our own vocabulary and experience, the cards are pieces of art created as a tool of symbols, and those symbols are signposts. Every card points to something different from another card: the Tower points to a more disruptive future than the harmonious 10 of Cups; the Knight of Wands refers to a totally different person than the Queen of Cups.

So, what does a card *mean*? Over time, a system—a tradition, almost—of meanings has been associated with the cards, and variations of it are used every minute in readings online and in person, by people and computers. If you open a fortune-teller app on your iPhone and get your card of the day as the 2 of Wands, you will also get a piece of text that says something like "A card of personal power; be bold and show originality today."

But how did those words and that meaning, get associated with that card? Furthermore, why could it not just as easily say the opposite, "A card of caution; take cover and avoid risks today"?

In this book, we are going to take you through time and incidentally discover how the cards in your deck became placeholders for hundreds of layers of meaning sometimes complementary, sometimes contradictory. We hope that it will first confuse you as to what a card may mean, and then clarify a singular thought—the cards do mean something, and what that thing is will vary in its delivery from time to time, place to place, and person to person.

We will return to answer the question of the meaning of the cards when we reach the end of our travels in this book.

In the meantime, you will learn tarot as it was developed, starting with an A-B-C of cartomancy with playing cards, then developing your language with Lenormand, using the right-left way of reading from vintage cartomancy. We will then practice with the Square of Seven, an extended method of cartomancy that will remind you of the Grand Tableaux of Lenormand.

You will then develop a more elaborate use of the language of correspondence through tarot and learn how to enter the cards as if they were landscapes of another world. As you experience the tarot as living ideas, you will then add esoteric and spiritual associations before applying them in a range of cutting-edge modern techniques we call *Tarosophy*. In doing so, you will re-create the journey of tarot through time and learn a little more about how it became applied to so many different purposes; from fortune-telling to spiritual development.

An Important Note on Lost Time Tracks

It would be impossible to collate and show the development of every deck and every author, teacher, and occultist who has developed the tarot story, so as we have mentioned, we will select only certain nexus points: big splashes and ripples. When an author or teacher has made a big impact on the card meanings (judged later vis-à-vis history), we have included them in our time travelling visits. We may have missed out big players such as Etteilla primarily because we have limited space to tell a connected story—our selections in this book were compiled to link together in a practical sense, and it might prove confusing to follow certain avenues that really deserve their own unique exploration.

Similarly, we have not attempted to collate card meanings across time, although we offer a Tarot Time Convertor in Appendix Two which provides several correspondences between playing cards, tarot and Lenormand. The reader can then determine if the 9 of Pentacles in their chosen tarot meanings matches to their chosen meaning of the 9 of Diamonds in playing-card cartomancy or the Lenormand's Coffin card. It would be overly confusing to present every parallel strand of history for card meanings across different types of playing-card decks, authors, tarot decks, Lenormand decks, et cetera, so we have presented them separately in their specific zones and chapters and then collated a selection in Appendix Two. If we were to add the 36 Kipper cards or try and align the 97 Minchiate cards to the 78 tarot cards, we would likely blow a gasket on our real-time travel device—our own mind.

We hope it will become obvious how other ripples have been created throughout time, and you may like to place whomever we have missed visiting in the timeline for your own studies and time travels. In that way, *Tarot Time Traveller* can serve as a framework for a full history and discovery of the mysteries of tarot.

To produce this book, we have taken a real-life journey through time over several years, accessing antique Chapbooks and collections of women's magazines; secret order documents and hand-written journals; visiting museums and archives around the world. We hope in your own tracing of this journey, you will agree with us that there is nothing new under the sun and that the tarot contains powerful echoes of the lives of real people across time.

Over time as well, your own readings will consolidate your specific "meanings" for your cards, which will also change in time—you too will become a tarot time traveller. That said, there is a mystery in this, which we will reveal at the conclusion of this present book.

Is it important to know the history of the cards? Well, we think so—our own reading of the cards, particularly the Waite-Smith Tarot, after thirty years, shifted massively after our writing of *Secrets of the Waite-Smith Tarot* (Llewellyn, 2015). When we get the 2 of Pentacles in a reading, that card is now (for us) far more about miscommunication—often deliberate—than the usual "juggling of resources" that many contemporary sources copy and paste between each other.

We trust this book will provide you an interesting range of layers to deepen your understanding of the cards as a divinatory tool. Let us begin at two personal points of time before stepping through the portals that contain all time and all possibilities: your tarot deck.

Preface

Marcus

Dawn, Friday, 17 June, 1983: Ambergate, Derbyshire, England

An eighteen-year-old boy sits out on the balcony of his bedroom in a little village nestled in the heart of England. He has just received a mail-order copy of the book *Practice of Ritual Magic* by Gareth Knight and is sat in a yoga position, meditating to the rising sun. His notebook records the appropriate correspondences for meditation; the god-name IHVH, the Angel Raphael and Paralda, Lady of the Sylphs, who he imagines he can see in the bright morning sky.

A few days earlier he had asked his homemade tarot cards a question: "How should I go about my studies in magick?"

The cards, twenty-two small pieces of cardboard on which he had pasted a photocopy of the major arcana taken from a Stuart Kaplan book in the local library some four years ago, were laid out in the Celtic Cross:

Devil (reversed), Temperance, Death, Hanged Man, Justice, Wheel of Fortune, Hermit, Strength, Chariot, Hierophant. [2]

He wrote dutifully in his journal his interpretation of these cards, that the reversed Devil signified ignorance but perhaps the dawn of spiritual seeking; that Temperance

---

2 From the personal journals of Marcus Katz, 1983. It is important to keep a journal as you never know how long the journey may be or when you may need to refer to something in your own personal history.

would be crossing him always, calling him to temper his life and responsibilities; that Death in the near future was a new beginning and an initiatory transformation; the Hanged Man below was "spiritual advancement" and so on to the final outcome card of the Hierophant; against which he wrote "social and material success." [3]

1. Original Tarot Deck created by Marcus Katz, based on IJJ Swiss Deck in Stuart Kaplan, *Tarot Cards for Fun and Fortune-Telling*, 1978.

3   *Ibid.*

We return to him sat a few days following that reading, as he was, meditating earnestly whilst contemplating the dawn light. Although he has been using his home-made tarot deck for several years, he still feels nervous about his knowledge and certainly his place in the world. It is a big step—an actual act of faith—to start buying occult books and contacting other magicians, witches, and occultists. He writes about his self-conscious lack of confidence in his journal.

A few days later he would leave high school and start a new life not just in work but also in magic, the tarot with him always, travelling at his side. They would travel in time together and divine nature in the journey becoming much like the Fool and his dog.

Some people wonder what the Fool, who is nothing and has no number, carries in his bag. The answer is that he carries everything—everything he has done, everything he has learnt and experienced, and his memories and past. The dog is his faith; and the last companion he must leave behind at the end of the path. The Fool is empty as his bag is full; he has come to the end, the realisation of everything and nothing, and that time alone is the secret—the secret of a life which is lived forever in an everlasting day.

Today, writing this, an older man looks upon the young man he once was. Ever the teacher even to himself, he gently looks over his shoulder and points out the Hierophant card. "You missed that," he says to himself, "the success is not social but perhaps in becoming the teacher you seek now in others."

I remember myself back then, and imagine that I look at myself now and reply, "Will it be worth it? All this work, all this learning, all this struggle to understand these mysteries? Really? Is it worth it? Is there any real meaning or pattern in life?"

I sigh; we both look at each other across thirty-three years of time and tarot; and for the first time I look at the date today in astonishment as I write this, and say, "Oh yes, there is a pattern, oh yes indeed."

—Marcus Katz, Dawn, Friday, 17 June, 2016: The Lake District, England

Tali

A young woman is dreaming on the night of the solstice, a powerful time when the sun appears to stand still and the night is at its shortest.

In the dream, she is returning to the family home at an earlier time, when her mother was still alive.

She stands across the road from the house and looks towards it longingly yet is unable to bring herself to walk any closer to the house. She holds a simple brown cardboard box.

With some bemusement, she turns to see on the side of the kerb, left of where she stands, is sat an Indian man wearing a white turban whose appearance she recognises as a secret master, guru, or swami.

She senses his presence but does not acknowledge him. Instead she crosses the road and enters the house. The house contains all her life, her past, and her memories. It is a warehouse of visions for the future held in the past, and past memories that may or may not have happened.

All she has come back for are the precious childhood photographs of herself and her now-deceased parents. She sorts through the photographs and piles them high into the box. She leaves the house carrying the box. As she walks away from the house, a wind begins to blow.

She looks and can see across the road, still sat upon the kerb is the swami. He looks intently at her, and for some reason this makes her feel angry. As she crosses the road, halfway across, the wind whips up into a sudden frenzy and blows the cardboard box high into the air. All the family photos are swept clean out of the box and scattered into the wind.

She panics and rushes to try to save the precious photographs, running this way and that, grabbing at the photographs as they spin through the air.

As she does, she notices something curious: when she plucks at each photograph, it turns into an illustrated card like some sort of playing card or the tarot cards she sometimes saw in her childhood when her mother used to go for readings. She recalls now that her mother always asked about whether she should have a long and healthy life, time and again. Yet her mother had died like her father, too soon and too early, leaving just these memories, these precious photographs that were now turning into cards.

She looked up from her mad dancing about the pavement, clutching at these falling cards, and still the swami was staring and now smiling at her. This infuriated her; she felt he was laughing at her in this desperate time when things could be no worse.

She walks up to him, letting the cards slip through her fingers to leave a trail of images behind her across the pavement.

"What are you laughing at?" she demands.

He stares back at her, and for a moment she thinks he will not answer. But then he does, with a voice that awakens her from her sleep and into the long day of summer ahead:

"You will heal. You will turn your life into cards one day. And you will heal others. You can call the Wind."

It is these words and this dream that would be realised twenty-eight years later into a new deck of tarot cards, the Tarot of Everlasting Day.

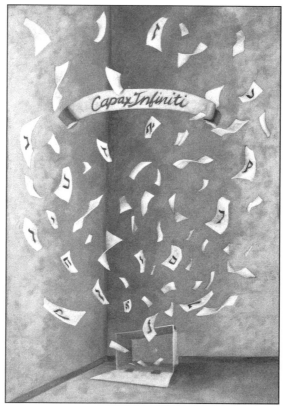

2. Ace of Swords from the Tarot of Everlasting Day/Union Deck, Janine Hall, Marcus Katz & Tali Goodwin, 2017 (in progress, unpublished).

The tarot is an illustration of not only our dreams but also of our future.

Now let us take you on your own journey through time, hopping into our tarot time pod and setting the dials for 1955. If you are ready, we will begin.

—Tali Goodwin, 22 June, 2016: The Lake District, England

1

Cartomantic Orientation

And it came to pass, as we went to prayer, a certain damsel possessed with a spirit of divination met us, which brought her masters much gain by soothsaying.

—Acts 16:16

11 February, 1955: Chicago, USA

We are time travelling! We have just touched down in our tarot time pod in mid-fifties America. It is a small jump by time traveller standards but one just right for beginners.

James Dean is still alive, and this year *On the Waterfront* will win the Oscars. As we arrive in downtown Chicago, we can immediately hear with some amusement the top hit of the day, "Melody of Love" by the Four Aces. Such resonances to our card deck show us that we are on the right oracular wavelength. In fact, it is when we recognise such synchronicities (meaningful coincidences) that we know our cards are leading us correctly. [4]

We overhear two men on the street corner in passing—someone called Lloyd Merriman has just been purchased by the White Sox from the Redlegs. As we walk by,

---

4   To listen to the soundtrack of this era, why not start out with the Four Aces' *Melody of Love* at www.youtube.com/watch?v=U6E5NGVbyCc. (Last accessed 27 September 2015).

they start to argue heatedly about left-handed batting. They are both wearing scarves across their faces, and it is curious to hear their muffled but insistent voices. It is cold here, and the wind is blowing hard from across the lake.

Our only task in this time is to simply purchase a copy of a magazine called FATE, so we locate the nearest newspaper vendor (seeing the headlines, "US Fleet Evacuates Chinese Nationalist Tachen Islands") and dig into our traveller's bag of time-variable coins to hand over 55 cents.

Without making too much contact with anyone, we hastily return to our time pod and put the little magazine on our shelf until we receive further instructions.

That was fun—we could get used to this!

The History of Tarot

We are not too interested in the history of tarot as we are tarot time travellers and will be experiencing that first-hand for ourselves on our journey. However, we should look briefly at what we might encounter according to those who have written about it in their own time or looking back as historians. The history of what people have written about the history of tarot is just as interesting as the history itself, if that makes sense. We will come across many such complexities, conundrums, and confusions as we wend our way through the time-streams. Let us first get a fix on the present.

At the time of writing (2015–2016 CE), tarot is being revitalised through "social media" as it is called at this moment. Future readers may vaguely remember something called "Facebook" and perhaps "Twitter," which were all the rage at this time. You may not believe it, but at the time, more than half the world's Internet population was connected to Facebook alone. It's true.

Tarot today is more easily accessible than at any time back down the time-stream, ahead of the forthcoming things you future readers already know when it really changed again. Our time-tenses will get a bit convoluted if we keep addressing you in the future from now.

At this moment, the information about the history of tarot is widely spread and includes unproven facts and guesses as well as the actual known history of the cards.

The tarot originated as a set of engraved and elaborate images held by a few noble families in Italy during the fifteenth century. It followed the arrival of card games in Europe and was *not* used by the Romani ("gypsies"). We will see how some of these legends arose during our travels. In the meantime, here is a traveller's checklist of misinformation:

- A man called Rider developed the major and minor arcana of tarot.
- The Romani came from Egypt, where tarot was used in ancient times.
- The tarot conceals a secret teaching of many ages.
- The tarot is evil, like the Ouija board.

The name Rider is the name of a publishing company, which first published the Waite-Smith Tarot; the "gypsies" (the story is more complex) originated in India; tarot was never used in ancient Egypt; tarot contains infinite teachings, not just one; and like the Ouija board, was originally a game.

The actual history of the tarot is fascinating and important to understand when we read the cards. In fact, it makes our readings even deeper and more flexible when we appreciate and can use all the layers of tarot through time.

As we will also see, the history of how people turned tarot to their own ends by creating fictional histories and stories of its past is also a part of our journey. We will discover these myths and then use them to help us create new and exciting ways of reading our cards.

Let us first consider a tarot timeline to identify a brief selection of the key nexus points, works, figures, and decks in cartomantic history. We might note the comparatively recent occurrence of tarot in the grand scheme of history; it really is at its infancy at the present time compared to other oracular systems such as the I-Ching.

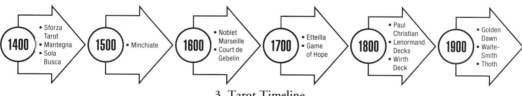

3. Tarot Timeline.

There are relatively few academic books on tarot history and we recommend all tarot time travellers to equip themselves with at least one of these as a companion in their journey. [5]

However, before we set our course into times long gone, we will begin by looking at contemporary tarot card meanings, and get to use our deck straight away in a modern style. We will return to this and develop it even further in our final chapter on Tarosophy, featuring cutting-edge methods.

Contemporary Time Meanings

If you are a new time traveller in tarot (because every reading is a form of time travelling) we advise pursuing the following meanings to get your bearings before we begin our journey. We have surveyed and observed some of the best and most experienced readers in the modern era and analysed their style to create this orientation guide.

A lot of students tell us that the two main difficulties for beginners are:

- Having difficulty applying a card "meaning" to a
  question (interpretation)
- Having difficulty putting the meanings together (delivery)

We have spent a lot of time listening to readers and breaking down simple skills that are universal to most readers, which we can then teach. It appears that by having just three essential meanings for a card, and one single sentence, we can get reading straight away.

We call this our three-minute method. Get ready.

You will discover that most tarot readings weave together a story from the cards using three simple points of reference that each card can give us:

---

5   We recommend Michael Dummett, *The Game of Tarot from Ferrara to Salt Lake City* (London, UK: Gerald Duckworth & Co. Ltd, 1980) although it is now difficult to acquire and expensive in hard-back. Another essential history is Ronald Decker & Michael Dummett, *A History of the Occult Tarot: 1870–1970* (London, UK: Gerald Duckworth & Co. Ltd, 2002) and Ronald Decker, Michael Dummett & Thierry Depaulis, *A Wicked Pack of Cards: Origins of the Occult Tarot* (London: Bristol Classical Press, 1996). An accessible overview is Robert M. Place, *The Tarot: History, Symbolism and Divination* (New York, NY: Tarcher/Penguin, 2005) and a wonderful compilation of contemporary research can be discovered in Emily E. Auger (ed.), *Tarot in Culture*, Vols. I & II (Valleyhome Books, 2014) which includes (Vol. I) a detailed tarot timeline assembled by Mary K. Greer.

- Resource

- Challenge

- Lesson

Every card, from the ten minor arcana (ace to ten) in each suit (pentacles, swords, cups, and wands), the four court cards (page, knight, queen, and king) in each suit through to the twenty-two major arcana (numbered 0 for the Fool, then I through XXI in Latin for the Magician to the World) can be read in the context of just those three essential themes.

First, each card can be seen to offer a resource. This can be easily imagined: if you plugged yourself into that card, what charge would it give you? A card like the Tower would charge you with sudden acceleration, for example, whereas the King of Pentacles would charge you slowly and surely. The cards contain these different energies and signify the resource or attitude they offer in a reading.

Similarly, every card is a challenge. In some cases, we could see this as the "reversed" meaning of a card, but we do not need to add reversals to our readings at this stage. If we imagined that each card was an obstacle—an image of a stage in a story that the hero or heroine must overcome—we can see these meanings. Again, the Tower would now be the challenge of a sudden shock to the system, striking like a lightning bolt and destroying everything, but the King of Pentacles would be a solid slow-moving person in the way of progress.

Finally, every card can be viewed as a lesson. There is no card that is not a lesson of some description. We might see this as the card being a teacher or summing up a moral at the end of a story. In seeing a card as a lesson, we can also practice getting an overall view of the card … and the reading itself. If we take the Tower again, we now see it as a lesson about renewal and moving onto new things, and the King of Pentacles offering us a straightforward lesson about patience and the reward of long-term work.

We have put together in Appendix 1 our own suggested list of universal keywords we find useful for this beginner method. We encourage you to consider each card in these three aspects and add your own words as you progress.

You are encouraged in your time travels to add constantly to this lexicon of card meanings under each heading—resource, challenge, and lesson—with your own meanings from other references and your experience.

Now that we have listed these universal keywords for the three essential aspects of every card, we will provide a quick method to get started reading tarot in just three minutes. Time will tell how we do when we come to practice our methods; however, first we want to jump-start our journey by being able to read right from the beginning.

How to Do a Tarot Reading in Three Minutes

In case we meet any emergencies in our time travel (or in life) we have a fallback method of reading tarot that works very well when we want to read for ourselves *and* for other people. It follows a script that's one example of what we call an *Oracular Construct* or *Oracular Sentence:*

In this situation, you are/I am challenged by [challenge] but can draw upon [resource] to learn [lesson].

When we want to perform a tarot reading, we simply draw three cards from our traveller's bag and read the appropriate word from our universal keyword list for this oracular construct.

Let us try it with a test question; "How will we learn best to do tarot readings by travelling through the history of the cards?"

We draw for our Challenge, Resource, and Lesson: Knight of Cups, Page of Pentacles, 8 of Swords.

If we look up in our list the Knight of Cups as a challenge, it is the challenge of temptation. Our challenge here is to not give in to thinking we already know the answers and remain open, perhaps.

When we put the other two cards into the sentence it becomes clearer:

In this situation, we are challenged by temptation but can draw upon steadfastness [Resource of the Page of Pentacles] to learn Autonomy [Lesson of the 8 of Swords].

We are being advised to keep at our studies and follow them through steadfastly to become free of previous feelings about the cards and learn our own meanings.

You can try this for any question that you have about your life right now and make a note of the answer to expand upon as you enjoy the rest of your journey throughout this book. As you continue to practice with this oracular construct, you will find your other readings becoming more flexible and fluid. You will be training yourself to read the essential context of the cards for any situation and delivering your interpretation in a consistent way.

Advanced Time Traveller Method

You can also use the three essential keywords and oracular construct with a past/present/future tense. So, you can say "In the future, you will be challenged by…" or "In the past you have drawn upon…and learnt…" As you get more practised, you will find it easy to lay a nine-card square down wherein the top three cards are the past, the middle row the present, and the bottom row the future. You can also then compare how the three challenge, resource, and lesson cards work through the person's past, present, and future.

Now that we have learnt to read tarot, we will look at one example of how the meaning of a card changes over time yet somehow remains the same. You will see from this how we have also roamed the time-streams to discover the essential keywords that remain the stable core of each card no matter how many years pass.

The History of a Minor Card

Having a time travel machine helps us see how the meanings of the tarot cards have come about. We will eventually look over every card, but for now let us take a detailed look at one.

In this section, we need a montage to tell our tarot story. In the 1930s and 1950s, the montage made its appearance in movies, having been popularised by Russian director Sergei Eistenstein in the classic silent film *Battleship Potemkin* (1925). We all recognise classic and clichéd montages these days, such as the training montage and the "getting ready for the heist" montage. However, we need to go all the way back to the old stand-by, the "calendar flipping" time compression montage for our story.

It is a common question students ask: "What does this card actually mean?" or "How can a card have many meanings?" Some students also become confused when they read "different meanings" in different books. Let us now explore this in our time travel device.

Taking a single tarot card and flipping it forward through time, rapidly, we see how the meanings of the same card have changed since it first appeared. This is also like watching the fashions change on the mannequin in the shop opposite the time machine in the original film, as Rod Taylor cavorts backward and forward in time.

We can use this montage method to really understand how a card can stand for one "theme" or "concept" across a wide range of different expressions.

This is also called "multivalency," where a card works to provide many meanings depending on the question and the situation. We will further see some surprising revelations when we do this in-depth for just one card—something that has not been done before.

We have chosen for our time travel card the **2 of Pentacles**, because it is such a unique image in the modern tarot since its depiction by Pamela Colman Smith. It was once wide open to speculation for a century until a reasonably definitive source was proposed in our own research, as "False Mercury" by Edward Burne-Jones.[6]

4. 2 of Pentacles, Llewellyn's Classic
Tarot by Moore and Smith, 2014.

---

6   Marcus Katz and Tali Goodwin, *Secrets of the Waite-Smith Tarot* (Woodbury, MN: Llewellyn, 2015), 38.

We will show how the meaning has been expressed from a large range of books in private collection and then highlight what this might indicate for the card's actual "meaning." In some cases, we have paraphrased the original text for brevity and consistency.

1888: Embarrassment, worry, difficulties. *Reversed:* letter, missive, epistle, message. [7]

1910: Card of gaiety, recreation and its connexions, news and messages in writing, obstacles, agitation, trouble, embroilment. [8]

We now see how these early meanings of communication and miscommunication disappear from the card as authors move towards interpreting the "juggling" nature of Pamela's 1909–1910 depiction and the nature of the Pentacles as representing money and business.

1941: Initiative, stability, practical sense. Diplomacy, adaptability, poise, and resourcefulness are the main factors of this character. The conflict lies between the desire for practical achievements and a restless instability of purpose. [9]

1951: Shared instances: divided money, shared accommodations, financial partnerships, division of possessions and or money, part-time income or work; part-time anything. Money; finances; securities; settlements. Financial or practical partnerships of any kind. [10]

1967: Money acquired by hard labour. Independence. Financial gain through ingenuity. Profitable partnership or marriage. Gain through unexpected social activity. Unusual courtship. Reward through mental effort. Romance hampered by coldness. Recompense for service rendered. Friendly gathering for scientific interests. Way out ideas. New methods in the working environment. [11]

---

7   Samuel Liddell MacGregor Mathers, *Tarot* (Brighton, UK: Unicorn Bookshop, n.d. originally 1888).

8   Arthur Edward Waite, *The Pictorial Key to the Tarot* (London, UK: Rider & Company, 1974), 278.

9   Muriel Bruce Hasbrouck, *Pursuit of Destiny* (London, UK: John Gifford, 1949), 146.

10   Ly De Angeles, *Tarot Theory and Practice* (Woodbury, MN: Llewellyn, 2007), 141.

11   Doris Chase Doane, *How to Read Tarot Cards* (New York, NY: Funk & Wagnalls, 1967), 127.

1970: Keeping two or more projects going or working towards two goals, at the same time. He embodies cleverness and the ability to keep a careful eye on more than one situation. Emotional ups and downs. Linkage between the material and spiritual aspects of our lives' activities. Flexibility in perspective. Physical dualities. Potential for transformation. [12]

1971: Juggling two propositions, trying to decide which to accept, ability to handle several situations or business proposals at a time. Maintain harmony amid change. New projects may be difficult to launch. Helpful message can be expected. Sea of (his) emotions is rough. [13]

1972: The Cycles of change at work in the world, natural fluctuations of fortune which must be allowed when planning ahead. Indicates movement and changes that are imminent. News, communications, journeys all connected with business/money, joys in the pleasures of society, knowledgeable manipulation of the rules of life. [14]

1972: Difficulty in launching new projects. Difficult situations arising. New troubles, embarrassment. Worry, concern. [15]

1979: Trying to cope with two situations, much more will be achieved if a decision is made. Essential that harmony is maintained. Expect to receive acknowledgment, reassuring news, small sum of money or a gift. [16]

1984: Constant fluctuation and change make new projects difficult to launch. Established business needs careful handling. A need to budget carefully. A warning to avoid purchasing on credit. [17]

---

12   Signe Echols, Robert Muller and Sandra Thomson, *Spiritual Tarot* (New York, NY: Avon Books, 1996), 116.

13   Eden Grey, *Mastering the Tarot: Basic Lessons in an Ancient, Mystic Art* (New York, NY: Crown Publishers, 1971), 33.

14   Alfred Douglas, *The Tarot* (Harmondsworth, UK: Penguin Books, 1981), 199.

15   Stuart R. Kaplan, *Tarot Classic* (New York, NY: Grossett & Dunlap, 1972), 160.

16   Eileen Connolly, *The Complete Handbook for the Apprentice* (London, UK: Thorsons, 1995), 127.

17   Emily Peach, *Discover Tarot: Understanding and Using Tarot Symbolism* (Wellingborough, UK: Aquarian Press, 1990), 89.

1985: The card stands for the necessity to keep several propositions going at once. The flow of movement, however, indicates that skillful manipulation achieves success. There is a change particularly with regards to financial matters, but also harmony within the change if the person can be flexible enough to keep everything flowing. [18]

1986: New inventions, investing effort in new projects, keeping (him) busy and active and willing to try several things at once. The 2 of Pentacles represents a state of change or fluctuation in material fortunes. Taking risks and using capital, rather than hoarding and saving at a time when new opportunities arise. Play with money. [19]

1987: A well-organised lifestyle, good social skills, the ability to remain calm on the face of change, a variety of activities. [20]

1987: Adaptability, mobility. Expanding your horizons. Change travel play. [21]

1988: Change that occurs slowly and in a balanced and orderly fashion. Planned change, alteration that is self-regulated and self-determined, rather than unexpected and sudden. [22]

1989: Entanglements and conflicts. When the 2 of Pentacles appears in a layout, it probably indicates that we are in danger of misinterpreting the meaning of events connected with the issue at hand. [23]

1993: Amusement, dissipation of resources, money. [24]

---

18 Juliet Sharman-Burke, *The Complete Book of Tarot: The Origins, Meaning & Divinatory Significance of the Cards & How to Use Them in Readings* (London, UK: Pan Books, 1985), 53.

19 Juliet Sharman-Burke and Liz Greene, *The Mythic Tarot A New Approach to the Tarot Cards* (London, UK: Guild Publishing, 1986), 174.

20 E.W. Neville, *Tarot for Lovers* (Atglen, PA: Schiffer, 1997), 109.

21 Mary K. Greer, *Tarot for Yourself* (Franklin Lakes, NJ: New Page Books, 2002), 221.

22 Emily Peach, *Tarot for Tomorrow* (Wellingborough, UK: Aquarian Press, 1988), 49.

23 Carl Japikse, *Exploring the Tarot* (Columbus, OH: Ariel Press, 1989), 159.

24 Melita Denning & Osborne Phillips, *The Magick of Tarot* (St. Paul, MN: Llewellyn, 1993), 212.

1993: Change. Understanding cycles of birth, death, and rebirth in the physical world; expanding awareness through change; recognising the idea of duality in life; agitation and duality. [25]

1996: The 2 of Coins represents movement from one financial or material condition to the next. [26]

1996: This is a time of balancing books, weighing choices, reflecting on a career and trying to create greater harmony in work. It shows a decision or choice in work or career needs to be made. A good time for thinking about contracts. [27]

1997: Manipulation, ingenious, knowledgeable manipulation of the rules of life, real operator both of human beings as well as of material goods /services, delicate balancing of resources, the ability to juggle simultaneously several projects. Travel or messages or hinted at by the ships. Far-reaching enterprises. [28]

1998: Change is the primary interpretation of this upright card, but not always for the better. Problems and setbacks are likely. Balance between competing demands. Financially, this is a good card but prudent management of resources is recommended. [29]

2000: Key phrase: Keeping track of many "irons in the fire." Major obstacle: Life out of balance. Here the consciousness maintains a certain equilibrium in the middle of opposing forces and the turbulent surroundings. The infinity symbol reminds us of endless cycles of change, and that sometimes life is like a balancing act. The old ying/yang. Pain and joy. Peace and interruption. Time budget and career, family and health and recreational

25 A T Mann, *The Elements of the Tarot* (Shaftesbury, UK: Element Books, 1993), 96.

26 Evelyne and Terry Donaldson, *Principles of Tarot* (London, UK: Thorsons, 1996), 79.

27 Adam Fronteras, *The Tarot: The Traditional Tarot Reinterpreted for the Modern World* (New York, NY: Stewart, Tabori & Chang, 1996), 83.

28 Sally Gearheart and Susan Rennie, *A Feminist Tarot* (Watertown, MA: Persephone Press, 1977), 30.

29 Rowena Stuart, *Collin's Gem Tarot* (London, UK: Collins), 221.

considerations can hit us all at once, sometimes forcing us to make choices per minute. [30]

2000: This card represents movement from one financial or material condition to the next. It shows us that we need to become more adaptable or flexible in what we do. That way, we can easily develop different skills, or relocate and work somewhere else, without any trouble or difficulty. [31]

2001: I know how to balance my money. Balancing health and money is an eternal struggle. Desire for material possessions, faith in future prosperity. [32]

2002: Juggling with money, robbing from Peter to pay Paul. Spreading resources of time, money, or energy very thinly. Sometimes this card represents a break of a relationship and the subsequent splitting of resources. [33]

2003: Juggling finances, need for flexibility, balancing multiple obligations, walking a tightrope, pulled in many directions, monetary fluctuations, a balancing act, splitting up resources, a change of job or environment, time is money. [34]

2003: The 2 of Pentacles is an atypical card in its air of fun and whimsy. It advises us to be flexible and adaptive so that we can keep things in balance, but it also seems to say, "Have fun while you are at it." This card indicates juggling various projects or tasks, but saying that we have a lot going on, but we will be able to handle it all if we keep our balance.

Advice: Balance your needs against those of other people. Whenever you are competing with someone else for resources, bring some balance into the situation. [35]

---

30   Stephen Walter Sterling, *Tarot Awareness* (St. Paul, MN: Llewellyn, 2000), 312.

31   Evelyne Herbin and Terry Donaldson, *Tarot* (London, UK: Thorsons, 2001).

32   Sylvia Abraham, *How to Read the Tarot: The Keyword System* (St. Paul, MN: Llewellyn, 2000), 35.

33   Sasha Fenton, *Super Tarot* (London, UK: Thorsons, 1994), 48.

34   Anthony Lewis, *Tarot Plain and Simple* (St. Paul, MN: Llewellyn, 2003), 139–140.

35   James Ricklef, *Tarot Tells the Tale* (St. Paul, MN: Llewellyn, 2003), 254.

2004: The two pentacles suggest the duality of this card. The 2 of Pentacles signifies equilibrium in the material realm, as well as both emotional and financial security. A young man is generally shown juggling two pentacles and, although the sea behind him may be turbulent, he appears happy and light hearted, for this indicates enjoyment of life. Balance is the most pressing issue when choosing the 2 of Pentacles. We find ourselves having to juggle different needs and finds ways of managing these conflicting aspects. Sometimes pressures of work or study conflict with need for leisure time. [36]

2004: You may need to seek balance in life. Trust and playfulness. Up and downs of material fortunes. Always attractive to have two of anything but keeping both in play can cause stress. Two or more jobs, homes, or demanding relationships or whatever you are trying to juggle can be hard at times, but the card conveys a sense of optimism and playfulness, but behind that a deep trust in the dance of life. [37]

2004: Financial stability or solvency, a boat or boat ride, eyeglasses. Near the Knight of Wands, it may mean a motor cycle or a bicycle; near the Ace of Swords it may mean an eye exam; near the Sun it may mean a pair of sunglasses; near the Chariot or the Ace of Swords it may mean a car needs a new tire or a wheel alignment. [38]

2005: Here we are faced with a physical or material decision that has emotional undertones. We are keeping our options open by juggling more things than we can really handle over the long-term. Meanwhile, we struggle with the internal process of what things to keep and which to let go. [39]

2005: The juggler is working hard to maintain a happy balance between competing forces. But he is in control and may even be enjoying the challenge of keeping more than one ball in the air at one time. If you get this card in

36   Annie Lionnet, *The Tarot Directory* (Rochester, UK: Grange Books, 2004), 124.

37   Philip and Stephanie Carr-Gomm, *The DruidCraft Tarot* (London, UK: Connections, 2009), 52.

38   Wilma Carroll, *The 2-Hour Tarot Tutor* (London, UK: Piatkus, 2010), 222.

39   Teresa C. Michelsen, *The Complete Tarot Reader* (St. Paul, MN: Llewellyn, 2005), 220.

a reading, you are likely to be juggling material or practical issues. Working out how to achieve a balance between career of leisure activities or making a choice between two job offers. [40]

2007: Recreation and celebration balanced against minor troubles and frustrations, the arrival of news or a message. Minor irritations and setbacks. A hectic schedule may force you to juggle more than one job. [41]

2009: Choices must be made. Juggling, resourceful, flexible, adaptable, accommodating, willing to please, managing priorities, displaying multiple talents, multitasking, keeping with change, juggling the demands of family, work, money, and relationships, having too many balls in the air, trying too hard to keep everyone happy. [42]

2009: A man juggles his coins as a ship in the background is tossed about carelessly by the ever-changing sea. Professional, not overly concerned, yet pensive, trying to find the perfect balance, ongoing struggle for balance through constant adjustment and analysis, ongoing emotional imbalance. [43]

2011: Learning to unite the forces of mind and body and bring balance to (his) physical and spiritual existence. The constant struggle to balance time and money, work and pleasure, and personal and professional obligations. [44]

2011: Successfully maintaining a balance. Juggling more than one project simultaneously—home/work balance, etc. Juggling finances. Juggling more than one project. [45]

2011: This card has connotations of equilibrium and harmony. Ideally everything will be in balance and be kept in that state—past and future, memory

---

40   Linda Marson, *Ticket, Passport, and Tarot Cards* (Melbourne, Australia: Brolga Publishing, 2005), 33.

41   Joseph Vargo and Joseph Iorillo, *The Gothic Tarot Compendium* (Strongsville, OH: Monolith Graphics, 2007), 197.

42   Paul Quinn, *Tarot for Life* (Wheaton, IL: Quest Books, 2009), 250.

43   Dusty White, *The Easiest Way to Learn the Tarot Ever* (North Charleston, SC: Booksurge, 2009), 210.

44   Corinne Kenner, *Tarot and Astrology* (Woodbury, MN: Llewellyn, 2011), 174–175.

45   Josephine Ellershaw, *Easy Tarot Reading* (Woodbury, MN: Llewellyn, 2011), 221.

and hope, sky and earth, privacy and openness. A mysterious light floods the darkness. Now that the one has become the two and new beginnings are afoot, endings are also possible. Unless we remember that all created things pass away, we only live in two dimensions. [46]

2012: Balancing financial or health issues, perhaps both. She may be juggling several jobs at once, at work or at home and personal projects. Market days or the Faire, generally happy days. Knows how to balance the problems of life with fun and socializing. Change in financial situation indicated. Balance, fun, and flexibility. Teamwork. [47]

We will now skip ahead to our recent re-casting of the card back to its original divinatory roots and true to Pamela Colman Smith's depiction of it.

2015: The image [which inspired Pamela to depict Waite's meaning of false communication is] "False Mercury," the poisonous flower also known as "Dog's Mercury." Burne-Jones describes this image as "The Dream-god shewing happy dreams of home to sleeping mariners at sea." Making contacts and socialising is good and beneficial to be happy and successful in life. However, on the downside, be aware of the more connections that you make with others, say through social media, Facebook, and on Twitter, may lead to communications being confused because as Waite says, "it is read also as news and messages in writing, as obstacles, agitation, trouble, embroilment." So, beware of Facebook trolling and miscommunications! From the reversal view Waite warns against "Forced gaiety, simulated enjoyment," so keep it real and authentic. [48]

We could now make a family-tree of meanings for the 2 of Pentacles, showing important branches of words and concepts, and when they originated. We can see clearly in our list that some words are like family traits, skipping a few generations only to later return. This may be evidence of the influence of previous authors upon following authors, or if they

---

46 David Fontana, *The Essential Guide to the Tarot* (London, UK: Watkins, 2011), 191.
47 Tessa Piontek, *Tarot for the 21st Century* (CreateSpace, 2012), 141–142.
48 Marcus Katz and Tali Goodwin, *Secrets of the Waite-Smith Tarot* (Woodbury, MN: Llewellyn, 2015).

were not aware of the earlier writings, it might be evidence of the *morphic field* said to connect information between us. As time travellers, we may even come to encounter these words floating around the *Akashic Field* or upon the *Astral Plane*.

You can see that certain concepts, whilst perfectly appropriate to the card, are time-based. The concept of credit-balancing only comes in after the 1950s, when credit became available to households on a mass scale. The idea of the card as signifying work-life balance is only a very recent meaning of the card.

The theme of unity is very much in evidence in the 2 of Pentacles as is the notion of juggling, be it of finances, ideas, the truth, or weighing projects.

Your Time Touchstone in Tarot

To ensure a safe journey through time and a return to the present, we need to calibrate ourselves to the current moment. We can do this by selecting three cards out of the deck to create a *time touchstone*.

Take out your cards and split your deck into three piles: the twenty-two major cards, the sixteen court cards, and the fifty minor cards.

Shuffle each pile whilst thinking about your past, present, and future. Then draw one card from each pile.

- The **major** card represents your "pattern" in time. This is the card that is presently influencing your life based on the decisions of your past and the consequences still to play out in the future.

- The **court** card represents your "being" in time. This shows who you can best be now to honour your past and best prepare your future.

- The **minor** card represents your "situation" in time. It gives a clue as to how the other two cards come together in real life and everyday events. It is the touchstone that tells you when to be more like your court card and recognise that the major card is active.

Look at the cards now and write down any meanings you have for those cards; any ideas, concepts, associations, or correspondences you might read for each. We can then compare that to how you might see them when we have finished travelling through time.

Now that we have established a touchstone, we will complete our brief survey of the cards with a brief look at the major arcana and then learn a method for getting a quick answer from the deck so we can safely commence our time travels.

The Major Arcana in Time

In 1781, during the first era of tarot, the twenty-two major arcana cards were an illustrated history of time, shrouded in secrets and lost in mystery. Comte de Mellet (1727–1804), writing in Court de Gébelin's *Le Monde Primitif*, presented the arcana as telling the story of the three great Ages: Gold, Silver, and Iron, in three series of seven cards.[49] We paraphrase his story as follows:

Gold: The Universe (World) gives birth to mankind (Judgment) and then are created the Sun (Sun), Moon (Moon), Stars, and fish (Star, corresponding to Aquarius). There is a fall from heaven (Tower), and the Devil (Devil) comes to end the Golden Age.

Silver: We are led by an Angel (Temperance) who teaches us to live and try and avoid death (Death) and accident (Hanged Man) now that we are no longer in the Golden Age. We are assisted in this by our strength to cultivate ourselves and resist our own wildness (Strength). In coming to realise we now live in an inconstant and changing world (Wheel), we seek (Hermit) Justice (Justice).

Iron: In the wars that follow (Chariot), we are caught between vice and virtue, no longer led by reason (Lovers). We raise religions and rules (Hierophant) and set Kings (Emperor) and Queens (Empress) upon the earth. This leads the people to pride, idolatry (High Priestess as Juno and the Peacock) and deception (Magician).[50]

---

49 Comte de Mellet, actually Louis-Raphael-Lucece de Fayolle, has taken these ages from Ovid (four ages) and Hesiod (five ages). See Farley, H. *A Cultural History of Tarot*, 104–106.

50 Comte de Mellet was likely using the Tarots de Besançon, identified by Helen Farley (2009) and Evalyne Hall (2016).

This leads to the eventual "madness" of our race, the Fool card, where the tiger biting at the legs of the Fool is viewed as our "remorse" as we try to delay our inevitable march towards folly and criminality.

5. Fool from *The Book of Thoth:*
Etteilla Tarot, Lo Scarabeo, 2003.

In weaving a story out of these twenty-two cards, we can also experience our own life story, as the pattern is archetypal, something universal which works at both a global and personal scale. Try this yourself: take out the twenty-two major arcana and place them in reverse order from the World to the Magician but do not include the Fool. Begin to match them to your own personal history and movement in time. Perhaps you will need to ask your parents about your family history or the moves of residence in your childhood, or your siblings about early school memories and friends. This can be a fascinating exercise to show how present our personal history is to our life.

An example might be:

I was born in central San Francisco (World) and my parents decided to move to a bigger house (Judgment) in Oakland. I had a great childhood there (Sun) and was always interested in astronomy (Moon and Star). However, when I went to school as a teen, things changed a lot (Tower) . . .

You must match your life to the tarot in their order, not the other way around—do not rearrange the cards but locate the events in your life that match them, perhaps having to go to minutes in time (or back out to years) to make a match for some cards.

If you naturally reach a card and it brings you up to the present moment, such as getting to the Empress and you are pregnant for the first time in the present, you can conclude the exercise at that point. Otherwise, work through the series as if the present moment is the Magician, the first numbered card.

It may also be that you reach the Magician at a particularly significant point that is still in your past, in which case you can re-commence the temporal mapping from the World again until you reach the present moment. The major arcana are a time-loop, woven through our lives in a spiral pattern.

Write this in your tarot time traveller journal and we will return to it at the end of our journey in our final chapter and see how the magic of tarot can help us create our future out of our past, as well as a mere prediction.

Intermediate Time Traveller Method

Use the twenty-two major arcana in this reverse order to tell the story of an event, a time in history, a situation in your workplace or other event. You may reach a card and realise that the story has reached only that point. This allows you to predict how the situation may develop and is a very advanced and powerful method for tarot time travellers to navigate their real life.

Now we will pack our last tool in our kit and go for a brief hop in our time travel machine before setting off for real in the next chapter.

Getting a Yes/No Answer in Tarot

Remember our first time travel escapade at the start of this chapter? Now for the instructions. Many querents—and sometimes ourselves as readers—would sometimes like to get a simple yes or no answer from the tarot. A reading is often packed with advice and general indications, but it is left to the reader to interpret the likely outcome of an event from the cards. Here in that 1955 *Fate* magazine we picked up at the start of our time travel, we will discover a method that purports to give a yes/no answer perhaps you can test.

When we return to the safety of our time pod, we can look over the cover and see something very important for all our trips and mental health—a tarot *anachronism*. This is when two things out of alignment in time are placed together, as if they are happening at the same time. These *anachronisms* (a word which literally means "against time") can confuse the time traveller into believing that what they are seeing is true or actually happened. The unwary traveller can then start to repeat these stories as if they are true, rippling out into the time-sphere to entrap other travellers.

What can we see on this cover in 1955? An image of gypsy dancers and a deck of tarot cards. The words "The Tarot: Secrets of the Gypsy Cards." However, as we will see, those cards in the picture were not published until December 1909. "Gypsy" is a generic (and these days considered impolite) term for the Romani peoples who likely originated in India and moved across Europe between the sixth and eleventh centuries.

Using cards for fortune-telling did not really become vogue until the sixteenth and eighteenth centuries. Furthermore, that tarot deck in particular could not have been used by "gypsies" until 1910.

There is confusion, and the minds of people unaware of these anachronisms still associate the tarot with gypsies. In fact, from the esoteric era of tarot, the deck was associated with ancient Egypt. This then got promoted even further in the "Egypto-mania" that swept late Victorian Europe and America, resulting in a widespread modern mistake that the tarot came from ancient Egypt via the gypsies.

6. *Fate* Magazine Cover, 1955.

A Spread from *Fate* Magazine (1955)

It is refreshing to go back to the 1930s and '50s and discover these rare curiosities, although as we have seen, we do have to take early writings with some caution as to their factual basis. In the article, we read about Irys Vorel's encounter with a Swiss Gypsy, "Boudrie," who used "colourful Tarots." The author goes on to talk about "pentacles" and the likely origin of Tarot in "the Far East" or "the land of Sumer," as well as their popularity during the "Middle Ages"!

Despite these romantic and untrue assertions, the article does contain a couple of gems. It introduces the idea of "assemblation," a term that denotes how a card is read in conjunction with the card next to it in a reading, and a Yes/No spread, reproduced here.

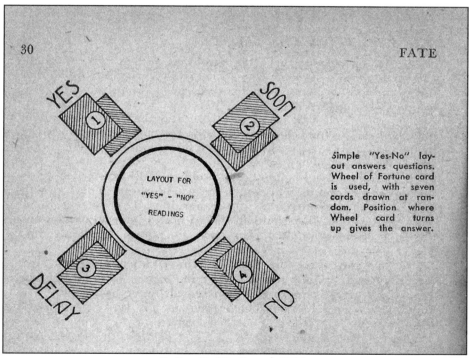

30   FATE

LAYOUT FOR "YES" - "NO" READINGS

Simple "Yes-No" layout answers questions. Wheel of Fortune card is used, with seven cards drawn at random. Position where Wheel card turns up gives the answer.

7. *Fate* Yes/No Spread, 1955.

1. Formulate the question that should have a yes/no answer.

2. Remove the Wheel of Fortune card and place it face up in front of you.

3. Shuffle the remaining deck and fan out face down.

4. Draw seven cards at random with your left hand.

5. Put these seven cards face down on top of the Wheel card.

6. Pick eight random cards, and turn the Wheel round so it faces as the others.

7. Shuffle these eight cards.

8. Lay out the top four cards as shown in a square face down: 1–2–3–4

9. Lay out the next four cards on top, fifth on the first, sixth on the second, seventh on the third, and eighth on the fourth.

10. You now have two cards in each corner of the Destiny Wheel.

11. Locate the Wheel of Fortune in the pairs and the position of that pair gives the answer: Yes, Soon, Delay, or No.

Even where there is a "No" answer, the skilled reader can look at the *assemblation* of the cards to divine what the obstacles and challenges may be to turn this into a positive result.

A Warning to All Tarot Time Travellers

We are about to set off on our journey through time but first—a warning about fake history. Throughout the ages, both friends and enemies of the tarot alike have sought to rewrite history. We must tread carefully and keep our wits about us as we venture into the past.

As an example, the contemporary time traveller may have seen in a recent film, *The Other Boleyn Girl*, a scene of Anne Boleyn reading a tarot card. She is rightly perturbed by the card, as it depicts a Queen without her head. Whilst this makes for a good story, it is a case of false history; the tarot was not yet popular outside of continental Europe at the time, and it is highly unlikely that Anne would have held a pack.

However, such false history does give us clues to time-tracks we might not otherwise discover. When following this false lead, we find that the story comes from Henry VIII's own writings but does not involve a deck but a book of "prophecy"; something Anne herself referred to in her own words as a "bauble." We will come to see how these Italian prophecy books are an early form of tarot and fortune-telling. In fact, we will turn this book into such a prophecy book as we go along.

With that warning in mind, we should certainly instead look for examples of tarot changing history as we go with factual evidence to back us up. The late Alec Guinness, English actor better known today for his part as Obi-Wan Kenobi in the original *Star Wars* trilogy, "experimented" with tarot as a young man. In his biography, *Blessings in Disguise*, Guinness writes about how he was introduced to it by a fellow actor. At odds with his cynical nature, Guinness seemed drawn to the esoteric, and quite spooky things happened to him. One such happening was when he worked with James Dean. Dean offered Guinness a ride in his new sports car. Guinness turned him down, and told him "if you get into that car you will die in it." [51] Dean died in that very car the next day.

Guinness's interest with the tarot was short-lived; he wrote that his Catholic wife did not approve of his fascination with the tarot. It was not long before he burnt the one and only deck he owned.

If Obi-Wan survived because of the tarot, let us also look forward to a long journey in tarot ahead. In the next chapter, we will get straight into our time machine and head to the perhaps unlikely place of Scotland at a time when the very first meanings were given to playing cards. We will then see how we can use some of the poetry and storytelling devices of the time to enrich our own readings both of playing cards and tarot.

---

51   Alec Guinness, *Blessings in Disguise* (Akadine, 2001).

2

Cartomancy Card Meanings

The whole adapted to the Entertainment of the humorous, as well as to the Satisfaction of the Grave Learned, and Ingenious. The like never before published.

—*The New Game at Cards* [52]

17 February, 1800: Edinburgh, Scotland

We are time travelling again. It is almost ten years since Robert Burns visited this city for the last time, and we walk by the Canongate Brewery which is being built by Steins. In just three years from now, William and Dorothy Wordsworth will visit the city. Meanwhile, the place is growing at a huge rate with more than 80,000 people overall and shortly there will be much demolition and plans for a second "new town."

We turn off Calton Road and continue under the arch reading "Campbell's Close" tucked beyond Cowgate and the Royal Mile. The air is dense with the sweet smell of barley being boiled and the more bitter aroma of boiling hops. Down the lane, we find a cart is being loaded with piles of freshly printed chapbooks; cheap pamphlets for sale across the city to a public hungry for accessible news and stories.

---

52 Title page of *The New Game at Cards; or, a Pack of Cards Changed into a Compleat and Perpetual Almanack.*

This particular cart is outside the presses of J. Morren and whilst no one is watching, we browse through the newly published pamphlets.

We first pick up a copy of a "full account" of the landing and arrival of the "Roman" prophet ENOCH—who apparently was brought from Rome to Portsmouth overnight by an Angel. Whilst intriguing, this is not what we are looking for today. A further look through the cart and we find our target; a second-edition copy of Flamstead and Partridge's *Fortune Book*.

It is unlikely that these names bear any relationship to the real author of the text—or authors—but that is to be expected at this time. One similar fortune-telling book in the cart gives a history of its author, Mrs. Bridget, or "Mother Bridget," as "someone whose name has been forgotten by history but is known to those who remember her." Bridget apparently lived in a hole in the ground and smoked a pipe, "of tobacco she was exceedingly fond." Visitors to her would be surprised by various small animals that would creep out of her clothing, and whilst she had "more money than was sufficient to maintain her," her later years were plagued by ill health and she cut a "terrifying figure" in her lonesome walks, surrounded only by dumb animals. There were many such Mrs. Bridgets at the time, fake people created just to sell a few more pages of their copied materials. [53]

There are many such copies and versions of these fortune-telling pamphlets: the *New Fortune Book*, the *Only Real Fortune-Teller*, the *Tree of Fate*, the *Spaewife*, and several more. Some would cover brief dream interpretation and the reading of moles, lines on the hand or on the face. We will also pick up a copy of the *Spaewife* in our time travels, as it includes a version of the symbolism of coffee grounds that we will meet in a later chapter on Lenormand cards.

For now, let us return to our time-pod and look over our second acquisition in our journey, this *Fortune Book* by Flamstead & Partridge.

Flamstead & Partridge

We could have chosen any time between the seventeenth and nineteenth centuries to visit Edinburgh and pick up one of these *chapbooks*—cheap and coarse pamphlets sold on the

---

53 We are also particularly fond of the Buzzfeed-type titles of chapbooks of the time, showing there is nothing new under the sun. Our favourite title is *HelioGabulus's Magic Tablets: A Never-Failing Key to the Future Fortunes of Enquirers. Also the Silent Language, or How to Discourse without Speaking, and Various Other Secrets Worth Knowing.*

streets for a penny or less. These booklets were popular until the mid-1800s when they were considered as certainly "ungodly" and as competition to religious tracts. Until that time, chapbooks provided the common folk access to sermons and prophecies, songs and ballads, almanacs and calendars, and instructional manuals. One such manual, the "Book of Knowledge" from c. 1800 includes instruction in "astronomy, astrology, geography, physic and surgery" as well as a guide to the fairs in Scotland that year.

Consider them the YouTube of their time and a prelude to the penny dreadfuls of later years.

There are several variations of this particular fortune book, which may have even been printed much earlier in the 1700s; however, we will use the one we have in our hands, purchased from the very streets of Edinburgh this day in history.[54] Here is how the book is introduced:

> Partridge and Flamsteads, new and well experienced fortune book: delivered to the world from the Astrologer's Office, in Greenwich Park. For the benifit [sic] of young men, maids, wives and widows, who by drawing cards according to the directions of this fortune book, may know whether life will be long o[r] short, whether they shall have the person desired, and what part of the world is most profitable to live in, and all lawful questions whatsoever. The signification of moles in any part of the body, and the interpretation of dreams, as they relate to good or bad fortune. To which is added The whimsical lady.

The Whimsical Lady is a brief story appended to the pamphlet, a practice common at the time. Whilst some versions of the pamphlet have instructions like the earlier Italian fortune books where the reader rolls a dice, picks a card from a deck, and follows instructions through the book to land on a final "oracle" or "fortune," this pamphlet has the first one-card reading method and a list of all the card meanings for us to study.

---

54 Some online versions are much the same; however, in a couple of cases, there are different interpretations caused by variations such as "Never will the truth forsake" compared to "For Ever will the truth forsake" for the 8 of Diamonds. We here use the original in the Museum of Scotland, which we visited several years ago.

The instructions and individual card meanings in the section below are drawn straight from the original text of Flamstead and Partridge.

The Instructions

Take a new pack of cards. Shuffle them well together, he or she that holds them spreading them on the table with their faces downward; then those who draw must shut their eyes and lay their right hand on their left breast, saying these words as they draw the card, "Honi Soit qui mally pense": Then look upon the number [of the card drawn] and have recourse to the book, so you shall have full satisfaction in good or bad fortune.[55]

Ace of Diamonds

Since this Ace it seems your lot,
You'll wed one that's fierce and hot;
But if woman kind draws it,
She'll have one with wealth and wit.

II

Hast thou drawn the number two,
Thou'lt wed one that's just and true,
But if a woman this shall have,
Beware of sly and cunning knave.

III

Having drawn the number three,
Honour will thy portion be,
But a maid who gets the same,
Must take heed of wanton shame.

IV

The man who gets the number four,
He must quit[e] his native shore,

---

55   The Anglo-Norman phrase is usually translated as "Evil (or shame) be to him that evil thinks."

If the same be drawn by woman,
She'll get a sweetheart out of hand.

V

He who draws the number five.
Where he lives he best will thrive,
But if drawn by woman kind,
They better luck abroad will find.

VI

He that draws the number six,
Will have silly and cunning tricks,
But if woman draw the same,
If doth shew them free from blame.

VII

Since the seven doth appear,
Crosses thou hast cause to fear,
Woman who the same do draw,
Fear no cross[s] of a straw.

VIII

Hast thou got the number eight,
Thou wilt be a cuckold great,
Females who the same do take,
For ever will the truth forsake.

IX

Hast thou got the merry nine,
Guineas will thy pocket line,
She that draws it with her hand,
Dies for love or leaves the land.

X

What the ten? 'tis very well,
None in love can the[e] excel,
But the girl who gets the ten,
Will be wed, but none knows when.

The King

This fair king of diamonds shews,
Thou wilt live where pleasure flows,
But when a woman gets the king,
Melancholy songs she'll sing.

The Queen

Now the Queen of Diamonds fair,
Shews you will some office bear,
Woman, if it comes to you,
Friends you'll get and not a few.

The Knave

Is the Knave of Diamonds come,
Then beware the martial drum,
If a virgin gets the knave,
She will better fortune have.

The Ace of Hearts

He that gets this ace of Hearts,
Will appear a man of parts,
She who gets it, I profess,
Has the gift of idleness.

II

He who gets the duce will be,
Full of generosity.

But when a woman gets this card,
It doth shew them very hard.

III
The poor man who gets this tray,
When he's bound he must obey.
Woman who do get this sort,
Will drink brandy by the quart.

IV
He that gets the four will make,
Faithful love for conscience sake,
But if drawn by a woman kind,
They'll prove false and sly you'll find.

V
Note the five of hearts declares,
Thou shalt manage great affairs,
But if got by women then,
They'll love any sort of men.

VI
Now the six of hearts foretels,
If a man here honour dwells,
If drawn by the other side,
It betokens scorn and pride.

VII
Now the seven I'll maintain:
Shews thou hast not liv'd in vain.
Thou wilt have the golden prize,
But with maids it's otherwise.

VIII

Having drawn the number eight,
Shews the servile born to wait;
But if woman draw the same,
They will mount on wings of fame.

IX

By this Nine be well assur'd.
Thy love pains must be endured.
But the maid who gets the nine,
Soon in wedlock bands will join.

X

Then the ten is a lucky cast
For it shews the worst is past,
But if girls the like do have,
Love will their kind hearts enslave.

The King

By this card it doth appear,
Thou shalt live in happy chear [cheer],
And if a female gets this card.
She'll soon likewise be preferr'd.

The Queen

By this Card it is well known,
Thou wilt still enjoy thy own,
Women if they get the same,
Will enjoy a virtous name.

The Knave

He that gets the knave of hearts,
It betokens knavish parts,

But if a woman gets the knave,
She will ne'er be man's slave.

The Ace of Spades

Thou who gett'st this ace of spades,
Shall be flouted by the maids,
When it is a damsel's lot,
Love and honour shall be got.

II

Now this duce betokens strife,
With a foolish whorish wife,
If a woman's lot it be,
Honour, love, and dignity.

III

Thou art happy in this tray,
And wilt wed some lady gay,
But girls who the same do take,
Shall wed with some poor town rake.

IV

Now this Four betokens you,
Must be of the horned crew,
Girls who get the like will meet,
With the height of joys complete.

V

This five of spades give you to know
That you must through great troubles go,
But if a virgin it foretells,
Her virtue others much excels.

VI

This six fortells when you do wed,
You'll have a cracked maidenhead,
But the girl this number draws,
She'll wed one with great applause.

VII

Since the seven's come to hand,
It doth entitle the[e] to land,
But girls by this shall wed those,
Who have no money, friends, or clothes.

VIII

This eight doth fortell you shall,
Wed a woman straight and tall,
If to a girl the like doth come,
She weds a brother of Tom Thumb.

IX

By this nine thou art fortold,
Thou shalt wed one lame and old,
Maids if they do get this chance,
May themselves to wealth advance.

X

'Tis seen by the ten of spades,
Thou shalt follow many trades,
Thrive by none. But women they
By this chance can't work, but play.

The King

By this King observe and note,
You on golden streams will float,

Women by the self same lot,
Will long enjoy what they have got.

The Queen

There's the queen of spades, likewise,
Thou wilt soon to riches rise,
Women by this same will have,
That they both desire and crave.

The Knave

This is a Knave then have a care,
That thou dost not make a pair,
Women who the same do chuse [choose],
Shall prove sluts, but that's no news.

The Ace of Clubs

He who gets the ace of Clubs,
Must expect a thousand snubs,
From wife. But girls again,
By this card will rise and reign.

II

Note this duce doth signify,
That thou wilt a Christian die,
Woman who the same do take,
Never will their friends forsake.

III

You who now this tray have drawn,
Will on cursed harlots fawn,
Women who do get this tray,
To their acts do answer nay.

IV

By this four we clearly see,
Four brats must be laid to thee,
She who gets the same must wed
Two rich husbands, both well bred.

V

By this five see that thou
Shalt join unto a dirty sow,
This drawn by virgins they
Will have husbands kind and gay.

VI

By this six you'll wed we know,
One that over you will crow,
Maids who get the same will be
Blest with husbands kind and free

VII

Thou that hath this seven drawn,
Must your breeches put in pawn,
Girls who get the same will wear,
Jewels rich beyond compare.

VIII

By this eight, though Whig or Quaker,
Thou wilt be a cuckold maker,
Maids who draw the same are born.
To hold fools and fops in scorn.

IX

That a nine? upon my life,
You shall wed a wealthy wife,
She who gets the same wilt have,
One who is both fool and knave.

X

Now this number half a score,
Shews thou wilt be wretched poor,
Maids who draw this number still,
Will have jobs and wealth at will.

The King

Here's the King of Clubs that shows,
Thou hast friends as well as foes,
Maids who the same do draw,
Shall have a man without a flaw.

The Queen

If the Queen of Clubs thou hast,
Thou wilt be with honour grac'd,
Women if the same they find,
Will have all things to their mind.

The Knave

Now the vainly knave appears,
He will cut off both thy ears,
Women when the same they see,
Will be what they us'd to be. [56]

---

56 Method and card meanings taken verbatim from a copy of Flamstead & Partridge, *Fortune Book*, c. 1800, in the National Library of Scotland, Edinburgh.

Pick a Card, Any Card

We can now commence our cartomantic journey with a simple one-card reading using a deck of fifty-two playing cards with the full ace to ten in each suit, and three cards for the court in each suit; the knave (jack), queen, and king. [57]

If you care to draw a card for yourself, you will also see that each card interpretation has two lines for each gender; the first is for a male querent and the second couplet is for a woman. This was also common at the time to provide different readings for male and female participants.

You might discover that the concerns of the time are not directly related to contemporary matters in all cases, and are very proscribed, particularly in the area of marriage. This was the very start of card interpretation, and we will trace how these cards became far more layered as time progresses; although, three in five questions—even in modern times—remain about relationship issues.

Having visited one of the very first occurrences of cartomantic meanings in print, let us now move forwards in time and learn how to use playing cards in a variety of ways for fortune-telling. We will just need to take a quick time hop. Watch out for the bicycle!

Tuesday, 25 June, 1935: Leeds, England

The bicycle swerves around the puddles along the cobbled streets. Luckily, the rider of the bike who is on her way home from the night shift at the Leeds Telephone Exchange is wearing culottes, saving her a pretty penny on laundry expenses.

She is on her way to the newsagents (which will soon be opening) to pick up her reserved copy of *Woman's Weekly*. This week it features a knitted jumper pattern with cable-stitched bands. She races by the Empire Palace movie theatre, hardly glancing at the posters for the latest Alfred Hitchcock film, *The 39 Steps*. She has other thrills and mysteries on her mind.

Last year, she, Judith Reid, aged 24, had been introduced to a whole new world. In the otherwise inconspicuous pages of *Woman's Own* magazine (13 January), for just 2d she had read how to read the cards and taken advantage of a rather special offer.

---

57 For an illustrated history of playing cards, including a selection of important and rare tarot and divination decks, see Catherine Perry Hargrave, *A History of Playing Cards* (Mineola, NY: Dover Publications, 2000).

She had learnt how to read the future in an ordinary deck of playing cards and had become rather good at it. This year, now that the girls at the Exchange were used to her reading their cards during cigarette breaks, she was about to branch out. The *Woman's Weekly* she was about to buy had a wonderful gift with it: a full deck of tarot cards.

Judith had promised everyone at work she would soon have them mastered and would be able to read even more for them. It was perhaps no coincidence that the story she was also following in the magazine in weekly installments was entitled "If This Be Destiny."

She turns a bit too sharply into Harrowgate Road, round by the Co-Op and brakes as she sees Wilson & Sons fruitsellers, already open. Dismounting quickly from her bicycle, she rushes into Harry Cleggs, local newsagent, and grabs her copy of the magazine from the piles newly delivered by the door.

"A treat every week," Harry jokes, handing her the deck of tarot cards, neatly packaged with the Thompson Leng publishing mark on the front of the box. Judith smiles politely but cannot contain her excitement. "It's the future, Harry," she exclaims, "just like them telephones!"

Cartomancy Basics

A Note on Keywords

Throughout our time travels, we will be referencing keywords and key phrases for not only playing cards but also for tarot and Lenormand cards. These assist us to unlock what we call the *cartomantic core* of each card. However, the keywords from one time zone to another may be different or even contradictory, as we will see. We advise all tarot time travellers to anchor themselves in **one** set of keywords that will maintain temporal consistency. As time goes on, your practice will modify the keywords as you unlock your own experience of the cards.

We provide variations of words throughout a card, as sometimes a slightly different way of wording the same thing, or almost the same thing, will unlock the card for you. E.g., "curiosity, learning, inquisitiveness, exploration" are almost the same things but one word will vibrate for you more than the others during a reading.

8. Thomson-Leng Tarot Cards, 1935.

The Decks

A playing card deck will vary from time to time and region to region. The study of the history of playing cards is even more dedicated than the study of tarot alone. We will provide an overview and recommend for those interested in further study the resources at the conclusion of this book, including playing card collector societies.[58]

The Pips

The amount of numbered cards used for playing can vary from nation to nation and region. This can be quite confusing at first when you look for the meaning of a card, say the 4 of Clubs, in an older German or English book and discover the book misses out the Twos to the Fives because it assumes a thirty-six-card deck.

---

58   Also see www.tarottimetraveller.com for an updated list of resources.

The common arrangements of decks are the full fifty-two-card deck (where the court is king, queen, and jack), the thirty-two-card deck (ace, 7 through 10, jack, queen, and king) used for games such as *Piquet* and the thirty-six-card deck (ace, 6 through 10, jack, queen, and king) which has the same number of cards as a Lenormand deck. There are many other variations of deck, such as the seventy-eight-card *Tarocco Piemontese,* likely familiar to those who use contemporary tarot for divination.

It is likely, for example, that both Casanova and Lenormand used a standard *Piquet* deck for most of their readings long before a totally different deck was given the name "Lenormand" as we will see in a later time zone.

The Black and Red

Some romancers (or *cartomantes*) use the black cards (spades and clubs) to indicate a more negative slant to the reading and the red cards (diamonds and hearts) to be positive. This can be used as a general guide; however (as with tarot), the individual cards and their combinations should dictate the overall interpretation.

The Suits

The four common suits vary by country and sometimes region; however, most will recognise their correspondence to hearts, diamonds, clubs, and spades:

English	Hearts	Diamonds	Clubs	Spades
French	Hearts	Tiles	Clovers	Pikes
German	Hearts (Roses)	Bells	Acorns	Leaves (Shields)
Spanish/Italian	Cups	Coins	Clubs	Swords

The Meaning of the Suits

There is a general agreement as to the overall theme of each suit, although there was little standardisation in early readings as information was either not shared widely or by word-of-mouth. The general themes for the four suits, which will later play into tarot are:

- **Hearts**: Love and feelings, family, home, emotions, positivity.

- **Clubs**: Resources, work, employment and career.

- **Diamonds**: Finances, money, communication.

- **Spades**: Argument, challenge, loss, negativity.

We can usually see the spades as being more negative than the hearts (usually positive).

The Meaning of the Numbers

Some cartomancers use a basic system of numerology to make correspondences to the pip cards and then combine that with the suit to get a bare meaning for interpretation.[59]

- **One**: Beginnings, starting, union, initiation, new plan

- **Two**: Partnership, duality, pair

- **Three**: Building, stability, growth

- **Four**: Structure, expansion

- **Five**: Movement, change (both gain and loss)

- **Six**: Balance, equilibrium, centre, diplomacy

- **Seven**: Spirituality, insight, mysticism, challenge

- **Eight**: Purpose, work, energy

- **Nine**: Novelty, pause

- **Ten**: Completion, ending, finality, results

So, the Ace of Hearts will be the positive start to a new relationship, just as we may read for the corresponding tarot card, the Ace of Cups. The 10 of Spades will be the ending of a challenge, or a loss in the final stages of a situation, just as might be the 10 of Swords in tarot. However, we should first learn cartomancy as a system to itself before learning tarot—or try and forget our modern tarot correspondences when we journey back down time to learn cartomancy.

---

59   See Johnathan Dee, *Fortune Telling by Playing Cards* (New York: Sterling Publishing, 2004).

The Court Cards and When Cartomancy is Better Than Tarot

In basic cartomancy, the court cards are people in the life of the Sitter or yourself. The jacks represent younger people and the queens and kings older people of their respective gender. We have always found that for situations involving lots of people, such as a workplace or family situation, or events revolving around a group of colleagues or friends, cartomancy with playing cards can be more useful than tarot. The earlier systems were naturally designed for a more gossipy and people-centric age, long before the meanings shifted towards introspection, self-development, and esoteric, psychological, or abstract concepts. We could argue, however, whether we have returned with celebrity culture to a more gossipy age—or perhaps never really left it.

Simple Readings

If we start up our cartomantic machine with just these simple cogs, we can easily perform our first reading with just one or two cards. As we will come to see with tarot and Lenormand, sometimes it is easier to learn with more cards rather than less, even if it seems more sensible to start with just one card of the day.

So let us ask our playing card deck the question, "Will I benefit from taking a new course of study this summer?"

We shuffle and draw a card: the 7 of Clubs.

This is the "insight" card in the suit of "work."

It would suggest a vocational course towards a career although it is not strictly answering the original question.

If we had drawn two cards and the second card was the 8 of Diamonds, we would read the second card as "purpose, work, or energy" in the suit of money.

So, the course would be profitable if we worked at it, and it would match our purpose if it was towards our employment.

We can now be confident that we have performed our first reading and precisely answered a question: "I have drawn the 7 of Clubs and the 8 of Diamonds.

This indicates that you will profit from a new course of study this summer if it is career-focused and you work at it."

A Note on the Ace of Spades

This card was originally the most ornate card of a playing card deck as it carried the emblem of the publisher for identification purposes. This was at a time when taxes were applied to card decks and so the Ace of Spades was often the card stamped or printed by the tax office themselves to show it had been paid.

The card also has the highest value in some games, so it became a lucky symbol. It was later used in the Vietnam War, where American soldiers used the card as a morale-boosting image that exploited a perceived superstition in the enemy.

It then began to be seen as a card related to death, a negative connotation carried to this day.

A Note on the 9 of Diamonds

The 9 of Diamonds has been called the "Curse of Scotland" since at least 1708, when a question was printed about it being so-called in *The British Apollo, or, Curious amusements for the ingenious.* In response to the question, it was alleged that it was a proverb arising from the apparent observation that every ninth king of Scotland was a tyrant. There have been several other theories since, but there is no definitive answer.

Odd Nicknames of Playing Cards

The time travelling cartomancer may pick up some strange slang and nicknames for their playing cards along the way. Here are just a few of the curious names you can call your cards.

Dirty Gertie	Queen of Spades
Time Travel	Any 8 card
The Devil's Bedpost	4 of Clubs
Laughing Boy	Jack of Diamonds

We encourage you to pick up more names during your travels and encounter the One-Eyed King and Calamity Jane amongst many other card characters.

Cicely Kent

One of the main sources for cartomantic re-discovery was Cicely Kent, who published *Telling Fortunes by Cards* in 1924. It is Kent who began to formulate much of the advice to the home-grown *cartomante* which is now repeated by most books about card-reading:

- Do not talk whilst shuffling.

- Only read and use one set of meanings at a time.

- Do not try and read when tired, sad, or irritable.

- Keep a clear mind ahead of a reading to avoid projecting your own concerns into the cards.

- Remove all distractions from the reading space.

- Do not mind difficult people or those opposed to reading, interpret the cards as you see them.

- Do not try to fit what you might know about the client into your reading.

- Keep one deck of cards just for your own readings so you do not influence readings for others.

She also discusses the frequency of readings, noting that "many authorities" suggest not reading more than once every three months, but she replies that she reads regularly and for herself, viewing the cards as friends, even if they give "inconvenient and unwished-for" statements. [60]

Her most succinct piece of advice is one that always stands to the true tarot time traveller, in whatever age they discover themselves.

"Your business is to read exactly what you see." [61]

---

60 Cicely Kent, *Telling Fortunes by Cards* (London, UK: Herbert Jenkins Limited, n.d.), 163–164.
61 Ibid., 23.

The Suits

As we have seen, the basic alphabet of the cards is composed firstly of the four suits. These provide us a general theme for that quarter of the deck. We give here contemporary versions of Kent.

Clubs

Business, reputation, organisation, authority.

Diamonds

Finance, decisions, risk.

Hearts

Emotions, satisfaction, love, contentment, home.

Spades

Negativity, failure, depression.

We can again see that the hearts are quite positive overall, with the spades being negative. The diamonds are slightly negative and the clubs are slightly positive. There is a far more definite meaning of good cards and bad cards in the early days of cartomancy, which we will see partially carried across into the Lenormand style of reading later in our time travels.

Clubs

Classic: Prognostic success, money, good luck.

Contemporary: Success predicted, security, wealth.

This suit indicates success in the material world, the appearance of clubs in a reading tells you about the practical side of life. Many clubs in a love reading speaks of physical passion or security.

Hearts

Classic: Sincerity in love, peace.

Contemporary: Committed to a relationship, compatibility.

Most hearts in a love reading speaks of love in abundance; you or somebody could be irresistible.

Diamonds

Classic: Precarious, dominated principally by the surrounding cards; they also predict money.

Contemporary: Uncertainty and risk, depending on the surrounding cards.

Most diamonds can either indicate a situation that comes with risk or it could mean that money is coming into your life.

Spades

Classic: Dark-haired people, widows and widowers.

Contemporary: Significator indicating that the person is dark haired. It can also signify loss in your life.

We will now add, with our own commentary (in brackets), Kent's card meanings for the Pip (numbered) cards into our card lexicon. These cards can be read both upright and with a reversed meaning which we have put in parentheses.

Clubs

Ace: Good news (papers or documents)

Two: Shaking hands—an agreement (an introduction)

Three: Letters, news (delayed or unwelcome news)

Four: A strange bed (bad dreams, insomnia)

Five: Talk, discussion (disagreement, argument)

Six: Vexation (disturbance)

Seven: Success (uncertainty)

Eight: Short journey (a walk)

Nine: Business (delays)

Ten: A journey (an outing)

Diamonds

Ace: A good present (a small gift)

Two: A surprise (gossip)

Three: A pleasant meeting (quarrel with a friend)

Four: A friend (money)

Five: Money settlement (annoyance ahead)

Six: Pleasure (boredom)

Seven: Animals (a bicycle)

Eight: Jewellery (clothes, furniture)

Nine: Money, business (speed, decision)

Ten: Money (pleasant outlook; with spades, pain)

Hearts

Ace: The home (great affection)

Two: Time, days (departures)

Three: Time, weeks or days (arrivals)

Four: Invitation (refusal)

Five: Present (domestics)

Six: Pleasure (social duties)

Seven: Lesser wish (jealousy)

Eight: Affection (friendship)

Nine: The wish (someone dear to you)

Ten: Happiness (lucky changes; with ace, marriage)

Spades

Ace: Sorrow (ace with 9, 7, 4, 2, of spades, death)

Two: Motor or carriage (a parcel)

Three: [with 3 of clubs] Tears (minor worries)

Four: A sick bed (trials)

Five: With 2 and 3 of Spades, sharp words (domestic difficulties)

Six: Child or relation (difficulties)

Seven: Removal (indecision)

Eight: A distance away (night)

Nine: Disappointment (loss)

Ten: Sea (illness)

An alternate system using a smaller deck is given below, where you will see similarities in the individual card meanings.

Clubs

Ace: Letters, papers, luck, riches (delayed letters, paper worries).

King: Generous man, straightforward (makes him handicapped in his desires, worried).

Queen: Loving, forgiving (troubled perplexed).

Knave: Lover (a young man).

Ten: Journey, luck (across water).

Nine: Will legacy (delays, troubled journeys).

Eight: Love of a young man (papers)

Seven: Victory (financial worries)

Hearts

Ace: House, love letter (change of residence)

King: Kind man (unreliable man)

Queen: Fair woman (revengeful)

Knave: Cupid (delays in love)

Ten: Corrective to bad cards, great affection happiness (birth, change)

Nine: Wish card, success (love)

Eight: Love, marriage (jealousy of men)

Seven: Inconstancy (jealousy of women)

Spades

Ace: Love business, high building (death, annoyance)

King: Widower, lawyer (enemy)

Queen: Widowhood (enemy)

Knave: Professional man (traitor)

Ten: Distance, water, journey (sickness, trouble, mourning)

Nine: Failure; if attended by hearts it represents an anchor (death)

Eight: Night, illness (deceit, immorality)

Seven: Determination (accident, loss)

Diamonds

Ace: Ring, bank note (money, good letter)

King: Grey haired man (treacherous man)

Queen: Widow, friend (coquette)

Knave: Military (treachery)

Ten: Money (journey)

Nine: Sharp instruments; with the 8 of Spades, cross words (coffin; with the 9 of Spades, danger)

Eight: Short journey, walk (spite)

Seven: Child, pet (small sum of money) [62]

We will also give below another series of keywords you may find more applicable to your readings. Our advice is to choose one system and work with it for a few weeks before trying any alternatives. You will soon find the right lexicon for the way your cards communicate uniquely to you.

An Alternate Meaning of the Cards

Hearts

Ace: House

King and Queen: Fair man and a woman

Knave: Thoughts.

Ten: Proposal

Nine: Wish, luck

Eight: Good heart

Seven: Night

Five: Strange bed

Three: Little boy, joy

Two kings coming together: A new friend

Two Red Tens: Marriage

The Four of Hearts coming between a King and a Queen: The marriage bed

---

62   All card meanings in this section drawn from Cicely Kent, *Ibid.*

Clubs

Ace: Letter

King: Darkish man

Queen: Darkish woman

Knave: Unfairness

Ten: Water, journey

Nine: Amusement

Eight: Impudence

Seven: Business

Spades

Ace: Sickness.

King: Very dark man, widower

Queen: Very dark woman, widow

Knave: Rogue

Ten: Distant journey

Nine: Affliction

Eight: Speedy

Seven: Removal

Five: Surprise

Three: Tears

The Ace coming with the Eight: Severe sickness

Diamonds

Ace: Ring.

King: Very fair man.

Queen: Queen very fair woman.

Knave: Knavery.

Ten: Money, town journey.

Nine: Money.

Eight: Money.

Seven: Money.

Five: Kisses.

Three: Little girl.

The 10, 9, 8, and 7, all touching, predict an inheritance.

A run of 7, 8, and 9 of clubs, hearts, or diamonds of a single suit or mixed, predict good changes of business, abode, finance, or a way of living.

A run of spades: Troublesome changes.

Three Eights: Changes.

Three Sevens: Marriage, changes.

With these alternate systems in our cartomantic journal, let us now look at a range of ways in which we can read them through a selection of vintage spreads and methods.

Reading Cards for Agony Aunt Questions

The tarot time traveller does not always have to travel in person; books are also time travel devices. In a collection of Agony Aunt letters, we can see that from 1855 onwards the questions asked by people echo all the way back to those asked to the Coptic magician and upon the shrines of Delphi. We will see how cartomancy can answer these questions and their contemporary equivalents.

These questions are modified from a few examples given in the book, *Never Kiss a Man in a Canoe* by Tanith Carey. She notes that the first Agony Aunt was a magazine publisher, John Dunton, who started answering readers with caustic and straightforward advice. He published in the *Athenian Mercury* in 1691. Roughly half were questions about romance and relationships. [63]

The popularity of answering questions from distressed ladies led in part to the first real women's magazine, *The Ladies' Mercury* in 1693.

Here is a question from that time period:

"I am afraid that as a rich widow, men seek to marry me for my money. Should I pretend to be a parlour maid and seek true love?"

Let us shuffle our playing card deck and select out two cards to answer this question:

King of Diamonds: Marriage; a fair person.

7 of Spades: Expectation.

We might word this as "You place your hope on a faithful man."

A modern-day version of the question could be; "I feel as if I am being forced into not being my authentic self and it is affecting my relationships. What should I do?"

Again, shuffling our deck and picking out two cards we receive:

9 of Hearts (rev): Tiredness, anxiety.

10 of Spades: Jealousy, tears.

This indicates depression (anxiety) caused by conflict (tears) when comparing one's own self and life to that of other people (jealousy). The advice of the cards is to stop the comparing, which will go some way to remove the conflict.

We can see in that question that the language and intention of questions can vary from time to time, but they all have a core similarity. We will look next at how we can translate questions—and card-meanings and their interpretation—across time.

---

63 Tanith Carey, *Never Kiss a Man in a Canoe* (London, UK: Boxtree, 2009), vii.

Releasing Cards from Their Time

The meanings and interpretations of early cartomancy can be very constraining, in some cases literally variations of "will I be married or not" meanings, scattered with the occasional "inheritance" card. The tarot time traveller will take these interpretations back to their original nature for more flexible readings. This can be done in four steps and allows any card to be read simply for any question.

Here we take a card meaning from *Flamstead and Partridge* for the 4 of Diamonds which is:

> The man who gets the number four,
> He must quit[e] his native shore.
> If the same be drawn by woman,
> She'll get a sweetheart out of hand.

Obviously, the answer cannot be to leave the country every time this card appears in a reading. These original meanings were meant to be read as a one-off parlour game or amusement, not for serious advice to be consulted daily for life.

We will break down the meaning to get to the *cartomantic core* for the card.

Step 1: Convert the card meaning to contemporary language.

Example: "must quit his native shore" is "emigrate."

So that is the first layer of the card, a literal reading of emigration. This may apply to a question such as, "Should I take the job offer abroad?" but may not apply to "Should I make a formal complaint at work about the bullying situation or take it up with the bully first?" It could do, of course; however, it would be a bit drastic to read it literally. It may shake up the person to suggest they leave their job, and it may help them connect to the value of their employment in a positive way.

Step 2: Extract the sense of the card meaning from the contemporary language.

Example: To emigrate is to move, to change location, and it comes from Latin, meaning "to move (out of) a place."

Now we see how this might apply to the question about workplace bullying. The answer is to move out of the situation in some way, not necessarily leaving the country or the job, but perhaps by moving out of the bully's reach. We could suggest a move of team or office, for example, in this card.

Step 3: Use the sense of the card as a symbol for action.

Example: Our sense of "moving away" on a more fundamental level brings us to the original question and as a symbol signifies that we must move away from whatever answer feels most like home. So, whichever action makes us most uncomfortable and moves us away from our comfort zone is the one we must take. Here we might suggest that taking it up with the bully first is the answer, if the reporting route was the "home" or originally preferred solution.

Step 4: Break it down to a simple yes/no or affirmative/dissenting response.

Example: The act of quitting one's home shore or moving away is a somewhat negative or dissenting route. The card is thus a more negative card more than a positive one. In our example question, if we were to take it as "Should I go and report the bullying before doing anything else?" then the answer still agrees with the other layers, which is no.

This method should always start at the top layer and work down until you get to the appropriate level for the question, even if it is simply a one-word answer of positive or negative.

We should note that the reading of the 4 of Diamonds for a woman is about "getting a sweetheart" out of hand, and that may indicate something about the bullying situation, strangely enough.

This four-step method allows us to take any archaic meaning such as, "You will die of the pox" through the levels and remain true to the cartomantic core of the card:

1. You will get ill and your health will rapidly become worse.

2. Whatever you are doing is making you uneasy and needs to stop.

3. The answer to your question is to not take that step and do something else.

4. No, do not do it.

Now that we can perform a one- or two-card reading, and translate our card meanings and questions across time, we can start to look at larger spreads and methods, and at interpreting the overall look of the spread before reading individual cards.

Overall View of Cards in a Reading

When we perform a reading, we can first take an overview of the cards to get a general flavour of the interpretation. Over time, we will begin to recognise patterns for ourselves, much like a chess master learns pattern recognition of openings, mid-game, and endings rather than every possible combination of pieces and positions. As a beginner, we can take these set positions on their word or as patterns to look out for in our readings.

These patterns are where they are found in the overall majority of a reading or as a pair, depending on the spread or method being employed.

- **Diamonds + Clubs**: Rapid success in financial or material issues.

- **Hearts + Diamonds**: Energy and pleasure, enthusiasm.

- **Diamonds + Spades**: Accident and negativity.

- **Clubs + Hearts**: Stable relationship and authenticity.

- **Spades + Hearts**: Regret and unhappiness in relationship.

The Qualities of a Cartomancer

The requirements to be a wholly proficient card reader in 1872 is a little different from what would be expected today, but at the same not so; certain phases and beliefs never wane. In the book *Fortune-Telling by Cards,* ascribed to a Madame Camille Le Normand by the publisher (Robert M. De Witt), it was said that to "acquire proficiency in the art of divination" that one would have to possess such qualities as "patience and the ability to study." They stress that this would be very much needed, as card reading was "based purely upon mathematical principles." [64]

---

64   Madame Camille Le'Normand, *Fortune-Telling by Cards* (New York, NY: Robert M. De Witt, 1872), 13. This book, like so many others of its kind, was not written by any relative of Lenormand.

However, the book does assure us that "it can be learned by any person of ordinary capacity." At the time, there was a movement to promote the art of cartomancy as a pseudo-science; they warned of the perils of being taken in by those who "assert it to be a divine gift" as they were "simply charlatans and mountebanks" who are after pulling the wool over the eyes of the unsuspecting public. The emphasis was very much put upon the importance of a sound education in divination, one that equips the student with the "fundamental principles of cartomancy."

We are made aware that the writer considers those who believe that they are "the seventh children of the seventh children" are in some way deluding themselves, and that the notion that the ability to use divination is a gift that is bestowed only on those who have acquired it from a "supernatural origin, are merely impostures, as anyone can become equally, if not better gifted through a careful study of the oracular science." [65]

At the turn of that century, cartomancy was both consolation and amusement; it was a social activity, and it was proposed that it was something that could bring recognition and esteem to the card reader.

In modern-day parlance, the qualities required for the successful study of cartomancy and tarot (and Lenormand and oracle cards and runes, and so on) are much the same as any skill:

- Application

- Practice

- Study

- Commitment

- Knowledge of symbolism

- Self-awareness

- Experience of life

- Curiosity

- Structure

---

65   *Ibid.*

We will add to this list in our final chapter, with the responsibilities and qualities expected of the reader.

We can learn cartomancy most quickly by learning the art as we would learn a language; starting with the basic alphabet, then making words, then forming sentences, and conversation. As we progress, we must practice—and practice more—to tune our language into how it should best be spoken and communicated. Again, we can only do this with practice. Study and practice.

The Cartomantic Language

Here is an example to which we might perhaps aspire in terms of its precision although as ever, it may be unlikely that this delivery of a reading was so accurate:

Now, madam, immediately after your marriage you will depart (8 of Clubs) for the country (8 of Diamonds), where you will be received with glee and merriment, for the Ace and the King of Hearts announce your presence at some scene of festivity, where you encounter a number of country gentleman (the two Knaves), one of them a young man (Knave of Clubs), who once inspired to the honor of your hand. This festival will be given at the house of a country lady (Queen of Diamonds), where you will meet with a lady, a brunette, of about your own age, an old friend of yours who for reasons best known to herself, has deserted the city to live apart from her husband.

Now then, madam, for your surprise. Take the surprise card (King of Clubs) and place on your last card to your left (Queen of Clubs). Ah then, how surprised you will be to find that your friend and her husband are reconciled, for the cards tell me that they, being both of the same color, are reunited. [66]

Let us prepare ourselves to be that accurate about the following types of questions, derived from the antique fortune-telling books and like those asked of contemporary readers.

List of Top Twenty Cartomantic Questions

1. What position shall I hold among men?

2. Will my circumstances grow better?

---

66   *Ibid.*

3. Shall I foresee calumny?

4. Will my expectations be fulfilled?

5. Will my journey be a pleasant one?

6. Will my experience avail me?

7. Shall I be sustained?

8. What position shall I hold among friends?

9. Is my principle virtue justice?

10. Is my principle virtue temperance?

11. Is my principle virtue reliance?

12. Is my principle virtue prudence?

13. What will be the result of a marriage?

14. Shall I have strength to carry out my plans?

15. Shall I regain health?

16. What do others think of me?

17. Will I die?

18. Shall I be deceived?

19. Will I be imprisoned?

20. Will I become rich?[67]

In our next chapter, we will look at a selection of spreads that will answer these and many other questions using the meanings we have now covered. Let us set our time-pod for an English summer at the beach.

---

67   Collated from several fortune-telling books in private collection.

3

Cartomancy Methods

The first step in reading cards is to learn their meaning by heart. Using an old pack for practice, write the meaning of each card on its face. These cards may be used until the meanings are thoroughly committed to memory. The mystifying part of reading fortunes is gained chiefly by being able to glance at ordinary playing cards and tell what they mean.

—Fortune-Telling, 1927 [68]

19 June, 1978: Blackpool, England

We are getting used to traveling in time now, and this trip is comparatively short. We arrive mid-afternoon on the shore-front road known as the Golden Mile, where the trams are busy competing with the horse-drawn carriages and donkey rides on the beach for the summer trade. Everywhere there are holiday makers, young boys in tracksuit tops, girls with their short-cropped hair or perms according to the weekly trend. Everyone appears to be wearing bell-bottomed jeans, and the guys all sport huge collars. The girls scream loudly as they rocket around the Wild Mouse rollercoaster.

Along the shoreline are lined booths for hoopla, candy floss, and bubblegum. But it is not these to which we are drawn—not only are these booths dotted with fortune-tellers carrying the Petulengro name, but behind the front, in the ordinary houses in

---

68   Ruth E. Trappe, "Fortune-Telling by Playing Cards" (Washington Bureau Bulletin, 1927).

the shadow of the amusement park are fortune-tellers of a more recent variety, the kitchen-table tellers. The Romany gypsies have been camped at Blackpool since at least the 1840s, settling to the fortune-telling trade in the 1960s.

However, we are observing a young girl and her mother arriving at a small brick-built terrace house behind the South Shore area. They are greeted by the woman of the house's husband who takes them through to the small kitchen area. There they meet an ordinary-looking and elderly woman who goes simply by the name of Mrs. T.

The process is always the same: a few cursory pleasantries and then a small payment. Mrs. T asks for an item and holds it tightly for a while in her closed hand, her eyes closed. The woman visiting looks nervously at her daughter...she never visits the gypsies on the pier because they are a little too mystical for her taste. She prefers a straightforward medium like Mrs. T.

The daughter waits for her mother to ask the same question she always asks while Mrs. T puts down the ring and gets out her playing cards, laying them in fans across the smooth plane of the kitchen table. Her mother waits until the cards are ready and then asks as she always does: "Can you see anything about my health? Will I live to see my children grow up?"

After the reading, the mother and daughter walk out into the afternoon sun. The young daughter has been very attentive to the cards and the way in which Mrs. T was using them to tell the future. The mother appears satisfied with the answers; although the reader appeared hesitant, she has taken what was revealed to bode well for her health. She looks down at her daughter and gives her 5p. She smiles and says, "Go on, Tali, go and get yourself an ice cream."

In this chapter, we will look at a selection of cartomantic methods across time, including stars, fans, pyramids, and squares, to encourage our practice of card-reading for questions both vintage and contemporary.

Writing on Your Deck

When you first learn to read playing cards, do not be afraid to write text on a deck of playing cards. This was done with abandon on a deck created by the artist and occultist Austin Osman Spare (1886–1956) who was born into a working-class background in the

Smithfield area of London. He began his early career with much success, but as his biographer Phil Baker wrote, his trajectory as an artist was in reverse of the usual rags-to-riches story; "he began as a controversial West End celebrity and went on to obscurity in a South London basement." [69] His downfall has been attributed to his insistence that his "mystical practices lay behind the production of his artwork." [70]

9. Playing Card with Handwritten
Notes, created by Marcus Katz, 1985.

69 Jonathan Allen, *Lost Envoy: The Tarot Deck of Austin Osman Spare* (London, UK: Strange Attractor Press, 2016), 13.

70 *Ibid.*

The mystical etchings Spare left upon his cards open a full deck of possibilities and give us license to create.

In the creation of his fortune-telling tarot-like deck, Spare was influenced by the French style of cartomancy; he uses the suit symbols of hearts, clubs, spades, and diamonds, rather than the Italian-style iconography of cups, wands, swords, and coins/pentacles. We can see the influence of both Papus and Lévi in Spare's work. It was also said that the young Austin Spare learnt the skill of cartomancy from a mysterious female figure during his childhood called "the Witch Paterson." However, this was a period when there had been a spate of "how to read the future by the cards" books; they were very much in vogue. Spare was likely to have read *What the Cards Tell* by Minetta and "Professor" P. R. S. Foli's *Fortune Telling by Cards*; we have seen already how these books collected and popularised cartomantic knowledge. [71]

The deck—like yours—should also be a "self-instructive deck" with the writing on the cards teaching you to remember every time you perform a practice reading. Spare, for example, on the Ace of Hearts, wrote "THE HOUSE" and "habitation, success, fortune, riches, good news, envy" as keywords to aid the learning process. He uses the word "house" from a French method written within Foli's *Fortune Telling by Cards*.

We can also see Foli's further influence on Spare's Ace of Hearts. Foli has a list of the cards for a game and the meaning he gives for the Ace of Hearts is "a new house." Spare has written on the card "The HOUSE," and the meaning of the card reversed is written as "Change of residence." On the card, Spare has also written "engagement in the family."

Spare's following of Foli continues on the 10 of Hearts and the 10 of Diamonds, where we see in Foli's list he has 10 of Hearts and Diamonds as meaning "marriage settlements." In these few examples, we can see how Spare was influenced by Foli and how by writing on his cards he created his very own effective self-instructive deck.

In fact, one of the founders of the Golden Dawn also wrote keywords on their first deck. Here we show an example of W. W. Westcott's own European deck (prior to the work of the Golden Dawn on the tarot) and see that he has also written keywords for the cards in pencil.

---

71 P. R. S. Foli, *Fortune Telling by Cards*, c. 1902. Professor Foli was the pseudonym of Sir Cyril Arthur Pearson (1866–1921).

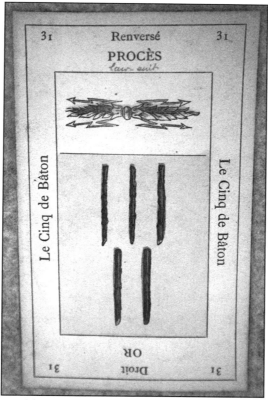

10. Tarot Card with Keyword written in the hand
of W. W. Westcott, c. 1888 (private collection).

We will now look at a range of spreads for cartomancy with playing cards. In any linear layout, emphasis is put more on the position of the card, rather than the card itself. The order of the cards can change the subject matter from being just about you and your action, to being all about the action of somebody else. Remember the card always influences the card next to it, right to left. We see this in the following example:

- **Ace of Clubs + Ace of Diamonds** = YOU will write a love letter.

- **Ace of Diamonds + Ace of Clubs** = A love letter will be written to YOU.

We will also introduce now the idea of a Significator, which is the card often used to represent the querent, querist, sitter, or client in the spread.

Choosing a Significator

You could say that the most significant part of a reading is the querent, and in cartomancy, this is decided by the querent choosing a Court card from the pack that most represents their personality. There are several ways of choosing the significator from the pack of cards, and we will provide one to time travellers as a basis. You are encouraged to explore alternatives in the future.

The way the significator is chosen is by matching their physicality and personality to the Court cards. In doing so, we consider age (maturity or youth), gender, physical appearance, profession, and personality. In later years, there are systems for corresponding the sun sign of astrology, the birthdate, or even the Myers-Brigg Type Indicator label to the court cards. Vintage methods are far less elaborate. As an example, "Minetta" wrote that "knaves … represent young men, soldiers, lovers and traitors."[72]

The spades are representative of "very dark people, widows and widowers" and clubs are "not so dark, brown eyes." The hearts have "fair, blue eyes" and diamonds are "very fair, red-haired, grey-haired, widows and widowers." Minetta also elaborated on this cartomantic profiling by saying "It is well to judge the Significator's coloring by the eyes." Further, "a club, if a widow, becomes a spade, and if a heart, becomes a diamond."[73]

The Significators

Spades: Very dark people, widows and widowers.

Clubs: Not so dark, brown eyes.

Diamonds: Very fair, red-haired, grey-haired, fair, widows and widowers.

Hearts: Fair, blue eyes.

Clubs

King: Generous man, straight-forward.

Queen: Loving, forgiving.

Knave: Lover [a down-to-earth character].

---

72 Minetta, *What the Cards Tell* (London, UK: 1896), 15.
73 *Ibid.*

Hearts

King: Kind man.

Queen: Fair woman.

Knave: Cupid [a romantic lover].

Knave of Hearts is of no sex, and always shows the **best friend** of the consulter. [74]

Spades

King: Widower, lawyer.

Queen: Widowhood.

Knave: Professional man.

Diamonds

King: Grey-haired man.

Queen: Widow, friend.

Knave: Military.

If you are reading for a child or a pet, use the 7 of Diamonds. [75]

We will now begin our spreads by looking at a basic method using the four aces. We will also make suggestions for using these spreads with tarot so you can revisit this chapter with tarot knowledge at any point in your time travels.

The Ace of Base

This technique uses the aces of the pack in a very simple way. [76]

We use a thirty-two-card Piquet-style deck for this method, comprising the French-suited deck of thirty-two cards, consisting of aces, 7, 8, 9, 10, jacks, queens, and kings.

---

74   *Ibid.*, 16.

75   *Ibid.*, 17.

76   This method adapted from Cicely Kent, *Telling Fortunes by Cards* (London, UK: Herbert Jenkins Limited, n.d.).

First, take the four aces out of the deck and lay them out into the position of a cross. Place the Ace of Clubs at the top, the Ace of Spades at the bottom, the Ace of Hearts on the right and the Ace of Diamonds on the left.

The remaining twenty-eight cards are then handed to the querent, and we ask them to focus deeply on the question they are asking the cards and to shuffle the cards well once more. When they are quite satisfied that they have forged a connection with the cards, take the cards back. Next lay out all twenty-eight cards, as follows: the first card on the Ace of Clubs at the top, the second card on the Ace of Spades at the base, the third is placed on the Ace of Hearts to the right, and the fourth on the left upon the Ace of Diamonds. Continue placing the cards down in this order until you have exhausted all the twenty-eight cards. There should be seven cards on each of the four aces.

We now turn over each of the four stacks and read the seven cards together.

If the Wish Card (9 of Hearts) and the Significator of the person (a chosen court card) appear in the same stack, this is a good sign of general success in the situation.

Tarot Version

In the tarot version of this method, we lay out the four aces in the same way, with the Ace of Wands at the top, the Ace of Swords at the bottom, the Ace of Cups on the right, and the Ace of Pentacles on the left.

We then lay out seven cards on each Ace in the same manner but from a shuffle of the remaining seventy-four tarot cards. Some time travellers may realise that this type of method is the pre-cursor for the Golden Dawn method called "Opening of the Key."

When we read the tarot in this way, we can correspond the four stacks to their themes and read the cards contained in each stack as applying to that aspect of our lives, making it a more rudimentary tarot spread.

1. **Ace of Wands (Fire)** = World of activity, enthusiasm, confidence, success, energetic attitudes, competitive nature, ideas, innovation, sleeplessness, living on nerves, highly strung, motivation, driven.

2. **Ace of Swords (Air)** = World of intellect, reasoning, decision making, organization, management, education.

3. **Ace of Cups (Water)** = World of emotion, over sensitivity, nurturance, worry, love, psychic ability.

4. **Ace of Pentacles (Earth)** = World of security, money, investment, training, application, practicalities, building, greed, banking, resources.

The Star of Fortune

This quick technique uses thirteen cards and divines for a person who is not present. [77]

Take a court card to represent the person for whom the reading is being conducted and place it central on your table.

Shuffle the rest of the deck and focus on the question while you do so. Then cut the pack into three piles, and turn them face-up. The three top cards can be read as an overall prognosis of the reading. Again, this is another element that is picked up in the later Golden Dawn "Opening of the Key" method.

Now collect together the cut cards into one deck again and lay out the cards around the significator as illustrated, creating a star. [78]

The original publisher of this method tells us that if the 9 or 10 of Hearts comes out as the thirteenth card, this is lucky, but not so the 9 of Spades, which would bring ruin to the situation. In early cartomancy, there was a clearer division of good and bad cards, and a more fatalist regard to their significance. However, mitigating that was a general idea that the cards were merely a parlour game and not to be taken seriously overall.

In the early version of this method too were indications of overall interpretations by suit and number, for example, if three nines appear, it shows delays and that patience will be required. Four kings would indicate good regard, social standing, and honors. The card at the top of the significator also has a large influence (as we see in our encounter with Lenormand cards in a later time zone) so we hope to get a heart card there, rather than a spade.

---

77 Kent, *Telling Fortune by Cards*.

78 Time travellers may also see some similarity of this layout to the "Celtic Cross" first published by A. E. Waite but also circulated in the Golden Dawn from where he published it. See *Tarosophist International* Vol. 2 for a full history of that spread.

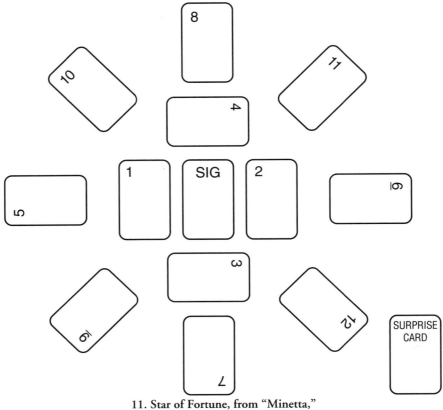

11. Star of Fortune, from "Minetta,"
What the Cards Tell, 1896.

Diamonds overall are most influenced by the cards near them, so they take on a negative aspect with spades, and a positive one with hearts. Clubs are generally positive.

The bottom of this spread relates to the past, and the top to the future, so if there are negative cards at the bottom and more positive ones at the top, it shows that someone has gone through a challenging time but is coming out of it. The reverse can also be the case.

As we will see in our Lenormand chapter, a significator or "key card" can be used for a specific subject rather than the person themselves. So, if we wanted to read for a question about an official matter, letters, awaiting contracts, etc., we would use the Ace of Clubs; for money matters, the Ace of Diamonds; and for the house or love, the Ace of Hearts. We would not use the Ace of Spades as it is a generally negative card.

The cards in this spread can be read in pairs, above, below, and to the sides of the significator, and as the single cards at the top and bottom, influenced by the cards paired to either side.

Advanced Method: Reading a Narrative

In this method, we simply draw cards one at a time and tell a story from their appearance, linking each card to another in sequence. This requires some reasonable knowledge of the cards, or plenty of time to piece the story together. Again, as we see with so many early methods, these were incorporated into the Golden Dawn and then re-surfaced in the twenty-first century with the refund popularity of the Lenormand. As both the Golden Dawn methods and the Lenormand were closer to early cartomancy, ironically, esotericists who were practiced in the Golden Dawn methods often found the transition to Lenormand reading a more natural process rather than straight tarot readers who were used to fixed spreads and positional meanings.

These tailored readings need to consider where the client is now; as a reader, you guide them through the narrative. It is more useful to find out from the clients as much as they are happy to divulge before commencing this style of reading.

Discuss with the client what is going on in their lives at present, do not focus too much on the past, but where they are now in their lives, and where they would like to be. Ask about family, friends, and romantic relationships. Encourage them to talk about the environment in which they live, work, and socialise. Discuss their likes and dislikes. Consider how they present themselves and their personality. As the original instructions often say about this type of reading, "make a smooth and interesting story."

The Name Method

This technique draws upon using the clients initials to construct a spread.

Take for example the three initials A V G, where someone has a middle name. Work out the three initials' corresponding order in the alphabet.

- **A** = 1
- **V** = 22
- **G** = 7

Shuffle your tarot deck well and then remove the first card from the deck, this represents the letter "A" of the client's initials.

Shuffle again and then remove the twenty-second card from the deck, this represents the letter "V" of the client's initials.

Shuffle the remaining cards one last time and then remove the seventh card from the deck, this represents the letter "G" from the client's initials.

Lay out the three cards in the form of a triangle (or the top of a pyramid), or as a pair side-by-side if there are just two letters.

Read these two or three cards together.

The Birthday Method

To use birthday cards, simply refer to the client's birthdate. We will use 8 May in our example.

We shuffle the deck and take out the fifth card to correspond to the month, and then reshuffle and take out the eighth card to correspond to the day.

We then read these as a pair.

Name and Birthday Combination Method

We can also combine the two previous readings doing both and by laying out the birthday cards beneath the name cards, forming a square or the base of a triangle.

Reading for a Dream

When cards appear in a dream, they have similar significance. These common interpretations ascribed to dreams in their relationship to our everyday lives are from a vintage teaching booklet from the "Washington Bureau":

Cards: To dream of playing cards denotes of wealth, love and marriage. Each card has the same significance as in fortune-telling. Many picture cards, a fortunate and wealthy marriage. Mostly diamonds, quarrels; spades, hard work; clubs, happiness and wealth; hearts, love, honor and prosperity. To dream of holding the Joker indicates a false friend.[79]

You can also read for a dream and its significance by choosing a significator that relates to a key item in the dream and then using any standard spread as may be relevant. So, a dream about discovering a strange house would be best read by using the Ace of Hearts. If you dream of driving in a car, we would use the 2 of Spades as a significator (see previous chapter).

Many of the kitchen-table readers throughout these years would have made-up meanings, learnt them from others, or gained them from the few books of the "Professor Foli" variety. However, there was another current that would carry cartomancy to the future, away from the esoteric orders and into the modern-day of the time—women's magazines. The history of cartomancy would be written across these magazines until the 1960s and the new era of tarot revival.

The "missing years" of cartomancy were being carried in plain sight through the 1930s to the 1950s by women's magazines, supplements, and—after awhile—mail order courses.

Here we see one example of the supplements that were so popular: "Palmistry and Fortune Telling at Parties" from *Woman Magazine*, 6 December, 1952. On the front cover of the pamphlet we have a blonde Grace Kelly look-alike who gazes longingly up into her partner's eyes. It is captioned: *Here's Magic!*

The magazine supplement describes the techniques within as "spell-binding," and that the sixteen-page supplement will "give you and your friends hours of fun." In fact, the social status of a reader is guaranteed: "Take your supplement to a party, and the guests will clamor for you to stay on and on!" What a brilliant marketing method.

Following the next two magazine covers, we present a summary of card meanings for your reference.

---

79 Washington Bureau Pamphlets in private collection.

12. Cover, *Woman's Own*, 13 January, 1934.

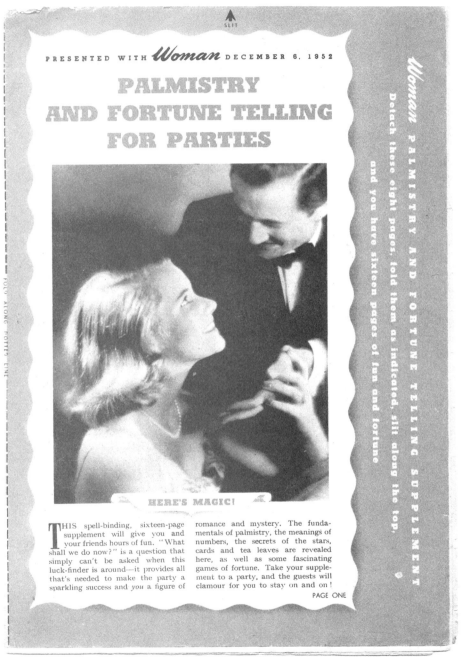

PRESENTED WITH *Woman* DECEMBER 6, 1952

PALMISTRY AND FORTUNE TELLING FOR PARTIES

HERE'S MAGIC!

THIS spell-binding, sixteen-page supplement will give you and your friends hours of fun. "What shall we do now?" is a question that simply can't be asked when this luck-finder is around—it provides all that's needed to make the party a sparkling success and *you* a figure of romance and mystery. The fundamentals of palmistry, the meanings of numbers, the secrets of the stars, cards and tea leaves are revealed here, as well as some fascinating games of fortune. Take your supplement to a party, and the guests will clamour for you to stay on and on !

PAGE ONE

Woman PALMISTRY AND FORTUNE TELLING SUPPLEMENT

Detach these eight pages, fold them as indicated, slit along the top, and you have sixteen pages of fun and fortune

SLIT

FOLD ALONG DOTTED LINE

13. Cover, *Woman Magazine*, 6 December, 1952.

What the Cards Reveal

Hearts

Hearts are the cards of love and friendship.

The Ace of Hearts indicates pleasant surprise connected with affection or love for someone.

2, 3, 4, 5, 6: These cards mean something to do with a friend that will not involve the emotions deeply. It may mean a letter, a present, or a visit.

7, 8, 9, 10: Love affairs. Watch for the wish card, **9 of Hearts**, (in the Waite-Smith tarot, the corresponding 9 of Cups denotes repletion, satisfaction, finding yourself in a very favorable position).

Clubs

The cards of travel, work, and business.

The Ace of Clubs signifies a long journey.

2, 3, 4, 5, 6: These cards suggest short travels (not outside the country); some change is likely about work and is likely to occur quite soon.

7, 8, 9, 10: These signify longer journeys, visits of considerable length. The 9 and 10 always indicate crossings by sea.

Diamonds

The cards relating to money matters.

The Ace of Diamonds means an unforeseen gift or a surprise legacy.

2, 3, 4, 5, 6: Indicate small profits, rises, bonuses, or any slight material gain. A heart card following foretells an unexpected gift from someone of the opposite sex.

7, 8, 9, 10: These show changes for the better. If next to the 9 of Hearts, expect money to come with marriage. The higher the card, the more prosperous the match.

Spades

The cards of trouble and disagreements.

The Ace of Spades indicate an unpleasant surprise of some nature.

2, 3, 4, 5, 6: These cards show a minor illness, disappointment, and misunderstandings. Work may be difficult and associates trying.

7, 8, 9, 10: These normally mean a more serious upset. Be careful if you are embarking on a new venture. Take special care of the health.

The Picture (Court) Cards: Represent the people in your life whose appearance you can guess by consulting the suit of the card.

The **Kings** signify older men, very often fathers or employers. They are usually in a positon of authority. The **King of Hearts**, a man of medium-fair coloring. The **King of Spades**, a very dark man. The **King of Diamonds**, a man with fair or white hair. The **King of Clubs**, a man with brown hair and eyes.

The **Queens** are the women in a person's life. Usually the **Queen of Hearts** signifies a fair, friendly woman, and the **Queen of Spades**, a dark or antagonistic woman. The **Queen of Diamonds** is a blonde with blue eyes. The **Queen of Clubs** is a brunette with dark eyes or a woman with red hair.

The **Jacks** are single young men. **Jack of Hearts**; a young man with light brown hair or grey or hazel hair. **Jack of Spades**; a man with black hair and dark eyes. **Jack of Diamonds**; fair and blue-eyed or with hair that is "carroty"; **Jack of Clubs**: a man with medium brown hair and deep brown eyes. [80]

Having added these vintage meanings to our cards, we will now turn to a fun cartomantic method for parties called "Make a Wish" and several other classic spreads.

Make a Wish

Ask a guest to make a wish, and the cards will tell if it is likely or certain to come true.

---

80   This set of meanings collated from various magazines of the time.

Give a full pack of cards to the wish-maker, telling him or her to make a wish while cutting the pack. Now deal the cards face downwards. As you deal, tell the wish-maker to pick out three cards at random. Put these three cards on the table, face upwards, in the order chosen. Counting tens and picture cards as zero, add up the value of the three cards. If the total can be divided by three or seven (lucky numbers), then the wish has a very good chance of coming true. If it can be divided by **both** numbers 3 and 7, it is almost certain to come true.

If unlucky, the wish-maker may make another wish and try again.

The Five Heaps

We will now describe a form of divination that furnishes the enquirer with answers under definite subjects.

The thirty-two cards must be thoroughly shuffled and handed to the enquirer to be cut with his or her left hand. While cutting the cards, they should, as ever, quietly formulate a wish of what they would like to know of the outcome. Now spread out the thirty-two cards out face downwards on the table and ask the enquirer to select thirteen of them. The remaining cards are to be set aside, while the thirteen cards chosen must be taken up, shuffled, and cut once more by the enquirer, again with the left hand.

The reader must then deal them out from left to right into five heaps, three of which contain three cards each, while the others have two cards. These heaps correspond from left to right in order, to the enquirer himself; their home and intimate circle; that which they expect to come about; surprise happenings; and lastly, the wish whose outcome they were anxious to have revealed.

An Old Italian Method

Here is another method, one that has apparently been used for centuries and enjoyed popularity among the gifted cartomancers of Italy.

After having shuffled the pack of thirty-two cards, request the enquirer to cut them with their left hand. Now turn up the first three cards on the top of the pack. If they chance to be all of one suit, lay them down one after another in a row from left to right and in the same order in which they appeared in the pack. If, however, they contain only two cards of the same suit, chose the higher of these two; but if the three cards are of different suits, they should be all thrown aside.

Thus, if the three cards taken from the pack happened to be the King, Knave, and 7 of Diamonds, they would all be laid in the row; if the Queen and the 9 of Spades appeared together with the King of Hearts, the Queen of Spades would be chosen; and if the three cards consisted of the King of Clubs, the 8 of Hearts, and the Ace of Diamonds—all different suits—they would all be discarded.

Go through this procedure with all the cards in the pack, taking them in threes. It will be found, of course, that only two cards are left, and unless these are both same suit—in which case the higher card is chosen—they should be discarded. Some authorities would reject these two cards in any case, and since there seems to be no outstanding reason why the portends should be affected whichever method is followed, the student may please himself regarding the course to adopt.

When the pack has been exhausted, the rejected cards must be reshuffled and the whole process repeated and so on until fifteen cards have been extracted. If more than that number are put down, reduce them to fifteen by taking away the requisite number from the left. It is important that these fifteen cards include the card of the enquirer (that is to be identified on the lines already described); if this card fails to appear, the whole divination must be repeated from the beginning—from the shuffling and cutting of the pack—until the required king or queen materialises.

When the fifteen cards have been assembled in a row, call the enquirer's own card one, and starting from it, from left to right, shift slightly out of the row the third, seventh, ninth, and thirteenth cards, reverting to the beginning of the row when you come to the last card on the right-hand side. Read the interpretations of these cards in order according to the tables given previously.

To complete the divination, take up a card from each end of the row of the fifteen, and read the meanings of the pairs together. Continue to read the cards in pairs until one card only is left—the "surprise" card, which should be regarded as furnishing the final revelation of the enquirer's fate and fortune.

The Rapid Method

The following is an extremely rapid method of revealing a person's destiny, though it is a matter of question whether it is as dependable as the more thorough methods we have given.

Request the enquirer to shuffle the cards thoroughly, cut them and hand them back to you. Now spread out the pack face downwards on the table, and ask the enquirer to choose thirteen cards at random. Arrange these cards in a row facing upwards in the order they were chosen, and read out their meanings. A second row of thirteen cards similarly selected and spread out below the first will serve to modify or confirm their predictions.

An even shorter method useful for deciding any single question consists of dealing the first seven cards of the pack in a row and reading the omens of the first, fourth, and seventh cards.

The Wishing Card Method

Hold the cards out in a fan shape face down. Ask the client to choose a random card from the deck. Take this card from the client, look at it and note it, then insert it back into the deck.[81]

The next step is to ask the client to shuffle the deck and focus deeply on a *wish* they would like to come true. Silence and focus is to be maintained during this time. When the client feels the wish has absorbed into the cards sufficiently, take the cards back and search through the deck for the original card they pulled from the deck.

Once you have located it, if it is within seven cards of the Ace of Hearts, the 9 of Hearts, or the significator card representing your client, their wish will come true. However, if the 9 of Spades is within seven cards of either side, even if the client's wish has come true, it will not come without complications. In fact, it may ultimately turn out to be not what they wanted, as the old saying "take care for what you wish for" cautions.

The deck can be shuffled a further two times and the process repeated with a fresh wish. When counting seven cards either side, you can tell or interpret as much or as little as you feel necessary. Even if the client is not successful in the pulling of their wish, you can still interpret the card on either side of the original wish card they selected and explain why they were not granted their wish.

---

81 *Woman's Own* magazine, January 1934, via Claire Langhamer, *The English in Love: The Intimate Story of an Emotional Revolution* (Oxford, UK: Oxford University Press, 2013), 202.

The By Fifteen Method

In this method, we use fifteen playing cards to look at the past, future, obstacles, immediate concerns, and the "luck" of a situation. This is the seventh method given by Minetta in *What the Cards Tell* (1896) and is to some extent a crude version of the Celtic Cross A. E. Waite used in *The Key to the Tarot* (1910) as is the second method, a Star Cross.

We will select a relationship question from 1956 given in *Never Kiss a Man in a Canoe* (2009), the collection of Agony Aunt questions compiled by Tanith Carey. This question was published in *Home Chat* magazine (published 1895–1959).

> **Q:** I am twenty-three and have had lots of bad boyfriends but have only just met one who wants to be serious. But I'm a bit afraid that he is old-fashioned in his ideas—he wants me to change my style completely. He says that I use too much make-up, smoke too much and drink too much; in fact, he describes me as "a sweet girl giving the wrong impression!" I'm rather in love with this boy, but I'm afraid that he is going to be too strict for me. [82]

The Method

Take a pack of ordinary playing cards, throw aside all the under-seven cards, reserving the aces. You will now have thirty-two cards.

Any cards that are the same both ways should be marked, as their meanings are changed when reversed.

> Shuffle your cards, having placed the significator on the table. Take three cards from the top of the pack; place them at the head for luck, three at the feet for the past, three on the right for the future, three on the left for the obstacles, and three on yourself for what is immediately crossing your path. [83]

Minetta states that it is a lucky omen if the 9 of Hearts or the Ace of Clubs (upright), crowns your significator.

I chose the Queen of Hearts as the significator.

---

82 Carey, 89.

83 Minetta, 35.

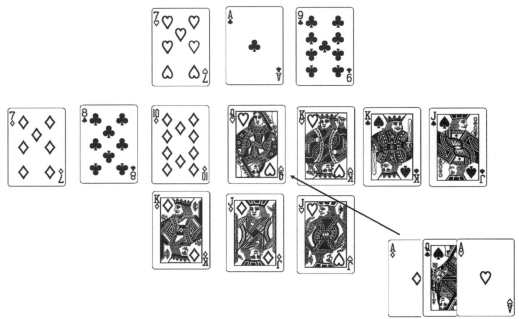

14. **By Fifteen Layout, from "Minetta",** *What the Cards Tell,* 1896.

Immediately in this reading we have a very positive omen with the Ace of Clubs, the right way up, crowning the significator.

The three cards at the foot of the spread are; King of Diamonds, Knave (Jack) of Diamonds, Knave of Hearts. These signify the past and we look at these cards first to look at how the present situation has arisen, and if there are any clues in the past to the future progression.

The appearance of the King of Diamonds literally at her feet signifies "a grey-haired man" according to Minetta (whose meanings we will adopt throughout this method). In doing so we can also see how stark and simple meanings do not have to be constraining and can be interpreted to any question or situation beyond their literal meaning. This is something that often confuses beginner cartomantic readers because they might not be able to immediately apply old-fashioned or one-word meanings such as "Cupid" or "Night" to a modern business reading, for example. In those cases, the card meaning "Cupid" could be read as "doing something you love as your business" whereas the second card might mean that there would be a period of stumbling about in the dark before the business made any progress.

If we look to the "cartomantic core" of any given card meaning, we can soon build up from it and apply it to any situation.

The King of Diamonds then is appropriate to our question as the enquirer talks about her new boyfriend's old-fashioned ways. Minetta also says that the card could "predict money." We take this to imply that the relationship will give her security in life. In fact, she will literally have security at her feet; it is a relationship based on a firm footing. But is that what she wants and at what cost?

We next look at the two cards of the same rank paired together, the Knave of Diamonds and the Knave of Hearts. In the pairings, we see that these two cards together mean "consultation." Having two Knaves together would also tell us that there is another man on the scene, probably one that would not be mentioned in a real reading situation.

This other man is the Knave of Hearts, which according to Minetta could be of a military background. In a contemporary setting this may still be the case or indicate a "martial" type of personality such as someone more aggressive or direct.

These two cards, both in the past position, signify that he is an old flame of hers, particularly as we know from the question that she has had a lot of boyfriends. The two cards in the past show us that she is torn between her old lifestyle and her future path.

We now look to her future cards, with the knowledge of the past to guide us.

The three cards that we have on the right, for the future, are the King of Hearts, King of Spades, and Knave of Spades. The King of Hearts touches the Queen of Hearts and is paired with the King of Spades; Minetta says that two kings together signify friendship. Here it is shown that in the future she should keep her new relationship on a friendship basis. She is certainly not a woman who drinks alone, going by the amount of court cards in this spread.

We now look at the obstacles before reading any further into the future cards. The three cards on the left, representing obstacles, are 7 of Diamonds, 8 of Clubs, and the 10 of Diamonds.

Minetta says that the 7 of Diamonds could signify a child or a pet, so it is now shown that the woman already has a child. The 8 of Clubs signifies a previous relationship, one that still attracts her, with "a man of clubs," i.e., described by the suit of clubs. This is most likely a dark-haired man, and the military man we have already seen on the table.

However, the obstacle here is also the man who offers her security, our King of Diamonds who lays security at her feet.

When we look next at the three cards placed directly on top of the significator, for what is "immediately crossing her path," we see Ace of Diamonds, Queen of Spades, and Ace of Hearts.

The first is "a ring" and "a bank note!" The Queen of Spades signifies widowhood, implying that she may feel like a widow if she marries the wealthy man who tries to control her life and does not allow her to truly be herself. We also see the presence of the Ace of Hearts, which signifies "house; love letter" and could imply that communications from the other man will prove to be an obstacle.

Finally, looking at the top three cards, for "luck" or opportunities, we can see that the Ace of Clubs does bring luck, and the two side cards are the 7 of Hearts and the 9 of Clubs. These variously indicate a business or long journey, with amusement (9 of Clubs) so that would indicate she should try and go on a business trip with the man and that will give the opportunity to resolve this matter. Similarly, the 7 of Hearts indicates that this is a matter of jealousy on his part; perhaps he wishes to live a freer life and is projecting resentment on her. We can see here again that sometimes Kitchen Table methods can be psychologically insightful.

Conclusion

In this chapter, we have looked at several methods that represent classic cartomancy and may be further developed as you practice. You can build up your repertoire with several spreads and then modify them once you have got the basics and found which keywords from the previous chapter work best for you.

In our next chapter, we will provide a vintage method that showcases many of the ideas about cartomancy, and provides a very performance-driven experience when you offer it to clients, friends, or family. We will set our tarot time pod with the key phrase "square of sevens" and see where—or when—it will take us.

The Square of Sevens

It is safe to presume that even the most inquisitive book-hunters of the present day, and few of the fellowship during two or three generations past, have encountered the scarce and curious little volume here presented, as in a friendly literary resurrection—Robert Autobus's "The Square of Sevens, and the Parallelogram…Its mathematical title hardly hints at the amusement that the book affords.

—*The Square of Sevens*, 1896

It seems our time travel is being interrupted or we cannot get a fix on our next acquisition. We are tracking the publication of a strange and detailed method of cartomancy, but our time-pod keeps shifting in its tracking across America and Europe through the late 1800s to the mid-1900s. Yet the method is said to have come from Cornwall, in 1731. Resetting our sensors, we are whisked to Lausanne, and then back in time to Madison, New Jersey, to the home of a Presbyterian minister in 1858. At no point are we locking on the 1700s. This is very strange. We end up at one point in Naples, 1908, locked on to the publication of a book called IMRE: A MEMORANDUM, which is said to be the first overtly homosexual novel (with a positive ending) and appears under a pen name: "Xavier Mayne." We are used to strange occurrences in our tarot time travels, but this one is very odd. We call up a time screen, and it shows that the author of this novel travels widely, writes for the *Independent* and *Harper's Weekly* amongst other publications, and was trained as a lawyer. We should set down our time-pod here in Naples, perhaps, and survey our machine for damage to its sensors.

When we time travel, we must be careful of false avenues, of which there are many in the cartomantic world. Equally, however, there is no such thing as an accidental oracle—everything comes from somewhere, even if we make it up.

One such avenue is the curious case of the *Square of Sevens*. This was a tract on a singular-card fortune-telling method written by Edward Irenaeus Prime-Stevenson (1858–1942), one of America's earliest gay authors, published in 1896. He wrote many different types of literature, under a bewildering range of pseudonyms, dealing with music, travel, poetry, and fiction—and children's books and cartomancy, the latter in the *Square of Sevens*. [84] He used literary devices in his works, often making use of translation between languages to make subtle allusions.

In the booklet, Prime-Stevenson alleges that a "Robert Antrobus" first published the method privately in 1735 based on an encounter of that man with a gypsy. It is the same type of story we have already seen repeated in 1955 by the author of the Yes/No method in *Fate* magazine.

He goes on to remark in the editorial preface that "Fortune-telling with cards and belief in fortune-telling with cards—like a hundred greater and lesser follies of the mind—were straws floating along the current of British life, intellectual and social, during the reign of George the Second." [85]

He calls the method "that most particular and potent method of prying into the past and present and future" and suggests that whilst it may appear complicated, it is effective:

And, by the way, the reader will please observe in his pages here following that though the method of "building" and so of forming the "Square," and of "reducing" it, seems at first glance bothersome and complicated, it is only a childishly easy performance in

84 See James Gifford, "Left to Themselves: The Subversive Boys Books of Edward Prime-Stevenson (1858–1942)" in *Journal of American & Comparative Cultures,* Vol. 24, Issue 3–4, Fall/Winter 2001, 113–116. Also see Mary K. Greer blog at https://marygreer.wordpress.com/2008/04/03 /a-hoax-revealed-update-on-the-square-of-sevens/for the debunking of Prime-Stevenson's fake history of the alleged author and history of the method (last accessed June 2016).

85 E. Irenaeus Stevenson, *The Square of Sevens* (New York: Harper & Brothers, 1896).

the way of making a square of seven rows of seven cards, and then of making the rows only three cards deep, at most![86]

We present here the method of the Square of Sevens, which we have also found "not ineffective in a drawing-room" and a condensed version of the *Tavola*; the table of meanings Prime-Stevenson provides from the almost-certainly fictional Antrobus. It also provides a perfect cartomantic bridge between our first chapters on standard cartomancy, our following Lenormand chapter and into the use of tarot in the final chapters.

Firstly, we will add to our suit lexicon:

- **Hearts**: Affections, passions, fancies, and feelings.

- **Clubs**: Judgment, intellect, will, mastery.

- **Diamonds**: Position, wealth, society.

- **Spades**: Doubt, risk, bad luck.

We now provide the meanings given by "Antrobus" in his *Tavola*, or table of meanings. Each card is given a meaning as a "Master-Card" and then separately, influenced by each suit and sometimes particular cards. These will become clear in the instructions for the method following the *Tavola*.

Hearts

The Ace

As Master-Card, a special Emotional Experience. Influenced by a king of like suit, there is figured an Intimate Friend, or one in whom the Querist is much bound. By a Queen of like Suit—an Emotion for a Woman of beauty and charm. By a Knave of like Suit, an Attachment to a Man younger than the Querist. Influenced by any high heart other than those above, an Amorous or Affectionate Temper of mind or body. By a low heart, an impressionable, kindly Nature. These are Five Special Interpretings. The more general are: influenced by a Diamond, Good Fortune in something, measured by the degree of the

---

86 *ibid.*

Influencing Card. By a Club, a Talent or Gift to be made much of. By a Spade, an Error, or Disappointment, in the degree of the influencing card.

The King

As Master-Card, is figured that the Querist deals or has had much to do with a Man of fair skin and light type, of good temperament. Influenced by an Ace of like suit, one notably unselfish. By Knave, a Lover, Husband, Friend. By a Queen, a Love-match. By a Diamond, a Man of Wealth or artistic nature. By a high club, a Man of Energy withal; by a low club, one of Prudence. By a Spade, a man of some defect of Temperament, or of a Chronic Malady or Blemish, ominous to him and others.

The Queen

As Master-Card, is referred to specially, an amiable, affectionate Woman, rather one sentimental than of intellect. Influenced by like suit, if an Ace, she is admired of many; if a King, she is wedded, betrothed, or beloved by one in especial. By a Knave of like suit, she is beloved by a Male Relative in especial, not of her own near family. By other cards of like suit, degrees of regard. By a Diamond, a Woman gifted, and esteemed much in Modish Life. By a Club, though not learned she appreciates knowledge in others. By a Spade, she is not of firm health; or not of wholly firm Virtue.

The Knave

As Master-Card—the Querist's closest Friend; yet likely held such because of feeling rather than judgment. Influenced by an Ace of like suit, there is no Inequality in the affection. By a King of like suit, Resemblance to the Querist in physique or mind or disposition. By a Queen of like suit, one with distinctively feminine traits. By another card of like suit, a popular man with his fellows. By a diamond, of wealth or social Position; but if by a 9 of Diamonds, not enduring in such Happy Fortune. By a Club, a Friend of judgment and good at advice. By a Spade, a Friend of not too sound health: or apt of offence.

Ten

As Master-Card, a general reference to Matrimony, as being ever the card-matrimonial. Influenced by like suit, a High-Marriage and that auspicious: by a low heart, a Marriage not one's first or first-wished. By a Diamond, a Marriage with money in it. By a Club, a Marriage of reason or of circumstances. By a Spade, an Interrupted or more or less Disastrous Match.

Nine

As Master-Card, a Card of Good Augury for what we wish for Another. Influenced by its like suit, an unexpected Meeting, with a person much affected or desired. By a Diamond, a Pleasure in store. By a Club, a Wish partly fulfilled, rather than wholly. By a Spade, a Wish fulfilled but followed by some detrimental Event.

Eight

As Master-Card, a Love-Interest. As influenced by like suit, an Interest of much Romance. By a Diamond, a Lost Article recovered. By a Club, the Victory in a difference or argument as to some plan or act. By a Spade, a Caprice to warm the heart; or a new Article of dress or household stuff.

Seven

As Master-Card: the Card of Trust and Confidence approved of. Influenced by like suit, honest Love, or Family regard. By a Diamond, wise Trust in a commercial or social step. By a Club, in a Secret. By a Spade, Confidence misplaced in a person or event.

Six

As Master-Card, a strong Inclination, a Desire, or Action is well rewarded. Influenced by like suit, it concerns another even more than ourselves, or as much. By a Diamond, a step of social or artistic or pecuniary vantage; save if the diamond be the nine, which leaves the result in Doubt of full success. By a Club, a Matter of Judgment and practical bearing, seen and discussed of others; or a Remark, or a Letter of more consequence than would appear. By a Spade, an Inclination or desire, not wholly honorable: or of brief realization.

Five

As Master-Card, an amusing and diverting Affair heard of, or entered into. Influenced by its like suit, a Feeling not hitherto returned is met at last. By a Diamond, a Success in something particularly wished. By a Club, a keen and shrewd Chance at a remark to be well caught. By a Spade, an Ache, Pain, or Breaking.

Four

As Master-Card, is figured the existence of an obstinate Sentiment toward one, or an Opinion not of our own building up. Influenced by the like suit, it is troublesome, causing thought, new to one, or burdensome. By a Diamond, it is known to others, or guessed. By a Club, it is apt to lead to acts officious or of manoeuvre. By a Spade, it is a Sentiment based on error and lack of full insight; or it will be abruptly weakened.

Three

An Act of Charity and Generosity, by or toward the Querist, if read as Master-Card. Influenced by like suit, Action in a matter of very confidential sort. By a Diamond, it is in part a Matter of Money or Office or from a Superior—and may be associated with an investment, a society, an entertainment. By a Club, it figures a Visit, or Visitor. By a Spade, a Change of Opinion in some near matter is enjoined, or the Loss of a good will; or a Surprise not welcome wholly.

Two

As Master-Card, favorable News, or a Letter acceptable. If influenced by its like suit, the Person from whom it comes, or also referred to in it, is much valued, or a near Relative. By a Diamond, a Present, a Visit, a Meeting of service, a Letter, respectively. By a Club, a "yes" in a matter open. By a Spade, it concerns Another more than the Querist; or else will not be altogether correct in statement.

Diamonds

The Ace

As Master-Card, a tangible and material Success in some Matter of Society, Money, Art, or Office. Influenced by a King of like suit, a Loss recovered. By any other card of like suit, Information and certainty of an Affair of purchase, bargain or sale, much to advantage. By a Heart, a wise Marriage, the settlement of a Difference, an open matter closed to satisfaction. By a Club, a prudent Choice. By a Spade, a Cost or expense, perhaps a loss, before a satisfactory and favorable Event, or in course of it.

The King

As Master-Card, is figured a brilliant, honorable and successful Man, of standing and perhaps of marked taste in art, belles-lettres and the like; and gifted in them. Influenced by its like suit, a Man with much original in him, shrewd in money or gift. By a Heart, a Male Character of kindly and humane traits; or one sensitive and easily moved in his mood. By a Club, a Man in professional life, and of good mental balance. By a Spade, such a life is threatened or broken, or not free from Self-seeking at others' expense.

The Queen

As Master-Card, is indicated the existence of a brilliant, gifted Woman; fond of social life and modish things, of dress or expensive and rare matters; perhaps of Talent in art or literature. Influenced by like suit, one of brilliancy rather than feeling or self-sacrifice. By a Heart, if high, of affection more than is thought; if low, beautiful. By a Club, a Woman executive; of some audacity; restless or self-depending: admiring intellect of solid kind tho' maybe lacking it. By a Spade, a Woman not devoted to benefiting others; and threatened by misfortune; or with a hidden Grievance.

The Knave

As Master-Card, is figured as within the Querist's life, a Relative, likely so made by birth or marriage; and ever disposed to use the tie for personal advantage. Influenced by like suit, the Relative is not remote, and marriage or love is so utilised by him, now; especially by weakness of judgment, or by over-affection on another's part. By a Heart, a shrewd Business Success. By a Club, a sudden Discovery as to a person. By a Spade, a Deferment of the Querist's prosperity in a matter.

Ten

As Master-Card, a brilliant, entertaining, but too trifling and irresponsible Man: or a vain and amoratious man if a knave of beads influence it, often is figured.

Nine

As Master-Card, a valuable Possession. Influenced by like suit, is concerned one intrinsically of value, as jewels, money or plate, a house or estate. By a Heart, a Secret: a Marriage. By a Club, the aforesaid or another Possession will be (or has been) won by special exertions of the Querist's abilities, or so to be kept. By a Spade, it is endangered.

Eight

This is the Unlucky Red Card if figuring as Master-Card; meaning a personal Event of importance going awry; a Subtraction that must be admitted to others. But if influenced by like suit, it is a favorable card and indicates a pleasing Journey, or Meeting. By a Heart, an Enemy or evil opinion altered in your favor. By a Club a Proposal of tempting kind. By a Spade, a Plan that in success is doubtful and partial, or troublesome to another.

Seven

A card of good omen if a Master-Card, in the Practical Affairs of life, business, society, or art, or one of them. Influenced by a like suit, in a Commercial thing; a Meeting wished; an influence desired. By a Heart, a wealthy and superior, or happy Marriage. By a Club, a Communication of importance or good. By a Spade, an Indiscretion that were better not committed by your fault; or a Negligence.

Seven (alternate)

As Master-Card, a commercial or social Step, a Purchase of importance; by the Querist. Influenced by like suit, attractive and unexpected. By a Heart, in regard to making a new Acquaintance, or bringing a Change of feeling toward someone. By a Club, a Matter of Necessity; or an affair dealing with a lawyer, doctor, clergyman, or servant: or a Step of wisdom as well as attraction. By a Spade, if high, a Loan of money: if low, a small Borrowing.[87]

Six

As Master-Card, the card of special Report, Conversation about one, or of Action by another; in a degree affecting one's outward affairs. By a Heart, from a near Friend. By a Club, where you esteem or respect. By a high Spade, with error or even untruth in it, mayhap not intended, but a pity. By a low Spade, it is somewhat written.

Five

A good omen; as a Master-Card, meaning a Gift to the Querist. Influenced by like suit, is figured a personal Ornament or convenience. By a Heart, a Gift is to be made. By Club, it comes with formality and after debate, and considering for some time, or for special circumstances. By a Spade, a Disappointment to another dear to you, is figured.

---

87 The transcription of this text gives two meanings for the Seven of Diamonds. We suggest testing which one suits your readings best.

Four

As Master-Card, an Honor or Favour or Compliment or bit of Luck. Influenced by like suit, in society, or art. By a Heart, long desired; and perhaps more pleasing than wise or useful. By a Club, due to one's own judgment and persistency. By a high Spade, entailing trouble or cost. By a low Spade, at the cost of another's misfortune; or not wholly our desert rather than another's; or brief.

Three

As Master-Card, a sudden Surprise in an event. Influenced by like suit, agreeable, and social or pecuniary or in the arts. By a Heart, Surprise, agreeable, yet not to one's interest or particular profit. By a Club, a social Responsibility. By a Spade, a Death or a Misfortune to another likely enters into it.

Two

A gift or fortunate Purchase, if a Master-Card. Influenced by the like suit, an Engagement or Burden happily broken or dismissed; a Good Riddance, a Disgrace or Plague ended. By a Heart, an Offer—in love, friendship, trade, travel, profession, or pleasure. By a Club, a Letter or Interview of consequence. By a Spade, a Service that one is glad of, or a Gift; but bringing obligation with it, sooner or later.

Clubs

The Ace

As Master-Card, is figured an Event of material weight, involving use of judgment, will, shrewdness, or decision. Influenced by the like suit, high or low, its effect is the more for our own making. By a Heart, is seen a Matter in which our Sentiments are specially enlisted, perhaps in contest with judgment or tastes or duty. By a Diamond, the affair is in society, artistic life, money, or responsibility to others as well. By a Spade, a Mischance or Disappointment is part of it; often faithfully hid, or to be hid.

The King

As Master-Card, our relationship to a strong mental or moral Influence of the male sex, respected and deferred to; or sure so to be. Influenced by its like suit, it is a cultivated and professional one, or involuntary. By a high Heart, it arises in a near relative or one for whom a special affection is felt. By a low Heart, it is either secret or remote; or it may be that it is religious, in part. By a Diamond, our outward life must have concern in it. By a Spade, the influence is of doubtful or worse healthfulness or profit to us.

The Queen

As Master-Card, a marked female Influence on the Querist, in the way of respect, judgment, advice, or authority: not necessarily as to a relative. Influenced by the like suit, a person of coldish and grave disposition. By a high Heart, of strong impulses and disinterested; by a low Heart, troublesome, often importunate and officious. By a Diamond, not married; and of wealth or social esteem; talented. By a Spade, not altogether open or disinterested; divorced or disappointed; according to the nature of the Card.

The Knave

As Master-Card, Relationship with a well-meaning, but over-rash and hasty or sanguine Man; not necessarily but likely quite youthful, and selfish in inclination, or too easily influenced by others of greater art: an Associate, partner, friend, or Employee in some matter of worth. Not to be relied on as one would gladly do. Influenced by his like suit, Circumstances assist him or make of less or more account his weakness or strength. By a Heart, he is inclined to be led by tastes and passions and by skilled flattery, or to overtrust. By a Diamond, he is in love with externals, fond of dress, or notice, or pleasure; ambitious. By a Spade, he meets with Losses to himself and the Querist, or he makes some particular Error or False Step.

Ten

As Master-Card, Success in a matter long pursued. Influenced by its suit, one of troublesome Conflict of conduct or advices. By a Heart, in an affair of love; or calling for courage; or for another, as well as oneself. By a Diamond, an Opinion or Prejudice overcome in others, through our persistency, or argument. By a Spade, an Inheritance; or a Matter needing much watchfulness and care, when known.

Nine

As Master-Card, the need of much Decision in our own judgments in an affair of importance; a need of disregarding counsels of Others. Influenced by the like suit, several persons or circumstances Oppose, perhaps slyly. By a Heart, there is a wounding of tenderer feelings or relationship in it. By a Diamond, the affair is of Estate, Position, Money, Comfort, or Purchase. By a Spade, beware lest so is assumed no greater Responsibility than can be easily carried; or acknowledged.

Eight

An absent Friend reflects on you in a particular matter. This as Master-Card. Influenced by like suit, a Conviction or responsibility of much weight laid on one. By a Diamond, a Choice of a wife, or precious article. By a Heart, Cause of Concern for a friend. By a Spade, you shall give Counsel not followed, and spend Thought thrown aside.

Seven

As Master-Card, a troublesome Situation dissolved. Influenced by like suit, a Secret imparted of interest and length. By a Heart, undo something very newly done. By a Diamond, beware of an Indiscretion or Error. By a Spade, a Neglect or piece of forgetfulness will be of cost to mend or replace: perhaps, if a high Spade, not to be mended at all.

Six

As Master-Card, cancel at once an Agreement, a Purpose, or wholly change a Decision. Influenced by the like suit, a card of fortunate aspect. By a Heart, the call to assist Another, near to one. By a Diamond, a Hazard, successful. By a Spade, a sudden Opposition.

Five

As Master-Card, a Guest, a Visit, a Letter, each needing exercising of prudence or self-restraint; but acceptable. Influenced by the like suit, a Proposal urged. By a Heart, a Wound or Bruise. By a Diamond, a strong Temptation, or a Journey. By a Spade, an Argument or Dispute on a matter.

Four

An important Request of the Querist, if read as Master-Card. If influenced by like suit, one not overmuch to your wish. By a Heart, you Sacrifice somewhat to grant it. By a Diamond, it involves anon a Change. By a Spade, the cost will not be valued for its worth.

Three

As Master-Card, a sad or serious Duty or Care. As influenced by its like suit, a Choice of two things; both desired much, but one to be dismissed. By a Diamond, Luck, or a forthcoming Pleasure. By a handsome Man or Woman to be met and attracted toward one. By a Spade, a Matter to make one angry, or heart-sick.

Two

A card of doubtful omen when a Master, figuring a grave Confidence, of interest to learn, but burdensome rather than easily to be passed by. By its like suit, some News. By a Heart, a Sentiment not wise though keen. By a Diamond, an awkward Meeting. By a Spade, a Piece of News acted on, and then found untruly reported: or Advice seemingly good, but not so.

Spades

(The Suit of Evil Omen and of Unwelcome Influences.)

The Ace

As Master-Card, the Ace figures a special Misfortune, Unhappiness, or Hurt to one's life, by no means avoidable, and perhaps not discernible at once. Influenced by the King of its like suit, sudden: by the Queen, long continuing ere complete; by the Knave, Fortune through Persons; by the ten, through concurrence of sundry events. By any other spade, sudden. By a Heart, Ill-Fortune in the Affection. By the Diamond, in the eye of Others, in society, money or art. By a Club, to our fear.

The King

As Master-Card is figured a particular Man, our enemy, resolute and powerful. Influenced by its suit, it signifies News of a Death: or of misfortune to others. By a Heart, it involves abuse of Trust or Affection. By a Diamond, is figured a Man of social station and wealth or talents. By a Club, a Man cautious and reserved, and hence perhaps unsuspected for his real Malevolency.

The Queen

As Master-Card, a Female Enemy, evil wishing or evil-working. Influenced by the like suit, known or soon to be shown as such to you, and the work. By a Diamond, comely and clever or gifted. By a Club, intellectual and audacious. By a Heart, her enmity arises in jealousy or vanity or in revengefulness or natural malice.

The Knave

As Master-Card, a Man having no love for you and inclined to wrong and hurt you; but happily limited in Opportunity. Influenced by like suit, often seen of you. By a Heart, abusing your Trust, smaller or greater. By a Diamond, adroit rather than bold. By a Club, cruel and slanderous.

Ten

As Master-Card, an Event or Project to your disadvantage and regret. Influenced by the like suit, a Disgrace. By a Heart, a Quarrel. By a Diamond, a Cheat. By a Club, a Hindrance.

Nine

As Master-Card, a Lie, or an unwelcome Meeting or Visit. Influenced by like suit, if a high card a Lie; if a low, a piece of undesired News or Letter. By a Heart, a sudden Alarm or Anxiety. By a Club, a Broken Promise: or a Secret told.

Eight

As Master-Card, an Illness. By a high influencing card of the suit, a long Illness: by a lower, a shorter one. By a Heart, an illness to Another dear to one. By a Diamond, a Misfortune in an affair. By a Club, an Accident.

Seven

As Master-Card, a tempting Proposal that must be declined. By the like suit, a Sharp Quarrel. By a Diamond, a Risk not welcome. By a Club, a Disappointment in a person or thing or event. By a Club, one arrives just too late for a certain Pleasure or Good.

Six

As Master-Card, a Disappointment. Influenced by its own suit, a Journey not of pleasure, or else unpleasant. By a Diamond, a fall. By a Heart, a mistake of inconvenience. By a Club, must be read an unfavorable Sign.

Five

As Master-Card, an Expense. Influenced by its own suit, a Neglect. By a Heart, a Worriment or Grief. By a Diamond, a doubtful Success. By a Club, a Death heard of.

Four

An unfavorable Master-Card, affecting some near Concern to the Querist; belike it shall end less well than was hoped. Influenced by like suit, a Separation not welcome. By a Heart, a capricious Change of inclination. By a Diamond, a Perplexity. By a Club, a Loss.

Three

As Master-Card, a suddenly changed Plan, a Discomfiture. Influenced by its like suit, a loss. By a Heart, a sudden Failure, a Doubt or Fear. By a Diamond, a Breach or Quarrel. By a Club, a sheer Folly, not to be warned away by a friend.

Two

As Master-Card, you must say "NO," when you would say "YES." Influenced by its like suit, a Displeasure. By a Heart, an Evil Habit to burden. By a Club, a Strong Effort of no use. By a Diamond, a Folly, or a Mare's Nest.

In this evil suit of Spades there be many other special Significancies; but they are not pertinent to this method.

Having now given all the card meanings according to this method, we will next provide the way in which the "parallelogram" is constructed. We will then give an example reading to show how this rather elaborate method can provide very specific divination.

Square of Seven

For this method, we use the standard deck of fifty-two playing cards, Ace to 10 in four suits (hearts, clubs, diamonds, spades) and twelve court cards of jack, queen, and king in each suit.

Shuffle the cards well, at least seven times in all; this adds to the mystery and magic of the occasion and helps to summon up the spirit of the cards as seven is a mystical number.

Making a Wish

Keep the cards face down so the identity of the cards is not revealed. Pass the deck to the person for whom you are conducting the reading, in old cartomantic speak we would call them *"querists."* Ask them to cut the cards three times and take the bottom card from each cut, and as they do so they may make a wish. Ask them not to look at these three "wish cards" and place them to one side until after the full layout has been interpreted.

Dealing of the First Seven Cards

You now have forty-nine cards remaining in the deck. Shuffle them well, face down, and then proceed to lay out the first seven cards face up. Lay them out one through seven in a stepped diagonal line, card one at the top to card seven at the bottom. Keep focused throughout, allowing no distractions as you go. [88]

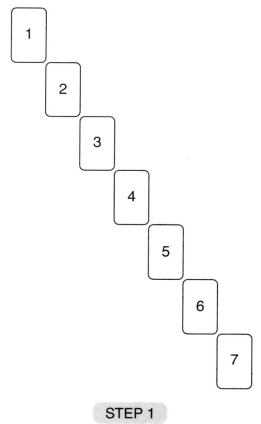

STEP 1

15. Square of Seven Step 1.

---

88 The original instructions state "avoid foolish conversation and sottish pleasantries with those about you."

The Next Six Cards

Shuffle the remaining cards again and lay out another six cards from the bottom of the pack, alongside the cards already laid out. As in Step 2, place the first of these six cards (the eighth card so far) squarely above the last card dealt, card seven on the base of our diagonal stepped line, and then repeat with the other five cards to the top of the stepped cards, card 13.

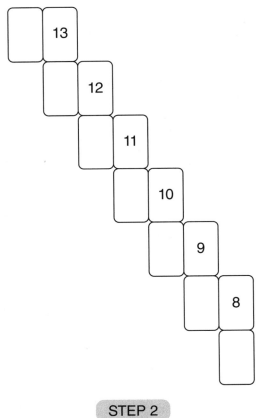

STEP 2

16. Square of Seven Step 2.

A Further Six Cards

Shuffle the remaining cards again because we are now ready to lay out a further six cards from the top of the pack. Lay the next card at the top of the step of cards, across one to the left and down one (diagonal) so it sits beneath card one. Then continue laying the next five cards out under each other in the same stepped manner. The last card is card 19.

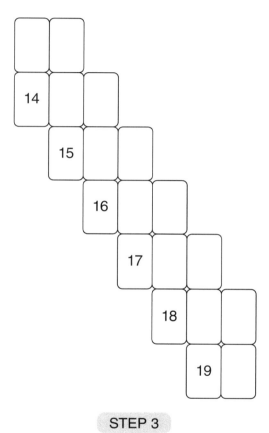

STEP 3

17. Square of Seven Step 3.

Another Five Cards

Shuffle the remaining cards again and draw another five cards from the bottom of the deck. Place card 20 over to the right of card 19 and two places up, then continue upwards in steps until card 24 is placed at the very top next to card 13.

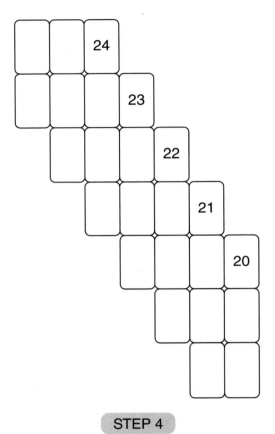

STEP 4

18. Square of Seven Step 4.

A Further Five Cards

Now shuffle yet again and lay out five cards from the top of the pack to make a left border, downwards as cards 25 to 29.

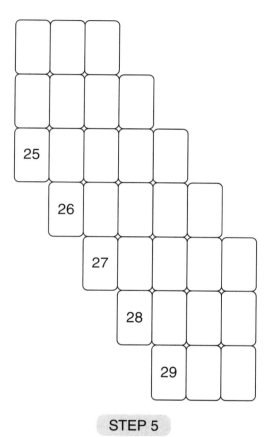

STEP 5

19. Square of Seven Step 5.

Now Four Cards

Shuffle and lay out four cards from the bottom of the pack, in positions 30 to 33. The original instructions suggest that it should now look like a tiled floor or ceiling pattern.

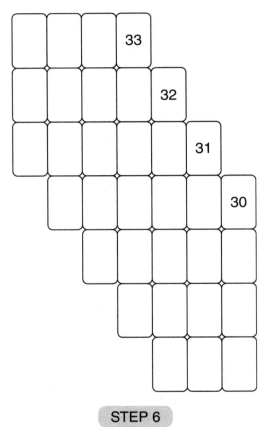

STEP 6

20. Square of Seven Step 6.

Another Four Cards

After shuffling the now-decreased deck, with thirty-three cards laid out on the table, from the top of the deck, now add four more cards: 34 through 37.

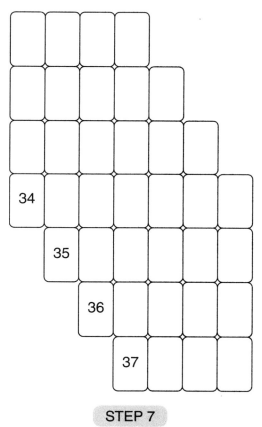

STEP 7

21. Square of Seven Step 7.

Prime-Stevenson suggests that the figure now contains a "fair cross," a good sign made of the four cards at the two borders and the seven cards across the middle and running through the middle of the diagonal. He says too that the "Square" is nearing its complete shape as the cards "equalise."

Now Just Three Cards

Shuffle what remains of the deck and lay out from the top, three cards in positions thirty-eight through forty.

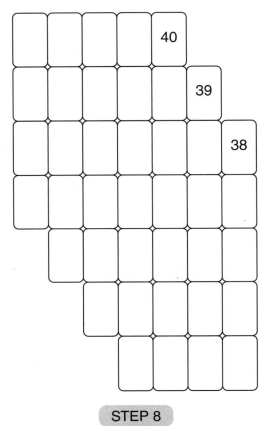

STEP 8

22. Square of Seven Step 8.

And Three Cards

We now shuffle and from the bottom of the few remaining cards, lay out three cards, almost completing our final shape, in positions forty-one through forty-three.

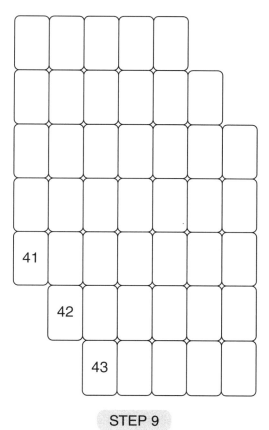

STEP 9

23. Square of Seven Step 9.

Two More

Mixing what is left of the deck, deal from the top two cards into positions 44 and 45.

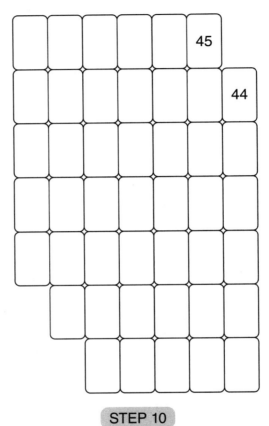

STEP 10

24. Square of Seven Step 10.

And the Penultimate Two

With the final four cards, after mixing with each other for a moment, lay two from the top into positions 46 and 47 to complete the imperfect square.

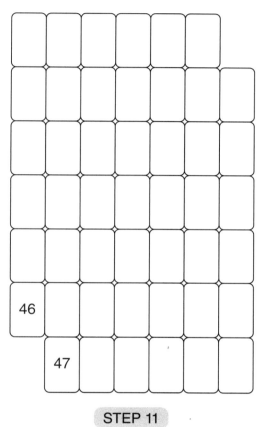

STEP 11

25. Square of Seven Step 11.

The Final Two Cards

The final two cards are placed into positions 48 and 49 to complete the square.

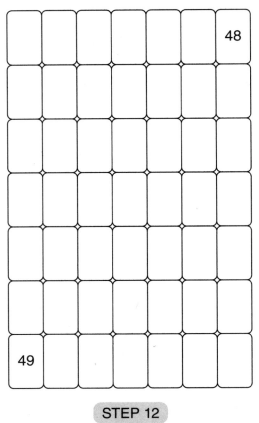

STEP 12

26. Square of Seven Step 12.

We might think that the perfect square of sevens is the final spread we could read from, like the method of the Grand Tableau in Lenormand reading and other cartomantic matrix layouts. However, Prime-Stevenson has a further process for us to follow which is similar to a card game called Patience and which he calls "formal reduction." This involves the master card of each row (across) and the "sacrifice."

He reasons this additional process as such:

You may indeed ask why so much Labour is made of building the Square only to reduce it, to despoil it, and to force it to hide or to part with so many of its Sevens—as by a sudden Slaughter or a Panic or a Plague. But it is held that by such prior Shufflings, Dealings, and Placings are much cherished the accidentall Declarings of Fates intelligence; and that by the other Processes, embracing The Sacrifice, there remain for Reading just the Cards decreed; free from disposition by light-fingered Craft, or from ticklish Arrangements by Skill.

The Master Cards

Throughout this reduction process the left column of cards is neither moved, nor any other cards laid upon them, and these seven cards are referred to as the master cards.

The Formal Reduction & Sacrifice

Step 1

Starting with the uppermost row, take the first card on the right and lay it on the nearest card of the same suit to its left. If there is no card of the same suit in the row (not counting the master card), leave the card where it is.

A suit is the hearts, spades, clubs, or diamonds.

Step 2

If there is another card of the same suit to the left of the piled two cards, take those two cards to the left and lay them on that card.

Step 3

Take the next suit in the row and reduce it to the left again if possible.

Step 4

Repeat steps 1 through 3 for each suit in the row. This may leave gaps between the piles.

Step 5

Repeat steps 1 through 4 for the other six rows.

Step 6

We now have the "reduction," so we close the rows together by moving the piles or single cards to the left removing any gaps. This should leave seven rows with the master card to the left in each row followed by up to four cards or stacks to the right. We are now only concerned with the cards we can see face up, not the cards underneath.

Step 7

Next remove all cards other than the master column and the first two columns; imagine that we are sacrificing all the cards to the right of the first three columns. You will now have seven rows of up to three cards face up, and this is our reduced and sacrificed layout that matches the querists situation perfectly.

We can now go about the interpretation of the cards we can see.

The Interpretation

Stage 1

Review the spread to see if there is a dominance of one color over another, red or black. Our example reading has a healthy balance of red and black, neither good or bad. Red cards are generally seen as the favorable color and if they are present as hearts this is very positive, whereas black is not so, particularly with a lot of spade cards dominant.

Stage 2

We next look at the suits and the following table gives the meanings of each suit majority:

- **Hearts:** Affections, love, passions, attraction.

- **Diamonds:** Social issues, standing and recognition, wealth, and security.

- **Clubs:** Judgment, ideas, innovation, dynamic behaviour.

- **Spades:** Disruptions and challenges

Stage 3

We read the card on the right column being influenced by the card on its left. In the example, we have the King of Hearts influenced by the Ace of Diamonds. If the *Tavola* does not describe a specific influence or combination, we can read the card alone, use our intuition, or apply keywords from our chosen cartomantic system. In this case, we have a specific mention in the *Tavola* of a diamond suit influencing the King of Hearts. This gives us: "a man of wealth or artistic nature." We can also derive this from the cartomantic core for the King of Hearts as an emotional man in the context of the Ace of Diamonds as social standing or riches.

Stage 4

We now read the middle column card as being influenced in turn by the master card to its left. So, the influence in the example is of the 9 of Spades upon the Ace of Diamonds. The glittery diamond is likely to be negatively influenced by the spade card; we can see this in the *Tavola* where we read "a cost or expense, perhaps a loss, before a satisfactory and favorable event, or in [The] course of it."

> So, an emotional man will bring social standing but there will be a cost to this, it will not be a straight-forward relationship.

We then go down each row, interpreting in the same manner.

In our example, the second row gives us the Queen of Clubs influenced from the left by the 2 of Diamonds; this gives us a woman of authority who is influenced by the card meaning "a woman who is not married; and of wealth or social esteem; talented."

So, this is possibly a single woman who will be in the client's life, but as yet we do not have any indication of what they bring, until we look at how the 2 of Diamonds is influenced by the master card.

We then see that we have the 2 of Diamonds being influenced in turn by the master card, the 9 of Hearts and this will result in "an offer—in love, friendship, trade, travel, profession, or pleasure."

> So, there is significant opportunity opening for our client in the months to come, from both a man and a woman who will make proposals, even if there is some cost to working with the man.

We then repeat this for each row, using a similar method of narrative and reading as we have seen in our previous cartomancy chapters.

The Wish Cards

If the three wish cards that we put aside earlier in the reading are more red than black, then it is said that the querist can make a wish for his overall well-being. This refers to the lines of the reading, so if there was something "negative" in the reading, they can make a wish that it be changed, if the Wish cards are favourable.

In the example, we can see that we have two clubs and one heart card. No wish can be granted. However, a wish can be granted for another person with the black cards present if there are either "court cards, aces, or above the eights."

In the example, we have the 3 of Hearts, 7 of Clubs, and 9 of Clubs; so, we can apparently grant a wish to another person, related to our reading.

Conclusion

Whilst this method appears to be complex, it is straight-forward in practice and a delight to perform as it takes commonly recognised methods, such as matching suits in a Concentration-like game to reduce to the final spread. It thus adds to the sense that we are divining down to something specific for the client, as Prime-Stevenson reasons in his tract.

It is often the case that "made up" methods draw on the same structure and patterns as those passed down, for in fact, all methods were "made up" at some point, and come and go throughout the timelines.

In the next chapter, we will take a brief stop to orient ourselves to one of the most important sources for tarot, the Tarot de Marseilles, or TdM as it has come to be known to new enthusiasts. This deck was one of the very first, and it continues to be one of the main cartomantic decks used across Europe. It is also presently undergoing a revival thanks to new teachers and popularisation by the film director, Alejandro Jodorowsky, who recently performed a public reading for James Bond actor Daniel Craig.

5

Tarot de Marseille

Thus, it may be more reasonable to think of the Tarot cards as a collective artwork evolving in marginal and half-legitimate popular circles, rather than as a sublime teaching kept in secret temples of wisdom and spirituality.

—Yoav Ben Dov, *Tarot: The Opening Reading* [89]

2:00 pm, 20 March, 1700: Paris, France

We find ourselves walking along the banks of the Seine towards a large governmental building. Louis XIV is on the throne of France, and will remain there for some fifteen more years after over seventy-two years of rulership.

However, all is not well in the city of the Sun King. We see poverty and misery behind every wide boulevard and under every grand archway. A series of unnaturally hard winters and terrible harvests are starving the city and its population. It will get worse: in nine years' time, the city will face *Le Grand Hiver*, a winter that will become a legend.

But today it is early spring, and the building we approach is not one of the new workshops for the poor, but a factory for a device that is still all the rage across every level of society—the deck of playing cards.

---

89   CreateSpace Publishing, 2013, 12.

We walk into the warehouse and are immediately assailed by the heat and the smell of paste. There is the noise of loud conversation and swift snickering sounds from huge pairs of scissors being used to cut individual cards from large print sheets.

We pass by a table where a workman is soaping sheets of cards with a rubber made of old hats sewn together. The floor is strewn with old cards and straw. Through another large archway, we see men struggling to make the last twists on large presses that are screwed down further every fifteen minutes.

It is hard work, and the entire place is full of people, cats, and a sooty dust that makes us sneeze. Trying to stay unnoticed, we come to stand alongside courtiers who have arrived by carriage and are waiting to pick up their orders, carried away by the armful.

There is no end to the work it seems, even in a time of poverty and uncertainty, the games must continue. [90] It is from this busy industry, not only in Paris but across Europe and throughout the century, that will arise the first phase of tarot, the Tarot de Marseille.

Whilst there are several variations and models for the tarot deck generally called the "Tarot de Marseille," it is usually accepted that a notable model for the deck was published in 1760 by Nicolas Conver in Marseille. [91] However, one of the more popular Marseille-style decks is that published originally by B. P. Grimaud, called the *Ancien Tarot de Marseille*. [92]

The TdM Major Arcana

The usual TdM pattern of major arcana contains several variations to what most contemporary readers see in a modern tarot deck. These are listed here:

1. **Card II** is the Papess, rather than the High Priestess.

2. **Card V** is the Pope, rather than the Hierophant.

3. **Card XVI** is the House of God, rather than the Tower.

---

90 Catherine Perry Hargreave, *A History of Playing Cards and a Bibliography of Cards and Gaming* (New York: Dover Publications, 1966), 297–300.

91 Yoav Ben-Dov, *Tarot: The Open Reading* (CreateSpace, 2011, 2013), 20.

92 Cherry Gilchrist, *Tarot Triumphs* (Newburyport, MA: Red Wheel/Weiser, 2016), 55.

Further, most often the Fool card is unnumbered as is sometimes the Death card, rather than being numbered 0 and 13, respectively.

A variant or parallel of the TdM sometimes termed the 1JJ or Swiss deck, replace the Papess and Pope with the less controversial Juno (with peacock) and Jupiter (with eagle). This replacement is also evident in the Tarot of Besançon, likely used by Comte de Mellet.

The TdM Minor Arcana

The Minor Arcana of the TdM are depicted as arrangements of the elements of the suit, usually in a *mandorla*-style, having an oval shape. So, the wands (or batons) make a cross-hatch pattern and the swords make a curved scimitar-like pattern. The cups and coins are placed much like traditional pips on a playing card.

There are a few distinct elements in the minor arcana of the TdM, such as the 2 of Coins usually being joined together by a wreath or ribbon on which is the name of the publisher.

Reading the TdM

When we approach reading the TdM, we should consider that we are moving forward in the timeline, so we have yet to encounter "scenic" illustrations for the pip cards as we find in the *Sola Busca* and later, the Waite-Smith Tarot. We should say the TdM does have illustrated pip cards, even if they are simply illustrated by their suit and floral decoration. This is an illustration from which can arise interpretation, even if it is not a symbolic scene such as a rotund merchant sitting in front of a canopy of cups or two mendicants struggling in a snowstorm. [93]

So, these cards can either be used as place-holders of significance, based on the suits and numerology, for example, or some given meaning from cartomancy—or they can be used to evoke an interpretation from their simple illustration and their context to the other cards in a spread.

Originally, these cards would have been read as any other playing card for cartomancy. We see later in our travels through time how the founder members of the Golden Dawn

---

93   The 9 of Cups and the 5 of Pentacles as illustrated by Pamela Colman Smith in the Waite-Smith Tarot, 1909–1910.

wrote on this type of European deck the "standard" meanings for fortune-telling from Etteilla.

However, contemporary readers have developed what might be called a "visual poetic" manner of reading these historic cards, particularly the work of *Tarology* by Enrique Enriquez. This approach is based on a background of poetry, literature studies, surrealism, and street magic.[94] It can also be seen in the work of Camelia Elias, who writes that "most of my method in reading three cards consists of noticing what turns into what…"[95] A similar approach is the "open reading" method adopted by Yoav Ben-Dov, a student of film director, tarot reader, and *psychomagician* Alejandro Jodorowsky.[96]

We will provide tarot time travellers an overview of the "numerology" method and the "visual poetic" Marseille reading, and open the avenues for much further discovery. These methods to some extent will also work with other decks of antiquity such as the Minchiate and Etteilla, which may be visited in the time travel of a future book.

Numerology Method

We can take a simple pattern running through the numbers one to ten and then apply it to the four realms governed by the four suits, which make up the pip cards of the TdM. This is similar to our ten-minute method covered in other books.[97] This particular version is based on Papus, who envisaged the numerology of the minors running through a triad composed of three repeating steps: commencement, opposition, and equilibrium.

We first look at the suits and suggest they are seen in the TdM as follows:

- **Coins:** Money and health

- **Cups:** Love and relationships

- **Sceptres/Staves:** Creative endeavours

- **Swords:** Struggle[98]

---

94   See Enrique Enriquez, *Tarology* (Roskilde: Eyecorner Press, 2011).

95   Camelia Elias, *Marseille Tarot: Towards the Art of Reading* (Roskilde: Eyecorner Press, 2015), 110.

96   Yoav Ben-Dov, 20.

97   See Marcus Katz, *Tarosophy* (Keswick, UK: Forge Press, 2016), 81–89.

98   See Fred Gettings, *The Book of the Tarot* (London, UK: Triune Press, 1973), 122–123.

We then cycle through the pattern of commencement, opposition, and equilibrium for their numerical sequence, replacing the words with the more accessible; starting, challenging and balancing as follows:

- **Ace**: Starting of starting

- **Two**: Challenge of starting

- **Three**: Balancing in starting

- **Four**: Starting of challenge

- **Five**: Challenge of challenge

- **Six**: Balance of the challenge

- **Seven**: Starting of balance

- **Eight**: Challenge of balance

- **Nine**: Balance in balance

- **Ten**: This card in each suit provides a summary of the cards around it, so is a completion or final word. As an example, if it were the 10 of Sceptres it would suggest that the reading was summarised by illustrating how the creative endeavours could come together successfully.

In this method, the majors simply represent their general or obvious meaning, such as the Moon being about dreams or the Tower being about destruction; they do what they say on the tin.

Similarly, the court cards are taken to represent people at various maturity levels in their respective realms: the King of Cups is an emotional man, and the Page of Swords is a young person engaged in struggles or with a temper.

If we drew a single pip card for a question such as "Will this business plan be successful?" and received the 7 of Staves, this would indicate a "starting of balance in the realm of creative endeavours." It would indicate that we are likely to be successful because already there is a coming together in what is being created.

If we added another card for "should I work with others?" and received the Queen of Cups, it would indicate that we would benefit from working with a sensitive woman.

Further, we could draw a third card to ask, "how would we work best together?" Should we receive the 4 of Coins, the indication would be "starting of a challenge with money." We should expect opposition to our financial plans, so prepare to have a solid business plan and savings *or* extend the timeline until we overcome what might have been unexpected challenges.

There are many variants to the meanings assigned to the number sequence of the pip cards in this approach, and whilst we ask our tarot time travellers to consider the Papus method first, we encourage you to explore other avenues for your cartomantic adventures in the future.

Visual Poetic Method

In the visual poetic method, we can lay out three cards. Some readers only read the major arcana of the TdM, and others read the entire deck; it is entirely up to you. We recommend trying both for a little while each and discovering which one works best for you.

We then look at weaving a story from the similarities and differences in the illustrations as if they were pieces in one narrative. We might further look at lines, shapes, and colours and how they change between the cards. Another visual cue might be the pose or glances of the figures.

In this three-card reading, we see the cards laid out for a business partnership. The question was about a quiet period in the business and what it might signify for the two partners.

The three cards drawn were: XI (La Force) + VII (Le Chariot) + VI (L'Amouruex).

We might read a story into these three cards as follows:

The woman looks to the man and the man looks to the woman. She tries to keep her mouth shut as he tries to drive forwards but only goes sideways. They must both look to the Lion and their own strengths to put their horses in order. They can bring themselves together by choosing to do what they love.

We can also look more in-depth with this approach by observing how the hands of characters move between the cards; in this reading, each pair of hands shows both one hand grasping and the other hand resting. This indicates the need to focus on what is important and what will not be lost by resting.

We can then apply this more directly to the context of the question or leave it with the client as a story or metaphor for them to process.

The Current State of Marseille

At the time of the writing of this book, in the early part of the twenty-first century, there is a renaissance of cartomancy where the "cards of antiquity" are being re-visited. The Tarot de Marseille (or TdM) is one of the several decks, alongside the Lenormand, Kipper, Sola Busca, Minchiate, and Etteilla, that are being re-interpreted and repurposed for contemporary fortune-telling and cartomancy.

A recent poll was taken on the largest social media group for tarot (and its sister group for Marseille) to discover the "top ten" of Marseille decks.[99] In the nine decks listed, the following were the top three chosen by Marseille aficionados:

1. **Conver Ben-Dov**: As illustrated here, a version of the original Conver deck by Yoav Ben-Dov.

2. **Jean Noblet TdM** (c.1650), editions 2007 and 2014 by the late Jean-Claude Flornoy.

3. **Jean Dodal TdM**, also by Flornoy.

The fourth position went to the ubiquitous B.P. Grimaud deck and included in the list was the Jodorowsky-Camoin deck of 1997 which has several unique variations to the TdM.[100]

---

99   The Queen's Sword review site at http://www.thequeenssword.com/top-9-tarot-de-marseille-decks/ (Last accessed December, 2016).

100   Alejandro Jodorowsky, *The Way of Tarot: The Spiritual Teacher in the Cards* (Rochester: Destiny Books, 2004).

There are, however, a great many artisanal TdM decks which can be discovered from creators both European and worldwide. [101]

Marseille Mushrooms

As we bounce around time with the Tarot de Marseille, we should briefly mention a strange signal coming from an alternative dimension: the rather unique book, *The Secrets of the Marseilles Tarot* by Namron. This was published in 1990 and is a riotous ride through the cards explained by the "Egyptian Spread," the Spider-Lady, the Sacred Mushroom, and sexual symbolism. It is one of the strangest books ever written on tarot and does contain half-page interpretations of each of the major arcana even if the rest of the text is obscure and mysterious.

Marseille Cats

As we hop back into our tarot time travel pod, we find that we have been joined by some unexpected companions—a group of cats. These felines are often attracted to astral activity and time-bending shenanigans, and they have made their way into many tarot decks, attracted by their common psychic energy.

As they bounce around our capsule, we check in our time-satchel and discover that they have also romped across an entire Tarot de Marseille. It appears that they are having fun adopting the poses of the Waite-Smith deck from the early 1900s within the designs of the Marseille deck from the 1700s for a deck available in the early part of the 2000s. This behaviour is typical of cats, as they have no consideration of linear space or geometric time.

Considering the deck, this may be a tool we can use to learn the Marseilles from our knowledge of the Waite-Smith deck—or you may choose to approach it one of the other ways we have covered in this section. Whatever the case, we clutch our satchel to our chest and set the dials for our next jump in tarot time.

---

101   See issues of *Tarosophist International* from the Tarosophy Tarot Association www.tarotassociation.net and review site www.thetarotreview.com for regular articles, including TdM decks.

27. Selected Minor Arcana cards from Marseille Cat Tarot (Lo Scarabeo), 2014.

Now that we have briefly pointed our sights at the Tarot de Marseilles, in the next chapter we will pass from France to Germany and the deck of cards known as the Lenormand. In doing so, we continue to track another contemporary revival that was also beneath most tarot travellers' time radars until just a few years ago. In fact, more Lenormand decks have been designed and pulbished in the last six years than in the last three hundred. Let us now change our hats and get ready to visit another way of reading altogether.

6

Lenormand

Fortune is far from frowning upon you, my dear lady, you have, indeed, the best of prospects, because, (14. [Moon]) your noble way of thinking will procure you many advantages, and you will particularly promote by it your easy circumstances, and make yourself friends, who shall contend to please you. Since nothing is perfect (30. [Insects and Pests]) on earth, you need not wonder, if there are little minds envy you, who being themselves without accomplishments, endeavor to lessen them in others.

—"Reading for a Lady," 1796 [102]

20 February, 1796: London, England

It is a few weeks after Queen Charlotte was hit by a stone in protest over the rising price of bread, and two months before Edward Jenner would administer cowpox to eight-year-old James Phipps, paving the way for proof of what he would later call "vaccine" for smallpox, after *vaca*, meaning cow.

On Jewry Street in Aldgate, behind the London Tower, we arrive to see a book being published amidst a whole selection of games and amusements from the same publisher, including the *Little Sorcerer*, *Combat with the Giant*, the *Magic Ring*,

---

102   Quoted in Marcus Katz and Tali Goodwin, *The English Lenormand* (Keswick, UK: Forge Press, 2013), 12.

and the *Pastora: or the Shepherdess of the Pyrenees,* described as "a diverting game calculated to kill care and enliven the dreary hours of winter." These are all listed as educational games, some obviously more so than others—the *Magic Ring* involves moving around a snail-shaped track encountering wizards and fairies whilst another game, *Le Petit Euclid,* is specifically to teach geometry to children. These games all come with a *tetotum* (a spinning dice),[103] tokens and small cases for "the pocket."[104] We add the tetotum to our growing collection in the time-pod.

The book, also listed under the education section in the *British Register* of the time, is *Les Amusemens des Allemands* (Games of Germany) and its author promises to unravel the mysteries of fortune-telling by means of thirty-two "emblematical cards." These cards are based on the symbols read in coffee grounds and are said to have first appeared in Vienna in 1794.[105] The author reports:

> In my late travels to Germany [footnote: 1793] I visited the library of a convent in that country, where I found a book of Egyptian hieroglyphics, which was said to have been discovered by the Emperor Constantine the Great in Egypt, in the year 320 after the birth of Christ. A translation of it in the Latin language being also shewn to me, I begged leave to make an English version of it, and copied the emblematic figures, in hopes of its being likely to become an acceptable present to my countrymen. This book, does not, properly speaking, teach the method of Fortune telling from the grounds of the coffee cup, because coffee was not in use at that time: but as sherbet is a very favourite liquor among the Egyptians and the people of the East in general; the art used to tell Fortunes from the dregs of that liquor, has been applied here to the grounds of coffee, which is drank in every country of Europe.
>
> With regard to the figures represented on the cards, it may easily be imagined, that they will not appear so plainly in the coffee cup, some degree

---

103 A slightly similar device to the spinning top called a "totem" used in the film *Inception* (dir. Christopher Nolan, 2010).

104 *The Monthly Magazine,* Or, *British Register,* vol. 4, December, 466.

105 This book was discovered by author Mary K. Greer and visited in the British Museum by ourselves to confirm that it contained instructions in addition to cards. The instructions contain the first definite proof that the Lenormand-style cards were derived from the symbols read in coffee grounds.

of resemblance being sufficient, and a fertile imagination will easily supply the rest. Thirty-two figures have therefore been chosen, though the grounds in the cup may perchance represent more. [106]

In this chapter, we switch our settings and add to our time-traveller tool-set a new deck of cards, but not yet the tarot; for now, we will add the "Lenormand Deck," a set of thirty-six cards carrying common emblems such as a "Dog," a "Key," a "Child," and other everyday symbols. [107] The Lenormand deck will help us bridge between cartomantic methods and tarot, although the method of reading is somewhat different to either, it uses layouts and methods that can broaden our cartomantic scope.

28. Dog, Key, and Child Lenormand Cards from The Original Lenormand (3rd edition), Marcus Katz & Tali Goodwin, 2016

The *Games of Germany* book in the British Museum comes bound with the whole set of cards on every page so they may be taken out and used in the fortune-telling parlour game. It is the first time that cards have been explicitly published for such fortune-telling and every card has two playing-card inserts; a German and an Italian playing card so the deck can be used to play Piquet and other card games. It is often thought that such "educational" or "fun" card games originated to provide decks for gambling during times when such activity was unacceptable or even illegal.

---

106   Marcus Katz, Tali Goodwin and Mary K. Greer, *The English Lenormand* (Keswick, UK: Forge Press, 2013), 8.

107   Lenormand decks are now plentiful on the market and you can purchase the original Lenormand from www.originallenormand.com (Last accessed 3 July, 2016).

During our time travels, we will see many esotericists allege that a secret teaching was passed down out of Egypt through the tarot cards, but the reality may be far more mundane; such symbolic and educational decks were a means of practising the real secret of life—gambling.

The instructions for use of the cards is as follows:

This pack of cards which is called the coffee pack, because the figures are borrowed from those represented by the grounds in the cup, is shuffled by somebody in company, who according to the sex, is to be called the cunning man or the cunning woman, cut by the person that demands to have his fortune told, and then laid down in four rows of eight cards each. If the person who wants to have his Fortune told be a man, he is represented by the male figure on foot; if a woman, the female figure will represent her. Every card therefore, that stands in the row of the pedestrian gentleman, besides all the cards immediately above or below the male figure, regards the person that wishes to have his Fortune told if he be a man, and if it be a lady that consults, the same rule to be observed with the cards in the row in which the female figure is, and with those immediately above and under it.

There are verses printed on each card also, similar to several other rare and unpublished decks in the British Museum (and likely elsewhere) that contain "speech bubbles" on the cards to give a direct message from the card itself.

Here is a list of the verses from this, the most original source of what is now called Lenormand:

The Coffee-Card Verses

1. **Crossroads/Fingerpost**: Excesses will certainly make you unhappy, avoid them therefore while it is time.

2. **Ring**: In the happy marriage which you are about to enter; avoid Jealousy for the sake of your own peace of mind.

3. **Clover**: You may be very fortunate indeed if you always discharge your duty with honour and integrity.

4. **Anchor**: A person as honest as you in his dealings, will never want a rich harvest of gain; your wishes too are likely to be accomplished.

5. Snake: A secret enemy endeavours to injure you; try by kindness to make him your friend.

6. **Letter**: You may flatter yourself with good hopes in your enterprise but act prudently and speak not always as you feel.

7. **Coffin**: You may rejoice at a considerable legacy, but many people will envy you for it.

8. Star: Do your part, and you will soon experience the good effects of it.

9. **Dog**: You will easily find better friends among strangers than among your own relations.

10. Lily: You wish for a virtuous wife, this wish may be granted if you requite the same for the same.

11. **Cross**: There is no misfortune however severe, that does not produce some good; hope therefore all will be for the best.

12. **Clouds**: Just as the clouds are dispelled, so let your anger vanish, then you will soon be superior to all vexations.

13. **Sun**: You will make an unexpected fortune, use it so that no body may covet it.

14. **Moon**: The liberality of your mind will always rather increase than lessen your prosperity; it will also daily endear you more to your friends.

15. **Mountain**: You may easily get in favour with the great, but remember always that the higher you rise the deeper you will fall.

16. **Tree** (3 Trees, two in sleeves): Never regret labour or pains; a good work is its own reward, be this your consolation.

17. **Child**: The consequences of the good education which you will give to your children, shall gladden your old age. You shall live to see much joy from them.

18. **Woman**: Gratify your partiality to the fair sex, but never offend decency.

19. **Man**: Depend upon receiving some good news; the loss you have sustained will recover likewise.

20. **Rider**: Despair not of Men's goodness for you shall have an unexpected proof of it; you may expect news, and restitution of that which you thought lost.

21. **Mouse**: Have a vigilant eye upon your servants, as your negligence may make an honest man a thief.

22. **Birch rod/Whip**: You are involved in disputes. Do not engage in them too warmly else your body will be afflicted with illness.

23. **Flower/Rose**: You sport with fortune, but whatever the cards refuse, your good sense, your skill, and learning will amply compensate.

24. **Heart**: You meditate a project of marriage, if you consult reason, you will abound with blessings.

25. **Garden**: You frequently go into company, if you wish to be benefited by it, hear much and say little.

26. **Bird/Turtledove**: You are very happy, but love entirely swayed by passion will render you very unhappy.

27. **Fish**: Don't let yourself be caught with baits like the fish; circumspection is very necessary especially on a long journey.

28. **Lion**: Be always on your guard; he easily believes is easily deceived.

29. **Tree** (Single tree, fully grown): The industrious, in whose number you are comprised, will never want for lucre and decent support.

30. **Insects and Pests**: Your unexpected good fortune will create you many unknown enviers, who shall grudge you it.

31. **House**: From the visit which you and your house will receive, great advantages must ensue, but let prudence guide your conduct.

32. **Scythe**: Wait quietly for the harvest, proportionate to your labour; for every one is the make of his own fortune.

We can see how these meanings barely differ from those which will be developed for the Lenormand cards as they begin their transformation through the timeline. However, it was not this particular deck of cards that would resurface a few decades later; rather it would remain consigned to a couple of museums for more than two centuries. In fact, the Coffee Card deck was not the only one of its type being produced at the time—let us travel just three years later and return to Germany to witness the actual nexus point of the Lenormand deck.

2 November, 1799: Nuremberg, Germany

A young man walks unsteadily along the square-cobbled streets of Nuremberg. It is early November and the snow is deep, muffling the sounds of his footsteps. It has been an atrocious winter in Europe and the man is coughing badly as well as itching, which has worried his wife.

They have a reasonable income from the brass factory of which his parents are owners, but his new ventures into game design have not yet brought them much additional income. Nuremberg is now the gaming capital of the world, with wooden toys and board games as much an industry as the brass factories which had been so busy creating musical instruments played across Europe. He has argued with his wife that in the future, games will be as much a part of household activities in the evening as musical recitals, but she is not yet convinced of his vision.

He looks up through the snow at the *Sinwellturm*, the Round Tower of the Imperial Castle and smiles grimly under his scarf—at least if he does not survive the winter, the tower will stand and it will also be forever on his latest deck of playing cards,

Das Spiel der Hofnung, or Game of Hope. He smiles again, ruefully; his first game had been called *Pandora*, a dice game with his favourite selection of jocular questions for the family; but it now seemed his last game would be one of hope.

Johann Kaspar Hechtel died one month later, likely of smallpox, leaving both his wife and his little game of cards behind him.

It was not until fifty years after Hechtel's untimely death that another death conspired to return his deck to the world—the death of Marie Anne Adelaide Lenormand (1772–1843), a self-made cartomantic celebrity who was the talk of Paris for some forty years. Within a few years of her death, two types of decks emerged from German publishers who were keen to capture the market with a new audience wanting details of Lenormand's fortune-telling methods.

The first was a fifty-four-card deck containing images of mythical figures, constellations, flowers, and other symbol systems. It was called the "Grand jeu de Mlle Lenormand" ("big game") and is a complex and somewhat confusing system of cartomancy. [108] Shortly thereafter a simplified version was published, the Petit Lenormand of thirty-six cards, which was actually a re-published version of Hechtel's "Game of Hope" with the same symbols and card inserts, only now given the name of "Lenormand," likely in the hopes of selling more copies.

So, a dead woman's name was put on a dead man's deck, to suggest that every purchaser could become a celebrity fortune-teller with the hidden secrets of Mlle. Lenormand herself. As it was the "little Lenormand" which more recently in our timeline has captured the popular imagination, it is to this version we will turn our attention. We will first note the differences of Hechtel's game (and hence the "Lenormand") to the original Coffee Cards which are parallel.

List of Lenormand Cards

To compare this earlier set of cards and instructions with the later Lenormand cards (originally Hechtel's "Game of Hope" deck), we present here a list of the 1796 coffee cards

---

108   It is hoped that the time traveller will return to this deck of cards at a later (earlier) date.

alongside the Game of Hope cards, this latter which was then used as the model for the petit Lenormand cards.

1799/1800 (Hechtel/"Lenormand")	1796 (Amusements)
1. Rider/Messenger	Roads
2. The Clover Leaf	Ring
3. The Ship	Leaf of Clover
4. The House	Anchor
5. The Tree	**Serpent**
6. The Clouds	Letter
7. The Snake	Coffin
8. The Coffin	Star
9. The Bouquet	Dog
10. The Scythe	Lily
11. The Rod/Whip	Cross
12. The Birds/Owls	Clouds
13. The Child/Little Girl	Sun
14. The Fox	Moon
15. The Bear	Mountains
16. The Stars	**Tree**
17. The Stork	Child
18. The Dog	Woman
19. The Tower	Pedestrian (Man)
20. The Garden	Rider
21. The Mountain	Mouse

1799/1800 (Hechtel/'Lenormand')	1796 (Amusements)
22. The Ways	Rod
23. The Mice	Rose/Carnation/Flower
24. The Heart	Heart
25. The Ring	Garden
26. The Book	Bird
27. The Letter	Fish
28. The Gentleman	Lion or any Ferocious Beast
29. The Lady	**Green Bush**
30. The Lily	**Worms**
31. The Sun	House
32. The Moon	Scythe
33. The Key	
34. The Fish	
35. The Anchor	
36. The Cross	

Hechtel possibly merged the four duplicate symbols out of the earlier deck (i.e., bush/trees became "trees" and worms/serpent became "Serpent") and then added six additional symbols, all of which are common to the symbols read in coffee grounds: Ship, Fox, Stork, Tower, Book, and Key. This would have been to create a deck more suitable for the common decks of the area which had thirty-six cards, not thirty-two.

These in part, we might suggest, are also iconic for the Nuremburg area, as the ship in Hechtel's deck features the flag of Nuremberg (half of a double-headed Eagle, a symbol used in the reading of coffee grounds), the Tower is modelled on the Nuremberg castle tower, the Stork and the Fox are both common and popular folklore creatures of the area (the tales of Reynard and the Frog-King tale), and the Book and Key may be simply personal choices.

In a **1763** German list of the symbols of coffee grounds, the additional symbols are all present, other than the Book. [109]

- **Ship**: Riches and Good Income

- **Fox**: Treacherous Person (or people)

- **Stork**: Moving (place of residence), travel

- **Tower**: Long life and happiness in old age

- **Book**: Not mentioned

- **Key**: Good career prospects (upright) and bad (reversed)

We will add to our list of Lenormand card meanings across time by visiting upon three unlikely sources; Cicely Kent, A. E. Waite, and C. C. Zain. All wrote about cartomancy, even if one used an alias at the time. We will then summarise the card meanings and provide spreads for their deployment.

Kent's Lenormand

Whilst not specifically writing about the Lenormand cards, Kent included a list of symbol meanings in her book *Telling Fortunes by Tea Leaves* (1922). We have selected out those which correspond to the Lenormand cards as currently used—some contemporary decks have added cards from the wide range of original coffee-grind symbols, dream symbols, or antique morality games which could have so easily been part of what is now accepted as a "standard" Lenormand deck. These include cards such as the Bridge card, the Dice, the Mask and others. [110]

1. **Rider/Messenger**: This brings good news from overseas of business and financial affairs.

---

109   To this and several other historical points we are indebted to the work of researchers at trionfi.com.

110   See Ciro Marchetti, original self-published version of the *Gilded Reverie Lenormand*.

2. **The Clover Leaf**: A very lucky sign of coming good fortune.

3. **The Ship**: News from distant lands; a successful journey; a voyage.

4. **The House**: A successful transaction, a visit, a new home.

5. **The Tree**: Good health and a pleasing assurance of coming prosperity and happiness.

6. **The Clouds**: These denote disappointment, failure of plans, and dismay.

7. **The Snake**: This is an unpleasant sign of treachery, disloyalty, and hidden danger, sometimes caused by those whom you least suspect; if its head is raised, injury by the malice of a man is predicted; it is also an indication of misfortune and illness.

8. **The Coffin**: A bad omen of coming bereavement.

9. **The Bouquet**: This is a most fortunate symbol of coming happiness, love, fulfilled hope, and marriage.

10. **The Scythe**: This sign foreshows grief and pain.

11. **The Rod/Whip**: To a woman this sign foretells vexation and trials in her marriage; for a man, it has much the same meaning, and severe disappointment will befall him.

12. **The Birds/Owls**: These are significant of happiness and joyful tidings.

13. **The Child/Little Girl**: This is a sign that you will soon be making fresh plans or forming new projects.

14. **The Fox**: This denotes that you may have an unsuspected enemy, possibly disloyal dependents; sometimes it means theft and trickery.

15. **The Bear**: A journey north, sometimes prolonged travel.

16. **The Stars**: A lucky sign; [if surrounded by dots in a leaf reading], wealth and honour are foretold.

17. **The Stork**: In summer, this bird tells you to beware of robbery or fraud; in winter, prepare for bad weather and a great misfortune; a stork flying predicts that whilst you hesitate in coming to a decision, a profitable chance is lost, the news of which will speedily reach you.

18. **The Dog**: This symbol has many meanings which must be read in accordance with the other symbols; in a general way, this sign indicates adverse conditions, the thwarting of life's chances, unfortunate love affairs, family misfortune and money troubles.

19. **The Tower**: This predicts an advantageous opportunity through which you may rise to a good position in life.

20. **The Garden**: Many pleasant meanings may be given to this symbol, good fortune, happiness, love, marriage, and a large circle of admiring friends, being among them. [We have used for this Kent's interpretation for "flowers" as distinct to "bouquet" as it carries the same meanings as the usual interpretations for "Garden"].

21. **The Mountain**: This gives promise of the realisation of a great ambition and of the influence of powerful friends; many mountains indicate obstructions and sometimes powerful enemies in your career.

22. **The Ways**: This symbol must be read in conjunction with surrounding symbols; it usually emphasises the importance of other signs; a broken signpost indicates that you take a wrong turning in your life and afterwards have much cause to regret it. [We have used "Signpost" here from Kent as carrying the same meaning as "Ways" or "Crossroads"].

23. **The Mice**: This invariably indicates that there is need for a trap to be set; it also gives warning that domestic worries are to be expected.

24. **The Heart**: A sign of coming happiness through the affections bringing joy into your life, or satisfaction through money, according to other signs near.

25. **The Ring**: [With dots around], a contract or a business transaction; with the figures of a man and woman, an engagement or wedding is foretold.

26. **The Book**: An open book shows a desire for information and a mind ever on the alert to understand new theories and facts; a closed book is a sign of expectancy.

27. **The letter**: These are shown by oblong or square tea leaves, initials near give the name of the writer; with dots around they will contain money.

28. **The Gentleman**: You may expect a visitor.

29. **The Lady**: [With bad signs, several women mean scandal]; otherwise, society.

30. **The Lily**: A fortunate omen of realisation, love, and marriage.

31. **The Sun**: This promises happiness, health, success in love, prosperity, and the beneficial discovery of secrets.

32. **The Moon**: A crescent moon denotes good news, fortune, and romance; for a man, it predicts public recognition and honour.

33. **The Key**: Circumstances will improve, things will become easy, and your path will be made smooth; you may hope for success in whatever you have on hand; a key at some distance from the consultant denotes the need for the assistance of good and influential friends in times of difficulty.

34. **The Fish**: News from abroad; with other signs of movement, emigration.

35. **The Anchor**: A pleasing symbol of good and loyal friends, constancy in love, and the realisation of your wishes; an emblem of safety to a sailor.

36. **The Cross:** You must expect to meet with hindrances and obstacles in the way of your desires; sorrow and misfortune are also indicated by this symbol.

We will next look at A. E. Waite and C. C. Zain and provide a summary of meanings for each Lenormand card.

A. E. Waite's Lenormand

One of the advantages of time travel that we can see from the future are the small events in the past which at the time were barely noted but have now become something far more than their original ripple in the timeline. We are never the best judge of our own time; history provides us many examples of this fact. When A. E. Waite and Pamela Colman Smith created their tarot deck in 1909, they had no idea what would become of it; Waite in fact called it nothing more than "a delightful experiment."[111]

Now that we are travelling back through time, with the benefit of knowing how the Lenormand deck will become a cartomantic favourite in the future, we can see the importance of Waite's writing on the symbolism of coffee grounds in his "fortune-telling" book, written under the pseudonym "The Grand Orient."

Whilst not comprehensive, it adds to our stock of card-meanings for the Lenormand, long before the Lenormand became a "thing" across social media such as Instagram and Tumblr.

> A cross denotes news of death, but three crosses in the same cup are symbolical of honour. A ring means marriage; if a letter can be discovered near it, that will be the initial of the name of the future spouse. If the ring be in the clear part of the cup, it foretells a happy union; if there are clouds about it, expect the contrary; if it chances to be quite at the bottom, the marriage will never take place. A leaf of clover or trefoil is a good sign, denoting speedy good fortune if at the top of the cup, and good fortune proportionately more remote as the symbol is nearer to the bottom. Flowers are commonly the signs of joy, happiness and peaceful life. A rose promises health; a lily at the top of the cup foretells a happy marriage, but at the bottom it portends anger. A shrub signifies delays;

---

111   A. E. Waite, *Shadows in Life and Thought* (London, UK: Selwyn & Blount, 1938), 184.

a single tree as a rule predicts a restoration to health, but a weeping willow is a portent of sorrow. A group of trees in the clear part of the cup betokens misfortunes which may be avoided; several trees wide apart promise that your wishes will be accomplished; if encompassed by dashes, it is a token that your fortune is in its blossom, and only needs care to be brought to maturity; if surrounded by dots, riches may be expected.

A tree beside a house promises you the possession of a country seat or cottage, according to size. A house beside a circle shows that the former will come into your possession. If there be an X near it, it will be situated in a city or town. If accompanied by triangles, it will be inherited or given to you. If it be surmounted by a cross, you will die in it. Mountains signify either friends or enemies, according to their situation. The sun, moon and stars denote happiness, success; clouds, happiness or misfortune—according as they are bright or dark. Birds are good omens; the appearance of one in the cup, typifies a sudden stroke of luck.

Quadrupeds—with the exception of the dog—foretell trouble and difficulties; reptiles mean treachery. Fish imply good news from across the water, but some authorities interpret their appearance as the presage of an invitation to a good dinner.

A serpent is always the sign of an enemy, and if in the cloudy part of the cup, gives warning that great prudence will be needed to ward off misfortune.

The figure of a man indicates a speedy visitor; if the arm be outstretched, he will be the bearer of a present. When the figure is very distinct, it shows that the person expected will be of dark complexion, and vice versa. A heart surrounded by dots signifies joy, occasioned by the receipt of money. A letter signifies news; if in the clear, very welcome ones; surrounded by dots, a remittance; hemmed in by clouds, bad tidings and losses; a heart near it, a love letter. An isolated line signifies a journey, its extent in proportion to the length of the line; dots or small branch-lines signify the obstacles which may be expected therein.

A circle enclosing four points foretells the birth of a child, and this emblem has a profoundly occult significance. A dog beside a human figure always has reference to a friend. A man mounted on a horse presages a male person who will powerfully espouse your cause. An anchor at the bottom of the cup denotes success in business; at the top, and in the clear part, love and fidelity; but in thick or cloudy parts, it means inconstancy.

A crown near a cross indicates a large fortune resulting from a death. A bouquet, composed of four or more flowers, is the most fortunate of all omens. [112]

A final stop in our time travelling overview of cartomantic meaning is with C. C. Zain, who we will meet later in our travels.

The Brotherhood of Light Lenormand

We are fortunate that Zain also wrote about the symbolism of coffee grounds and hence the modern version of the so-called Lenormand cards.

He also provided good direction for those wishing to read coffee grounds or tea leaves, which suits the tarot reader as well as the Lenormand reader of today:

> The skilled cup diviner, however, does not leap from one symbol to some other on the far side of the cup. He starts in with those symbols nearest the brim of the cup, and nearest the handle. Often there will be a chain of symbols reaching from near the brim down into the bottom of the cup; reaching from the present into the very distant future. He permits his attention to follow these symbols in the order in which they occur, and strives to perceive the exact relationship of each symbol to the next one in the series, and perhaps how the symbols on one or both sides influence it. As he passes from one symbol to another, observing the influence of adjacent symbols, he endeavours to weave the whole into a connected story. He seeks to point out how one event follows another, and what causes each. Instead of a disjointed account he strives to knit together the **influences** and **persons** and **events** represented into such a connected narrative of the future that it brings out all the important facts and relationships. [113]

He also makes a fascinating observation in that class that some people will have specific experiences with common objects, animals and events used as symbols which give those things specific meaning to that one person. Zain suggests that the soul uses these specifics in

---

112   A. E. Waite (as "Grand Orient"), *Complete Manual of Occult Divination, Vol. 1* (New Hyde Park: University Books, 1972), 220–223.

113   From Course XI, Divination and Character Reading, Chapter 2 (Serial Lesson 119), 1940.

communication, over and above the more commonplace meanings—making every oracular moment unique.

He then returns to the common or universal meanings, saying:

> The tree, because of its strength and long life, is usually interpreted as a symbol of health and vitality. The dog, because of its faithful companionship with man, is usually interpreted as a friend. And a railroad train, because it is commonly used for transit, is usually interpreted as a journey. [114]

Regarding these meanings, Zain notes that:

> To the soul, in its code messages to the physical, an emblem symbolises that which it is most strongly associated within the unconscious mind. This usually, though not always, is that event, or quality, or thing, which most readily comes into the mind next after thinking of the emblem. Usually, as in most of the above examples, the relationship between the symbol and that which it signifies is quite clear after a moment's reflection. [115]

Here are the specific symbols Zain gives that relate to Lenormand:

- **Cross**: Hardship & Suffering
- **Fox**: Trickery & Cunning
- **Bird**: A message or messages
- **Mouse**: Small difficulties & petty annoyances
- **Fish**: Gain & Money
- **Baby** (Child): A new enterprise (project)
- **A Ship**: Approaching wealth

---

114 *Ibid.*

115 *Ibid.*

- **Ring**: Marriage

- **Flowers** (Bouquet): Expression of goodwill and kindness, happiness.

We can now use our Lenormand meanings with a model derived from Zain, and provide a method of reading Lenormand in three minutes. In a similar manner to how we engineered the tarot into three aspects in our orientation guide at the front of this present book, we can also see every Lenormand card in three ways: as an **influence**, an **agent**, or an **event**.

If we consider the Tree with its usual meaning of health, then its **influence** is a healthy one, promoting growth and stability; if it is acting as an **agent**, it would be someone in the family tree or a healthy diet, and if it were an **event** it would be something long-standing and seasonal, or something healthy like a spa day or retreat.

We provide below a key to these three aspects for every card and an oracular sentence to easily place these cards together into a three-minute instant reading.

Lenormand in Three Minutes

We have used the core cartomantic meanings of 1796 and extended these into the three aspects and provided the meaning of the card most popular through the little sheet that often accompanied the "Lenormand" deck under the name "Phillipe Lenormand."

1. Rider/Messenger: News.

Influence: Novelty, Newness, Originality.

Agent: A person revealing something or carrying a message on their own behalf or that of another.

Event: Receiving News, a new proposal or a delivery (but of something totally unexpected, unlike the Stork).

2. The Clover Leaf: Good luck.

Influence: Luck in a little sense (compared to the Sun, which is bigger fortune and opportunity).

Agent: The right person at the right place at the right time, lucky meeting (with the Park/Garden).

Event: A chance occurrence, a piece of good luck, slight unexpected change for the better.

3. The Ship: Wealth, investment, travel.

Influence: Exploration, Discovery, Adventure, Risk, Investment (with Fish).

Agent: A traveller or someone outside your usual circles.

Event: Journey (Holiday with Sun, Business trip with Fox).

4. The House: Prosperity, the home.

Influence: Home, security.

Agent: family member.

Event: Family gathering.

5. The Tree: Health.

Influence: Health.

Agent: Doctor.

Event: Health check.

6. The Clouds: Trouble, delay, confusion.

Influence: Uncertainty, confusion.

Agent: Change; with Fox, it would be job uncertainty; with Mouse and Fox, job uncertainty and loss.

Event: Redundancy if with mouse and fox, job redundancy.

7. The Snake: Misfortune, betrayal.

Influence: Betrayal, traitorous behaviour. Snake, heart, ring = commitment, union and betrayal.

Agent: Tempter/temptress, traitor, a hypocrite.

Event: Betrayal, Marriage/relationship breakdown.

8. The Coffin: Serious illness.

Influence: Endings.

Agent: Time.

Event: Leaving home, with the House/coffin, with Heart/coffin, is endings of love union.

9. The Bouquet: Happiness, gift, proposal.

Influence: Gift, generosity: Bouquet/ring = marriage proposal.

Agent: Giver, suitor, lover. Bouquet/whip = trouble maker.

Event: Birthday, anniversary, engagement, presentation.

10. The Scythe: Danger.

Influence: Shock, surprise, change, Stork/scythe = Shock/surprise pregnancy, mountain/scythe = sudden obstacle, Tree/scythe = shock with health, Tower/scythe /fish = Money shock from bank.

Agent: Competitor, rival, ill health, stock market, banks, politicians.

Event: election, referendum, stock market crash.

11. The Rod/Whip: Argument, sorrow, disagreement.

Influence: Strife, conflict, anger, back-biting.

Agent: Jealous person, nasty person, peevish person.

Event: Workplace, marriage/relationship, divorce; Whip/Tower/ring = commitment to institution brings strife; or Whip/mice = loss of strife, however with the combination of whip/rider/mice/heart = love or union loss brings strife.

12. The Birds/Owls: Brief difficulties.

Influence: chatter, communication.

Agent: telephone call, skype call.

Event: Group discussion, friends talking at a bar, conference call, meeting/discussion, people gossiping., birds/moon = recognition verbally; in that people are talking about something or somebody. Birds/key = unlocking communication.

13. The Child/Little Girl: Good friends.

Influence: childlike behaviour, innocence, authenticity, new enthusiasm.

Agent: Child or childlike person.

Event: Birth of new idea, newcomer (with Rider).

14. The Fox: A deceiver or trickster.

Influence: Ambition, completion, greed.

Agent: Rival, for example somebody who is after your job.

Event: Successful plan, job or project success, promotion opportunity. Fox/fish = money work, work you do will bring money. Fox/ring = work commitment, Fox/book = knowledge work; this is as simple as working to get educated, going to college.

15. The Bear: Happiness, but warning about the jealousy of others.

Influence: authority, legality, strength.

Agent: Strong male figure, boss, bank manager, authority figure.

Event: Meeting with your financial advisor or bank manager. Bear/letter = written advice, perhaps a legal letter. Bear/mountain = obstacle authority figure; somebody is going to stop you getting your own way.

16. The Stars: Extended luck.

Influence: Guidance, advice, clear direction is brought to the situation.

Agent: Handbook, google, navigation, satnav, map.

Event: Trip, consultation with an astrologer, lawyer, accountant. Stars/woman; this is wise woman.

17. The Stork: Change of residence.

Influence: Return, habit, displacement.

Agent: Someone from the past returns.

Event: A repeating event.

18. The Dog: Faithful friend.

Influence: Loyalty.

Agent: A close friend.

Event: Trustworthy advice.

19. The Tower: Healthy old age.

Influence: Bureaucracy, organisation, control.

Agent: A social worker, bureaucrat, official.

Event: Authorisation, passage.

20. The Garden: Good friends.

Influence: Social connections.

Agent: Many people, connections, a networker.

Event: Social event.

21. The Mountain: An enemy in your way.

Influence: Obstacle, detour.

Agent: Someone in your way.

Event: A problem, a challenge.

22. The Ways: Misfortune.

Influence: Gives freedom, choice, opportunities ahead, opens the situation.

Agent: Someone asks for a decision or forces a choice.

Event: Things come to a head and cannot go forwards in the same way.

23. The Mice: Theft, loss.

Influence: A reducing of things, a nibbling away, biting into the situation.

Agent: Others are being left alone too much and taking to their own devices.

Event: Something, even if just your time, is taken from you in small ways.

24. The Heart: Union, bliss, harmony.

Influence: Love, good feelings and blessings, strong emotion is brought to the situation.

Agent: Someone who cares about you, literally has your best interests at heart.

Event: A declaration of love, support or trust.

25. The Ring: Good marriage.

Influence: Union, agreement.

Agent: Someone who agrees with you, someone close.

Event: Contract, agreement, marriage.

26. The Book: A secret.

Influence: Secrecy, knowledge.

Agent: An expert.

Event: Knowledge, a secret revealed (with Key), new information (with Rider).

27. The Letter: Written news.

Influence: Recorded information, archive.

Agent: Someone who remembers.

Event: Written communication, email, text, etc.

28. The Gentleman: A man.

Influence: Masculine.

Agent: A Man.

Event: A male partner.

29. The Lady: A woman.

Influence: Feminine.

Agent: A woman.

Event: A female partner.

30. The Lily: Virtue, good living.

Influence: Time, age, sexuality, purity.

Agent: An older person.

Event: A good deed, a virtuous action.

31. The Sun: Happiness, encouragement of growth.

Influence: Expansion, growth, success.

Agent: An optimist, someone who has big plans.

Event: Success, good luck, a big opportunity to grow.

32. The Moon: Honour.

Influence: Recognition.

Agent: Someone with influence.

Event: Promotion, announcement, award.

33. The Key: Success.

Influence: Unlocking, opening, revealing.

Agent: Someone with influence, a decision-maker or deal-maker.

Event: A revelation or opportunity, success of a plan.

34. The Fish: Fortune.

Influence: Acquisition of resources, finances.

Agent: A wealthy person (in time, resource or actual money).

Event: The availability of money.

35. The Anchor: Faith, success in business and love.

Influence: Long-term, stability.

Agent: A long-standing member of a group, etc.

Event: Setting a long-term plan in motion.

36. The Cross: Misfortune and suffering.

Influence: Hardship, discomfort, difficulty.

Agent: A depressing or negative person, complainer, trouble-maker.

Event: An adverse change in circumstances.

Lenormand Oracular Sentence

We can now use these keywords within those aspects of the cards to create an oracular sentence or oracular construct, as we term it. The straightforward grammar of these three aspects is that "an event is caused by an agent, bringing the influence of the third card to the situation."

We can write this out in the construct:

When [Event] By [Agent] It Will Bring [Influence].

We can see that this works as well when reading "right to left" as Influence acts on Agent to cause Event.

We always place the cards into context with a question in Lenormand, which is very different than tarot in this respect. In Lenormand, the cards act as symbols or emblems rather than in tarot where the cards are complex metaphors, having multiple symbols on one card.

This construct, with the context of the question, allows us to perform a simple three-card reading with Lenormand that respects the way of reading larger layouts and helps build proficiency in the method. We will start with three-card readings but recommend that the reader quickly moves to nine- and thirty-six-card layouts even if you only choose to read sections of the larger layout. In our experience, it is easier in the long run to start with the full "grand tableaux" of thirty-six cards and work backwards with Lenormand.

Having said that, here we provide the shortcut three-card method to get you up and running quickly.

We will ask the cards as an example, "What will happen if we request a delay to the project?"

We shuffle our thirty-six cards and receive:

Heart + Mouse + Ways.

When [Heart/Event] by [Mice/Agent] it will bring [Ways/Influence].

"When there is a declaration of trust, by the people who have not been trusted, it will bring new opportunities ahead."

We should consult and involve in the project anyone who has felt excluded from it, explain the reasons for wanting the delay, and this might even bring new ideas and plans for the future.

We can now turn this into a more direct oracular, predictive or fortune-telling script by simply putting it into the future tense like so:

There will be [Event] by [Agent] Bringing [Influence].

If we received the cards:

14 + 17 +16

Fox + Stork + Stars

"There will be a successful job opportunity through/by a person returning to a place they have been before which will bring clear guidance."

Another example would be:

"How should we launch the project to make the most of the newly changed situation?"

14 + 2 + 7

Fox + Clover + Snake

"There will be project success by connecting with the right person through networking, but be warned that this may bring betrayal at a later date."

So, we should look to capitalise on the connections, and then go it alone as soon as possible, or have a cast-iron contract or loyalty agreement, perhaps. Once we had made that change, we could then consult the cards again to check that we had removed or mitigated against that risk.

We will now travel along the timeline and recover questions from across time to show how the Lenormand, using the keywords given throughout this chapter, can resolve any situation no matter the era, culture, or language.

Lenormand Answers to Questions Through the Ages

I am twenty-three, engaged to a young man I love very much but he is very mean. He hasn't even brought me a ring. He lost both parents in the war and he says he is saving to buy our own house as he is sick of lodgings. But is it true that mean men make jealous husbands?[116]

---

116 *Mirabelle* magazine, 1956.

If we were to rephrase this in a contemporary manner, perhaps what she is asking is, "Am I with the right man and should I marry a man like this? Is he worth marrying or should I cut my losses?"

We perform a simple three-card spread for the question and receive:

Lily (30) + House (4) + Letter (27)

The first card here is the Letter, and as we see in the Square of Seven in our cartomancy chapters, the cards can influence one another from left to right, or right to left, depending on how you choose to read.

The Letter card corresponds to "written communication" and suggests that until the man about whom we are asking the question (therefore the question's subject) has a contract in his hand securing a house, he will not be content.

The House is literally the house that he wants to buy, whereas the Lily is about age and retirement—long-term security. So, there is a letter about a house and a long-term plan.

The answer to the question is that he is only interested in his security and not much interested in romance, as the woman suspects. This does not look as if it is going to change in the long-term. The biggest concern here is that he is not going to provide any romance in the relationship. So perhaps if this relationship is not fulfilling her needs she should cut her losses and end the relationship.

If we were performing a reading for a real person, it may be that there are issues with the loss of the parents affecting the man's ability to seek intimacy, a matter we could explore with the cards. What indicates this situation is the Lily (a flower sometimes associated with mourning) at the left side of the reading, which the other two cards are affecting. It is not true that Lenormand can only read mundane matters; it is quite capable of communicating psychological and spiritual concerns.

We now turn to another relationship question, as three out of the five questions asked of every cartomancer are about relationships:

Pete and I have only been married for a year and already I am just an old housewife to him.

He scarcely speaks in the morning and never takes me anywhere, and more and more he goes out with the boys before coming home. What can I do about it?

Our contemporary rephrasing of this is "My husband has gone off me and I am worried that he is having an affair. What shall I do?" The cards we draw are:

Snake (7) + Mountain (21) + Garden (20)

Reading from right to left:

Garden: Meeting place + Mountain: Obstacle + Snake: Betrayal/other woman.

The Garden, a meeting place, and then the Mountain which signifies that it is an obstacle in this marriage. On the left, we have the Snake lying in the garden. Betrayal is indeed as old as time itself—like all these answers, we have drawn cards at random from our deck, not deliberately selected them for the question.

Even down the ages, oracular moments are still being picked up down the timeline. This question was a real-life question of a young woman from 1958. To an oracle, all time is one and the same. We wonder what happened to this young woman, and whether she found happiness in life? Out of curiosity we pulled another three cards to see:

Rider (1) + Whip (11) + Letter (27)

From right to left it reads:

Letter: Written communication + Whip: Strife/conflict + Rider: News.

Here we have written communication, most likely a legal letter, and the presence of the Whip indicating much strife in the marriage. Then we have the Rider (most likely bringing the *decree nisi*) to state the end date of the marriage.

From this reading it does not look like the marriage survived much longer than the one year.

Next, we will look at a more existential question, and one no doubt that is asked by querents in every day and age:

I expect you will think that this question is foolish, but it worries me so that I have to thrash it out. Why is it I feel like life is just pointless? I work, come home, have my meal, go to the pictures or a dance, and then go to bed.[117]

In modern terms, should it be needed: "What is the meaning of life, have I got a greater purpose?"

The three cards pulled for our demonstration are:

Ship (3) + Lily (30) + Mountain (21)

From right to left, they read first from the Mountain, an obstacle that blocks, but with retirement (lily) on the other side, in the sense of "taking time out." This will bring about travel. The cards suggest that over time the person discovers a new experience (Lily) through travel (Ship).

In this next and closing example, we will take a situation and answer it by splitting it into two related questions, performing a three-card reading for each question. Whilst there are many methods for carrying out a full-scale reading for a complex situation (such as the Grand Tableaux, or "big table"), we can begin by building up sets of three-card readings.

I have two lovers, writes Crushed Strawberry, and I like them both equally. One is liked by my mother but disapproved of by my father, and the other one my father favors and my mother does not care about. What am I to do? If I take either, it will be in opposition to the wishes of my parents. It makes me extremely miserable and I don't know what to do?[118]

---

117 Carey, 171.
118 Ibid., 27.

There are two issues in this question and thus they need addressing separately. In modern parlance, we can ask:

1. I am torn between two lovers. What shall I do?

2. I let my parents control my life. If I carry on like this, where will it end?

Question 1

We ask the first question and receive the three cards:

Tree (5) + Cross (36) + Garden (20)

From right to left we read this as "We have a meeting place (Garden), where the relationship will be brought out into the open, which in turn will cause suffering (Cross), and this will affect your health (Tree)."

Question 2

We ask "I let my parents control my life. If I carry on like this, where will it end?" and receive:

Heart (24) + Child (13) + Ring (25)

Here we have, from right to left:

The (Ring) will commit you to a (child)-like state of (Heart) emotional union.

The cards are saying in their literal and direct wisdom, that if you do not take control you will be committed or bound to a child-like relationship with your parents.

In summary, the cards are simply confirming the obvious health issues that the stresses of indecision and parental authority are causing the querent. The advice is to bring the situation out into the open, otherwise there will be increasing risks to health.

If these two rows of cards were laid one above the other, we would see how the Tree (Health) was above the Heart. This would indicate the nature of the health issue that might be increasing in risk. Similarly, the Cross is above the Child, indicating that the main cause of all the suffering is the childlike relationship with the parents, and the Garden is above the Ring, meaning that the lover who should be chosen is whomever proves ready to commit (Ring) in public (Garden).

Lenormand Nine-Card Square

As we have just seen, the positions of cards above and below each other as well as to each side can also add to our reading. We can now slightly re-word our oracular construct and easily create a comprehensive nine-card reading by laying out three rows of three cards in a nine-card square.

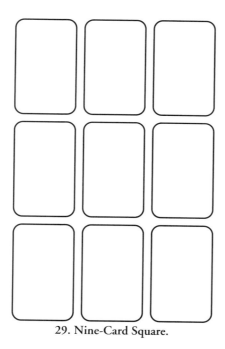

29. Nine-Card Square.

First lay the man or woman card as appropriate in the center of your table and then place eight cards around them.

The first (top) row can be read as "What is over me?" It indicates issues that are influencing your situation and over which you have less control or are in the hands of other people or processes.

The second (middle) row is read as usual with direct regard to your question.

The third (lower) row is read as "What is below me?" It indicates those things upon which you can act or change most readily.

You will soon find with a bit of experience that using the nine-card square after just a few practice three-card spreads rapidly becomes second-nature. You can then quickly move to laying out all thirty-six cards even if you start reading it in 9 x 9 sections as described below.

Intermediate Time Traveller Method

If you have a specific question or situation that can be represented by one of the cards—for example, a money question (Fish), a big business question (Tower), a love question (Heart)—then place that card instead in the center and read as usual. This practice also prepares you easily for the Grand Tableaux, which builds up from this technique whilst adding additional possibilities for interpretation such as the distance between cards, a factor that changes their effect and influence.

Advanced Method

Lay out all thirty-six cards in rows of eight. This is called the Grand Tableaux and is one of two main layouts when using the whole deck. Start reading the cards about the Gentleman or Woman card as you have done with the nine-card method, then read in lines above and below in a similar way. You can then consult the same layout without moving any of the cards to look at your health by reading around the Tree card, your love life by reading around the Heart, and so on. [119]

---

119   See Marcus Katz and Tali Goodwin, *Learning Lenormand* (Woodbury, MN: Llewellyn, 2013).

7

The Pioneer Years

The Tarot of Etteila is of no symbolic value; it is a bad mutilation of the real tarot.

—Papus, 1899 [120]

2:30 pm, 2 March, 1899: Paris, France

We walk amongst men with straw boater hats, who tip them in acknowledgment as we pass, and women in black bustled dresses, themselves tipping umbrellas to the afternoon sun. The scent of horses, leather, and lavender pomanders barely covers the rotten smell from the sewers that would assail Paris for several years.

As we turn a corner to 26 Rue Racine, behind the Odéon-Théâtre de l'Europe, we hear carts, horses, carriages, buckles, and harnesses, the sounds fading slightly as we leave behind the main squares and avenues of the city. The preparations for the grand *Exposition Universelle* world fair are already underway, which will be the talk of the city from May until it closes in October.

At Rue Racine, we locate the publishing house of Ernest Flammarion, founded in 1876, and see the gilt gold lettering spelling *Librairie* above the door. It is here that

---

120   Proof that "hating on" other tarot decks or works is nothing new. See also Crowley's acerbic review of A. E. Waite & Pamela Colman Smith's deck, quoted in Marcus Katz & Tali Goodwin, *Secrets of the Waite-Smith Tarot* (Woodbury, MN: Llewellyn, 2015).

an author named Gerald—better known by his nom de plume, Papus—will come to deliver his manuscript for *Tarot of the Bohemians* later this week.

We continue by the publishers and find the author's apartment nearby. He is finishing his preface in a small room lit by gaslight. A worn rug covers most of the parquet floor upon which stands a decorative high table and a simple chair with an embroidered cushion and a fur throw. Across the hall through an open door, we catch the opening piano notes of Debussy's first arabesque as a young pianist practises for the spring season.

The late afternoon light streams in through an arched window where curtains are tied back on a series of rings. Above, decorative tiles adorn the window-frame, one small nod to the new elegance becoming now popular in late Victorian Europe, the avant-garde.

By the fireplace squats a three-legged round table with a vase of flowers upon it, and Papus himself sits writing at a small desk pushed against the wall.

Above the heavily bearded thirty-four-year-old author are portraits, perhaps of family members or great figures of the past—we cannot see at this distance without disturbing him. He signs off his preface for the manuscript and gathers it together. He goes to get his coat. Whilst he is occupied, we begin to scan his work. We want to see if we can learn what Papus wanted to do with tarot. As we continue our travels along the time-stream, we will see if he accomplished his ambition.

In this chapter, we will explore the pioneering work on tarot along with its mistakes, which was created in the late 1800s. This drew on the first writings on tarot and consolidated many of the strange theories about its purpose and origin. However, at the same time, it developed the teaching work of Etteilla, and authors such as Papus created the bedrock of what became modern tarot.

In learning from this era, we will learn the tarot before the Golden Dawn took it even more esoteric, before Waite revealed and hid its mysteries at the same time, and before Crowley showed how individual a deck could be created. We will learn tarot in a half-way stage between pure card-reading, fortune-telling, and heavy esotericism.

We will begin by looking at the card decks that were available to us in this time. It is sometimes difficult to consider what it might have been like when there were only rumours and suggestions about tarot, and less than ten tarot decks in the world you might likely manage to obtain, after much searching and word-of-mouth—or the occasional advert in underground esoteric pamphlets.

Tarot Decks of the Era

In this era, Papus conveniently lists the tarot decks available to readers across Europe, from the publisher M. Pussey, on the Rue de La Banque, from whom a deck could be purchased for 4 Francs, or George Redway publishers in London, who would later publish his own book, an English translation by A. P. Morton in 1896. [121] The decks, less than ten, were as follows:

- The Tarot of Etteila

- The Italian Tarot

- The Marseilles Tarot

- The Tarot of Besançon

- The double-headed Tarot of Besançon

- The Tarot of Watillaux

- The German Tarot

- The Tarot of Oswald Wirth

Papus takes a large creative leap and whilst firmly rooted in the misguided notions of "ancient Egypt" and "Kabbalah," spins some useful interpretations, methods and tables of correspondence that would quickly re-surface in the occult era of the Golden Dawn.

Time Traveller Visitors' Book

After visiting this era of time, we can now also time-skip a hop backwards and locate the people who we hear Papus talking about to his own friends and colleagues. He is at least

---

121   You can visit 20 Rue de La Banque in Paris, just down from the *Bourse* or historical stock exchange and see the archway through which the doors to the apartments are reached. It is rather fittingly designed with ten Rose emblems.

someone who also mentions those who have influenced his work in his own book, so we can use this as a time traveller guidebook for our next adventures in the tarot.

The names of those who most influenced Papus are:

- Eliphas Lévi

- Stanislas de Guaita

- Oswald Wirth

- Court de Gébelin

- Fabre d'Olivet

We would encourage all time travellers to visit these personages whenever they have time to explore these many further tributaries for the tarot time-streams.

Using Kabbalah and Tarot

When we pick up Papus's manuscripts from his table, we see immediately the wealth of diagrams and notes mentioning the Kabbalah, Hebrew letters, and numerology. There are annotated circles and triangles, and all manner of tables. It is all completely overwhelming, and we can perhaps see why he suggested his book was for "initiates only," although he did devote one chapter on using the cards for fortune-telling "for the ladies."

Papus drew his Kabbalistic work from d'Olivet, Lévi, Paul Christian, and the original work of Kircher, who influenced the Golden Dawn. As time travellers, we can see immediately why this is important to us as it re-surfaces in the major arcana of A. E. Waite and Pamela Colman Smith and is then the most powerful stream of symbolism coursing through the veins of every tarot deck since that time. [122]

We can see it here as we hold it in our hands and smell the very parchment as the ink dries. The very first layerings of Kabbalah into symbols and spiritual teaching through tarot are here in our hands. Let us look closer to try learning some new methods while the ideas are freshly forged.

---

122 See Marcus Katz and Tali Goodwin, *Secrets of the Waite-Smith Tarot* (Woodbury, MN: Llewellyn, 2015).

Papus's Hidden Resonances

Locked away in Papus's work is a powerful pattern of tarot reading we can learn and apply to our cards. We use it to determine how court cards affect the answers to questions when they interact with other cards in the spread. [123]

As an example, we might have the King of Cups in a reading and the 4 of Wands, one of the specific cards Papus links with all the Kings. This sets up a resonance we call "reconciliation" or "getting the feeling right for everyone." The 4 of Wands is traditionally about invitation, but we have discovered that many readers also see it as "an appropriate response." [124]

When we combine that with the King of Cups, who is known for his emotional depth and compassion, we get an invitation to be compassionate, empathy, and the idea of an "appropriate response (4 of Wands) to compassion (King of Cups)" or "empathy (King of Cups) invited by others (4 of Wands)." We put this into our mental mixer and come out with the single keyword or concept "reconciliation." You will find that we have done this for all the hidden resonances Papus discovered through his analysis of Kabbalah.

Although the method is based in Kabbalah, we do not need Kabbalah to use it. We will provide a separate section below for advanced time travellers who want to look under the hood of the method. We call this method "hidden resonances" because it shows us lines of force interacting in a reading. It applies to the court cards in combination with specific cards.

When one or more court card appear in one of your readings, consult these lists and see if there are any of the other cards listed also appearing in your reading. You can then read and apply the appropriate resonance to further deepen your interpretation.

Intermediate Time Traveller Method

As a method for reading for yourself, to get a direct and clear answer, use this technique which we call "Resonant Response." Pick out the court cards in one pile and all the minor cards listed that follows. Shuffle the court card set whilst considering your question.

---

123 This method is developed from Papus, *Tarot of the Bohemians* (Hollywood, CA: Wilshire Book Company, 1973), 62, where Papus lists "affinities."

124 See Marcus Katz and Tali Goodwin, *Tarot Flip* (Keswick, UK: Forge Press, 2010).

Turn up the top card from the court card set. This indicates the force that is active and is seeking expression in your situation.

Remove from the minor cards the three cards listed under that court card. So, if you receive the King of Cups (or any king), select the Ace of Wands, the 4 of Wands, and 7 of Wands.

Shuffle these three minor arcana cards while looking at the court card.

If you have received a page, you need only select the 10 of Pentacles to place next to the page. Being simple forces, pages are only paired with that card.

Select the top card from the minor arcana set and place it next to the court card. This indicates how the expression of the court card is being filtered, constrained, focused, or even blocked.

Consult the resonant combination listed here and read the interpretation.

Continuing our earlier example of the King of Cups, if you then received the 7 of Wands from the three minor cards that would be "instinct." The interpretation is that whatever you deeply feel about the situation is likely to be the case.

King of Wands

+ **Ace of Wands**: Ambition

+ **4 of Wands**: Autonomy

+ **7 of Wands**: Arrogance

Hyperactive, restless, arrogant, control freak.

King of Cups

+ **Ace of Wands**: Legacy

+ **4 of Wands**: Reconciliation

+ **7 of Wands**: Instinct

What we drive against, rebel or fight. Instinct/instinctual, savvy, common sense, perceptive.

King of Swords

+ **Ace of Wands**: Determination

+ **4 of Wands**: Negotiation

    Brainstorming, a lecture, debate, discussion.

+ **7 of Wands**: Diplomacy

    Warfare, warrior king, war campaign, keeping order through instruction and ideas.

King of Pentacles

+ **Ace of Wands**: Security

+ **4 of Wands**: Consolidation

    Financial consolidation, buying a house, setting real boundaries.

+ **7 of Wands**: Budgeting

    Resisting temptation to spend. Auditing, accountability, responsibility

All four aspects of the King + Aces for a monarchy to survive.

Queen of Wands

+ **2 of Cups**: Union

+ **5 of Cups**: Courage

    Initiation, accountability in the face of adversity.

+ **8 of Cups**: Motivation

    Positivity in the face of adversity.

Queen of Cups

+ **2 of Cups**: Compassion

+ **5 of Cups**: Melancholy

Dark night of the soul.

+ 8 of Cups: Nurturing

Queen of Swords

+ 2 of Cups: Negotiation

+ 5 of Cups: Regret

Recrimination.

+ 8 of Cups: Revenge

Revengeful, bigoted, bitter, vindictive.

Queen of Pentacles

+ 2 of Cups: Collaboration

+ 5 of Cups: Practicality

Reality check, nurturing, support. As the saying goes, "fall seven times, get up eight." Find a new state of balance. Earth and water do complement, can turn into mud, and then bricks to build again.

+ 8 of Cups: Relocation

This combination deals with commitment in various forms.

Knight of Wands

+ 3 of Swords: Frustration

+ 6 of Swords: Moving on

Migration.

+ 9 of Swords: Suppression

These are all states of mental anguish. The Knights are showing us four different ways in which these states manifest in our personality or projects. The minor cards act as a filter to the court cards' natural state of expression, page = impulse, knight

= force, queen = containing, king = controlling. So, the King of Pentacles is controlling earth, and through the 4 of Wands, for example, that control would be expressed as a bouncer-like energy.

Knight of Cups

+ **3 of Swords**: Treachery

Irresponsibility/breach of contract, at best indifference/Commitment phobic/heart breaker.

+ **6 of Swords**: Acceptance

Five stages of loss and grief.

+ **9 of Swords**: Delusion

Psychotic, behaviour, beleaguered, harrowed, troubled, restless.

Knight of Swords

+ **3 of Swords**: Conflict

+ **6 of Swords**: Eloquence

Verbally expressive.

+ **9 of Swords**: Fear

Fraught and fought, thought.

These are hardly the best of combinations to see in a reading.

Knight of Pentacles

− **3 of Swords**: Stubbornness

Fixation.

+ **6 of Swords**: Stamina

+ **9 of Swords**: Burden

The Pages are pensive in four elemental ways.

Page of Wands

+ **10 of Pentacles:** Folly

Page of Cups

+ **10 of Pentacles:** Speculation

Gambler.

Page of Swords

+ **10 of Pentacles:** Prudence

Page of Pentacles

+ **10 of Pentacles:** Investment

When reading these resonances, also contrast the position in which the cards fall.

Also, when reading several resonances, consider them like ripples in water.

For Advanced Time Travellers

You will see in this method that there are connections to both kabbalah and numerology. This is because Papus used these systems to construct all his methods, only briefly touching on cartomancy or traditional card-reading towards the end of his work. This is an approach we see throughout this era, all the way down the timeline to A. E. Waite. It was only after these eras of esotericism that fortune-telling returned into vogue.

Tarot and Initiation [125]

One of the people we see in Papus's life was a steady presence in the esoteric scene of the time but about whom little has been written. He is mentioned in *Tarot of the Bohemians* as F. Ch., which was short for his pen-name Francois Charles Barlet, real name Albert Faucheux. He also wrote under the pen-name of Glyndon and appeared in occult groups, magazines, and reviews of the era. He covered theosophy, initiation, Gnosticism, and all forms of esoteric studies, perhaps influencing Papus's view of initiation in tarot.

---

125   See also Naomi Ozaniec, *Watkins Tarot Handbook* (London, UK: Watkins, 2005).

Papus tells us that initiation is the means of instruction by which we are enabled to "draw near to [these] transcendental realms of perception," guarded from illusion and able to converse with the beings we encounter in these planes. [126] He sees our state as ascending but caught halfway between the beast and the angel in a dead-stop without special work—that work being initiation, the "instrument that facilitates the development of the human butterfly." [127]

In this method, we will draw on the plan that F. Ch. and Papus lay out for us and recreate a modern form of initiation with our twenty-two major arcana. This method is suitable for both individual and group work.

We will see that Papus believed that because we are in a state of devolution, the first steps on our initiatory path are to "re-descend" and become re-acquainted with all the "degrees and forces" through which we have already passed (and forgotten) on our journey. Not only that, but we should master each so we become free of our former state and can ascend to our higher state.

The Twelve Hours of Initiation

The twelve hours of initiation, illustrated by the tarot major arcana, allow us to re-experience all the forces that create our instincts, desires, and passions. In observing them, we become more aware. As we become aware, we can formulate our next experiences with more insight, gaining a little illumination on our path. This is the process of *initiation*— changing our state of awareness in progressive steps.

Papus and F. Ch. teach that the tarot can be compared with the "twelve hours of Apollonius," a series of teachings by a Greek philosopher of Tyana. Our time-travel machine may one day take us all the way back to see if Apollonius was born at the same time as Christ as is said, but for now we will simply take his writings as seen by Papus. These twelve sentences are also referred to as the *nychthemeron*, a word composed of the two Greek words for "night" and "day."

---

126 Papus, 255–256.

127 *Ibid.*, 261.

The sequence starts with the Wheel card, Atu X, and because it uses the Marseilles Tarot, has Strength for card XI, not Justice. It is seen that the previous cards 1 through 9 show the descent stage, here we are only interested in making our ascent.

The First Hour [The Wheel]
Here the Neophyte praises God, utters no injurious words, inflicts no more pain.

This whole experience will take twelve hours, so we recommend commencing it in the morning, at 8:00 am or sunrise, whichever may be convenient. The sentences and activity appropriate to each hour can be written on index or reminder cards, or created as reminders on your mobile phone or other device.

Each activity is cumulative and should be completed before commencing the next. If you cannot complete a particular activity within the given hour, abandon the exercise and restart it another day. As all initiatory work, it should prove a challenge; the gates of heaven are not stormed easily.

You may find surprising coincidences or experiences arise during this type of work, which is a specific example of a "gated spread" where a sequence of tarot activities is engineered to create challenge and change in your life. If you journal the experience, you may also discover that some things happened or you changed as a result without noticing at the time because the experience is immersive.

The first hour is called by Papus an "hour of preparation." If you would like to perform a visualisation for each hour, we have provided text at the end of each section. However, the main activity for this first hour is silence. Whether you wish to offer silent praise to a deity is an individual choice but the main requirement in this hour is absolute silence. If you speak during the first hour, you must recommence the whole practice on a different day.

You can also practice any form of mindfulness, contemplation, or meditation during this first hour, whether you are to spend the remainder of the day in work, with family at the weekend, by yourself, or on vacation.

If possible, attempt to clear your mind of any negative thoughts towards other people or situations in your life. If these arise, let them pass through your mind and continue the silent contemplation of the world.

Your attention should be brought to the simple experience of being in the world itself, aware of time passing and all the changes and transitions the Wheel brings to us. Every moment is a revolution.

This is the preparatory experience of the first hour. Once completed, you can move on to the next hour.

Visualisation of the First Hour

The visualisation for the first hour is of approaching a vast gate or portal at which sits a sphinx, guardian of the mysteries of initiation. As we gaze upon it, we consider that its head says to us, the neophyte: "First acquire the knowledge which shows the goal and lights the way to it."

The heavy thighs of the sphinx, like a bull, are the image of the rough, persevering labour of the farmer and worker, and we consider the words that arise in us: "Be strong and patient in thy work."

The paws of the lion say to us, "Thou must brave all, and defend thyself against every inferior force."

Finally, as we prepare to pass by the sphinx, wondering at its teaching, its eagle's wings say to us: "Thou must will to raise thyself towards the transcendent regions, which thy soul already approaches."

We pass by the sphinx as a neophyte through the first portal of dawn and into the second hour of everlasting day.

The Second Hour [Strength]

The abyss of fire—the virtues of the stars close as a crown through the dragons and the fire.

Immediately switch off the silence of the first hour and enter fully into the practice of the second hour. It is rare in life that we undertake such a deliberate re-visioning of our daily life, so throw yourself into this experience and you may experience marvellous results. At the very least, you will have an interesting day if you give yourself to it completely.

In this second hour, you must do something brave, something that requires a little strength to do. It can be one little action or a big one, but it must be done. Take something that you may have been putting off for a while—say, a difficult conversation or a risky proposal—and just do it.

If you would like a magical suggestion, take the following seven cards corresponding to the planets and their virtues, from your tarot deck, shuffle them, and then select one to suggest a relevant action.

- **Sun** *[Sun]*: Perform an action that is true to yourself, despite fearing the outcome of expression.

- **High Priestess** *[Moon]*: Act according to a deep feeling about something you have put to one side.

- **Magician** *[Mercury]*: Create something or start something new despite not knowing where it will lead.

- **Empress** *[Venus]*: Take time to care about something in a practical way which you have previously seen as an unwelcome obligation.

- **Tower** *[Mars]*: Something very out-of-character or unusual for you that will take someone by surprise or shock others in your direct action.

- **Wheel of Fortune** *[Jupiter]*: Take a moment to gamble on something without concern of the outcome.

- **World** *[Saturn]*: Do something that starts to relieve a heavy burden upon you, even if you cannot tackle it all or resolve it completely.

VISUALISATION OF THE SECOND HOUR

The visualisation for the second hour is that of an open hand over which is the symbol of infinity. As we approach the hand with its open palm, we realise that the symbol of infinity contains all space and time in an endless loop.

A voice says to us: "Behold, that which receives and restores every variety of form." We begin to hear the mighty roar of a lion as the symbol spins and loops in endless waves.

The Third Hour [Hanged Man/The Great Work]

The serpents, the dogs, and fire.

After performing an act of minor or major bravery in the second hour of this magical day, the third hour requires you to release a habit. This could be a habit of speech or a bad habit such as biting your nails. If you do not think you have any habits, ask your friends and family in the week prior to performing this gated spread if they can point out any.

You may also choose to avoid doing something inconsequential such as raising your right hand above your head at any time during the hour. This exercise promotes a certain watchfulness as we try and suspend ourselves in our action.

We may also consider our habits and unquestioned viewpoints in the symbol of the Hanged Man and the serpents, dogs, and fire Papus assigns to this hour.

VISUALISATION OF THE THIRD HOUR

The visualisation for the third hour is a simple geometric shape: an equal-armed cross under which is attached an equilateral triangle pointing downwards. This is a simple glyph of the Hanged Man yet also the reversed alchemical symbol of sulphur, the symbol of the soul.

As we gaze upon this symbol, we hear a voice: "This is the absolute submission of all to the divine fire."

The Fourth Hour [Death]

The Neophyte wanders in the sepulchre, and it will injure him; he will experience horror and fear of visions; he should devote himself to magic.

Having successfully avoided a habit or other chosen action in the prior hour, we now take a big step and spend the next hour imagining that we are a spirit in human form and that all others are likewise. During this hour, avoid material activities such as eating or sensual pleasures. We act as if we are in the world but not part of it. Imagine you are a time traveller visiting this time and place, yet with no real connection to it. This can be an unsettling experience if done correctly, and you must hold the state for the entire hour without forgetfulness before continuing to the next gate.

Visualisation of the Fourth Hour

The visualisation for the fourth hour is that of an endless field from which arise parts of the body, many arms and hands, legs and feet, and heads. This macabre scene is suspended under a dark night sky, without stars. We realise as we see this scene that it is one of endless generation and not death.

A voice whispers in our ear, "This is the place of all regeneration and all transformation, of one thing into the other."

The Fifth Hour [Temperance]
The waters above the heavens.

Having released ourselves, albeit briefly from personal habit and then our habitual engagement with the world, in the previous gate, we now spend an hour along with Temperance. In this hour, we simply go with the flow with no disagreements or resistance to anything that takes place in this time.

During this hour look for signs and symbols as if the universe was guiding you. Take the path of least resistance in all cases.

Visualisation of the Fifth Hour

The visualisation for the fifth hour is a scorpion eating fruit between two rivers that flow into each other. Above is a golden sun in a clear blue sky. There is a sense of peace and power in the scene and that all is a combination of danger and peace, of poison and passion. A voice informs us as we gaze upon this strange image, that "the genius of the Sun pours the fluid of life from a golden vase into one of silver." We take time to wonder what this enigmatic statement might mean to us.

The Sixth Hour [Devil]
Here one must remain quiet, immovable through fear.

Having gone through the previous hour, we now reverse tracks. During this hour, do not be swayed by anyone or anything for any reason. This is absolutely the opposite state of the previous hour and may come as a shock in contrast. Do not fall for marketing, adverts, persuasion, or subtle suggestions of any kind.

Notice any fear that arises during this hour as you hold your ground, particularly in cases where you may have usually not done so. Papus sees the Tower of hour seven as the result of the work of this hour and the Devil card.

Visualisation of the Sixth Hour

The visualisation for the sixth hour is that of a cube inside a circle created by a serpent eating its own tail. Upon the cube is an arrow, spinning restlessly in an endless spiral motion. It signifies the constraints of time and space upon the soul that resides in matter.

A voice speaks clearly to us and says: "This is destiny, which circles the world in its embrace."

The Seventh Hour [The Tower]

Fire comforts every living creature, and if some priest, himself a pure man, purloins and uses it, if he blends it with holy oil, consecrates it, and then anoints some ailing limb with it, the malady will be cured.

Arising from the challenges of the previous hours, we now turn outwards to consider others. In this hour, we look to help or heal the concerns or worries of another person in our life. We can conduct a random act of kindness, aid, donation, or any similar help. We should consider in this hour that our own suffering and challenge reflects that undergone by all people, and we have due consideration for others in our own work.

Visualisation of the Seventh Hour

The visualisation for the seventh hour is that of the actual tarot card that corresponds to the hour—that of the Tower, or the "Fire of Heaven." Visualise the image with note of the crown being struck by lightning. Consider what this might indicate in terms of initiation and your experiences so far during this day. Then consider what the two figures falling from the Tower may represent.

A voice informs you, "As this is the Materialisation of the Divine, so it is our own Condition."

The Eighth Hour [The Star]

The astral virtues of the elements, of seed of every kind.

Having assisted someone else in the previous hour, we now return to our own centre (if we have continued to abide by the conditions of each gate). During this hour, attempt to rest within yourself and get a true sense of what it is you seek in life. Make of yourself the centre of the universe and presume that everything else is in your orbit. Consult your astrological chart if you have one, or take a psychological profile test or similar self-assessment online.

Consider that your own will is the seed from which all is formed in your world. This hour should feel slightly "trippy" as it does not require any outwardly directed action. We are now two-thirds of the way through this initiatory challenge; if you've come this far, you can congratulate yourself briefly.

VISUALISATION OF THE EIGHTH HOUR

The visualisation for the eighth hour is a butterfly hovering over two jars suspended in the heavens underneath a single bright star. They pour their waters endlessly into two streams upon the earth, forming the symbol of Aquarius. The butterfly is a symbol of the soul.

A voice whispers kindly to us, "There is hope; the fall is not irreparable."

The Ninth Hour [The Moon/Twilight]
Nothing is finished here.

Continuing our contemplative gates, imagine for this single hour that all reality is based on a hidden pattern just beyond our view. Observe for this hour what this hidden reality might be trying to teach you through the day's events. Take every situation as a symbol, lesson, or example of a divine pattern. This hour may be extremely significant and powerful if you have fully engaged with the previous gates and experiences, giving an indication of what initiatory experience within a magical order can truly bring to your daily life. [128]

VISUALISATION OF THE NINTH HOUR

The visualisation for the ninth hour is that of an endless field of poppies over which shines the full moon. There is no direct light in this place, rather it is reflected. Everything conspires to forgetfulness. We feel as if we could become lost in this endless field without horizon.

Somewhere, we hear a voice say, "Nothing is finished here."

---

128   See www.westernesotericism.com (Last accessed 6 July, 2016).

The Tenth Hour [The Sun/Resplendent Light]

The gates of heaven are open, and man is born again, docile in the lethargic sleep.

Following all your previous experiences of the day, imagine for this hour that you are eternal, that your light will never die. How might you act if you knew this were the case? Spend the hour as if it were. If practical, light a candle for this hour.

Papus points out the initiate now only has two steps to go.

VISUALISATION OF THE TENTH HOUR

The visualisation for the tenth hour is that of the glorious sun. Imagine to yourself a light that is endless and infinitely radiant. Visualise being absorbed into that light until it becomes every bit of you.

See the words in the light simply writing, "The spirit is awakened in this light."

The Eleventh Hour [Judgment/Awakening of the Dead]

The angels, the cherubim and the seraphim fly with rustling wings, there is joy in heaven, the earth rises, and the Sun, which issues from Adam.

In this penultimate hour, we begin to perhaps realise our sacred responsibilities and profound depth of this experience. We might wonder how our everyday life compares to the ways in which we have conducted ourselves through this initiatory experience. During this hour, seek to bless others. Treat them as fellow eternal beings. Become a priest of the universe, even if just for an hour. If you have performed all the previous tasks and passed through the gates, you will find that there is a movement towards such expression as you now begin to conclude the experience.

VISUALISATION OF THE ELEVENTH HOUR

The visualisation for the eleventh hour is of an empty tomb.

A divine voice above says, "Life renews itself by its own motion." We realise that this applies to our experience of this day in full.

The Twelfth Hour [The World/The Crown of the Magi]
The cohorts of fire rest.

In this final hour, take time to rest and recover from your experiences of the day. You may choose to write about them, make notes, listen to music, or otherwise conclude the day normally.

VISUALISATION OF THE TWELFTH HOUR

The visualisation for the twelfth hour is that of a cross within a circle. It is a complete emblem of our gated spread for the twelve hours of initiation.

THE TAROT OF THE HOLY KINGDOM

"To attain the Sanctum Regnum, in other words, the knowledge and power of the Magi, there are four indispensable conditions—an intelligence illuminated by study, an intrepidity which nothing can check, a will which cannot be broken, and a prudence which nothing can corrupt and nothing intoxicate. To Know, To Dare, To Will, To Keep Silence—such are the four words of the Magus, inscribed upon the four symbolical forms of the sphinx."
—Eliphas Lévi, *Transcendental Magic*[129]

We must now take a couple of mid-chapter time travel-hops, so hold on tight and bear with us. The history of tarot is very busy during this time, so we will often get caught in time-vortices.

10:00 am, 3 December, 1861: Paris, France

We arrive in time to locate a young English man walking down the Avenue du Maine, just as he turns into block number 19, a well-appointed brick building of three stories, with a small garden area, porters lodge and a pillared front tower almost symbolic in its nature. We follow the young man as he asks the porter for directions—it seems as

---

129 Eliphas Lévi, *Transcendental Magic* (London, UK: Rider & Company, 1896), 30.

if he speaks French as well as his native English—and makes his way to the first floor. He walks along a narrow corridor and turns to the fourth door on the right; at which is a small card sign declaring in Hebrew characters the name of the occupant and the sacred word *INRI*. The man smiles as he sees that the letters are all drawn in the three elemental colours of red (fire), yellow (air) and blue (water).

He knocks on the door and we wait silently behind him. Shortly, the door is opened by a short and stocky man with what his visitor will later describe as a "rubicund complexion." He has a thick black beard and moustache as well as a felt hat upturned at the front. The man takes it off in greeting and we see that at some point he has had a tonsure on his scalp, over which new hair is now grown.

After entering and making pleasantries, the two men sit down and talk business; the young man tells his host that he has been collecting much information of the occult game of tarot, and asks if the older man intends indeed to issue a complete set of tarot cards, as he had read in one of the man's previous books. His host gets up from his chair and takes out from a pile of manuscripts a small volume which contains "twenty years' of work"; sketches of all twenty-one cards and the Fool amongst other occult symbols and text. He offers it to the younger man with his assistance should his visitor decide to publish a set of tarot cards in England.

The man is Eliphas Lévi. His visitor is the Freemason Kenneth Mackenzie, member of the S.R.I.A., and the most likely author of the manuscript that will be the basis of the Hermetic Order of the Golden Dawn some twenty-seven years after this meeting. [130]

As Lévi proves to be such an important nexus in our time-stream, we will also hop to 1896, where we find his work is being appreciated by a later founder member of the Golden Dawn.

---

130   Mackenzie recounted his visit in detail in *The Rosicrucian and Red Cross*, May 1873, and it is reproduced in full in Christopher McIntosh, *Eliphas Lévi and the French Occult Revival* (London, UK: Rider & Company, 1975), 117–122.

6:00 pm, 7 February, 1896: London, England

We find ourselves stood again in a small apartment, this time in London rather than Paris, watching a man complete a manuscript ready for publication. We are beginning to realise that the history of tarot is being written at many such desks as much as across the tables of actual tarot card readers, who are now in a parallel stream to such esoteric writing.

The manuscript is an edition of Eliphas Lévi's *Magical Ritual of the Sanctum Regnum* (Holy Kingdom), and it has been translated and prepared for publication by W. W. Westcott, one of the three founder members of the Golden Dawn, who is sat at his desk even now, completing the preface.

He completes his writing by hoping that his "little volume" will have a "cordial reception" by a "large [a] circulation" in readership. Unfortunately, we know from the future that such a readership will not be found for this work, other than a few members of the Golden Dawn, including a certain A. E. Waite, who will write that Westcott deserves praise for his rendering of Levi's work, which Waite sees might provide a "kind of syllabus" for Lévi's later books.

The volume also contains eight coloured plates, several of which illustrate images that Waite would draw upon soon for his own "delightful experiment" in the tarot. One of these is a hand holding a sword out of a cloud, illustrating "the magical sword." Another direct influence is the illustration of the "Wheel of Ezekiel" which bears the letters TARO, the alchemical symbols, and other design features Waite will copy in his own designs given to Pamela Colman Smith.

However, there is a deeper influence; in one illustration, "Le Cherub de Jekeskiel," found in his *Magical Ritual of the Sanctum Regnum*, Lévi hand-wrote upon the illustration the names of the sephiroth of the Tree of Life. These indicate that the image corresponded to (or was drawn deliberately with) the locations of the Tree of Life matching sections of the image. This is a central idea picked up across the Golden Dawn materials and by Waite himself, a fact more clearly evident in his second tarot, the Waite-Trinick. In that deck, the illustration designs are overlaid onto a secret template of the Tree of Life. [131]

---

131   See Marcus Katz and Tali Goodwin, *Abiding in the Sanctuary* (Keswick, UK: Forge Press, 2011).

Tarot materials were in short supply at the time for the members of the Golden Dawn, and Westcott's list of references shows us how the time-stream of tarot is connected at this point and passed onto the English esotericists: Court de Gébelin, Etteilla, Eliphas Lévi, Paul Christian, Papus, and Oswald Wirth.

There are also two interesting historical compendiums listed by Westcott: *A Descriptive Catalogue of Playing and other Cards in the British Museum,* by W. H. Wiltshire in 1876, and *Facts and Speculations on the Origin and History of Playing Cards,* by W. A. Chatto, far earlier in 1848.

Before we look at Lévi's work and its influence on Waite—and on Crowley—we note that Westcott states clearly (for his likely intended audience in the Golden Dawn) that "the twenty-two Tarot Trumps bear a relation to numbers and to letters" whilst suggesting that the attributions given by Lévi, Christian, and Papus are incorrect when compared to what he certainly alluded to the Golden Dawn teachings in the Cypher manuscript.

A Doctrine of Tarot

It is not often mentioned that Lévi also made his living for a while as a poet and originally as an illustrator. He could deftly summarise the correspondences of kabbalah and tarot, and in doing so, created a template for the Golden Dawn teachings and inspired Crowley's later mystical poetry where it was often based on a tarot or Kabbalistic correspondence.

We will here list Levi's correspondences for the twenty-two letters and tarot cards.

1. [**Aleph**] A conscious, active cause in all we see.

2. [**Beth**] And number proves the living unity.

3. [**Gimel**] No bound hath He who doth the whole contain.

4. [**Daleth**] But, all preceding, fills life's vast domain.

5. [**Heh**] Sole worthy worship, He, the only Lord,

6. [**Vau**] Doth his true doctrine to clean hearts accord.

7. [**Zayin**] But since faith's works a single pontiff need,

8. [**Cheth**] One law have we, and at one altar plead;

9. [**Teth**] Eternal God for aye their base upholds.

10. [**Yod**] Heaven and man's days alike his rule enfolds.

11. [**Kaph**] In mercy rich, in retribution strong,

12. [**Lamed**] His people's King he will upraise ere long.

13. [**Mem**] The tomb gives entrance to the promised land,

Death only ends; life's vistas still expand.

These doctrines sacred, pure, and steadfast shine;

And thus we close our number's scale divine.

14. [**Nun**] Good angels all things temper and assuage,

15. [**Samekh**] While evil spirits burst with wrath and rage.

16. [**Ayin**] God doth the lightning rule, the flame subdue.

17. [**Peh**] His word controls both Vesper and her dew.

18. [**Tzaddi**] He makes the moon our watchman through the night.

19. [**Qoph**] And by his sun renews the world in light.

20. [**Resh**] When dust to dust returns, his breath can call

20 or 21. [**Shin**] Life from the tomb which is the fate of all.

21 or 22. [**Tau**] His crown illuminates the mercy seat,

And glorifies the cherubs at his feet. [132]

    We will see how these correspondences can be used following a brief overview of the minor arcana.

---

132   Eliphas Lévi, *Transcendental Magic: Its Doctrine & Ritual* (London, UK: Bracken Books, 1995), 124–125.

The Kabbalah of the Minor Arcana

Levi also provides a further analysis of the minor arcana of the tarot with the kabbalah. He creates a correspondence between the four suits and the letters Yod + Heh + Vau + Heh which make the divine name YHVH as follows:

- **Clubs** *(Wands)* = Masculine Yod [Creation, Man]

- **Cups** = Feminine Heh [Mercy, Love, Woman]

- **Swords** = Vau, the conjunction of Yod and Heh [Force, Child]

- **Coins/Pentacles** = Heh (final), circle [Completion, World]

We have added a selection of contemporary keywords in square brackets above to provide a straightforward way of blending the suits with the card numbers as we will describe below.

Having created these correspondences, he is then able to extend them into the ten sephiroth of the Tree of Life through the ten cards in each suit. In the list below we have amended the names of the sephiroth to keep them consistent in this present book, as Lévi had a few alternative spellings. In square brackets, we have added keywords which will prove useful in the following exercises.

1. Kether [Crowning, Point, Unity, Source]

The four aces.

Four brilliant beams adorn his crown of flame.

2. Chokmah [Wisdom, Duality, Pair, Energy, Father, Force]

The four twos.

Four rivers ever from his wisdom flow.

3. Binah [Intelligence, Understanding, Structure, Mother, Form]

The four threes.

Four proofs of his intelligence we know.

4. Chesed [Mercy, Love, Expansion, Boundless]

The four fours.

Four benefactions from his mercy come.

5. Geburah [Justice, Severity, Organization, Power]

The four fives.

Four times four sins avenged his justice sum.

6. Tiphereth [Beauty, Harmony, Balance, Self, Centre]

The four sixes.

Four rays unclouded make his beauty known.

7. Netzach [Conquest, Victory, Nature, Cycles]

The four sevens.

Four times his conquest shall in song be shewn.

8. Hod [Triumph, Reverberation, Echo, Thought]

The four eights.

Four times he triumphs on the timeless plane.

9. Yesod [Foundation, Dream, Image, Vision]

The four nines.

Foundations four his great white throne maintain.

10. Malkuth [Kingdom, Matter, Material, Action, Manifestation]

The four tens.

One fourfold kingdom owns his endless sway,

As from his crown there streams a fourfold ray. [133]

---

133   *Ibid.*, 126–127.

Having laid out these two systems of correspondence between the Suits and the ten cards in each suit, Lévi is then able to provide a "Kabbalistic meaning" for each card, and thus set the template for the Golden Dawn, Waite, Crowley, Zain, Case, and all similar systems down the time-stream.

He gives the example of the 5 of Clubs, which by correspondence is the "Geburah of Yod," or the "justice (Geburah) of the Creator (Yod)" and on a lesser plane, the "wrath of man." He suggests this system allows us to "understand how the ancient pontiffs proceeded to make the oracle speak."[134] We can see how the Golden Dawn later arrived at the title "Lord of Strife" for this card and it passed on to Crowley in the Thoth tarot as "strife," and to Pamela Colman Smith as an image of her friends trying to erect a trellis-work together in mock theatrical and good-natured argument.

Similarly, then, the 7 of Cups will be "the victory (Netzach) of Mercy (Heh)" or "the triumph of woman"; which becomes more negatively in the Golden Dawn, "illusionary success." The Golden Dawn *Book T* description of the card includes "violence against women" although Crowley turns this around again in his own card, "Debauch," a self-imposed weakness arising from a lack of balance, even "prostitution" in its widest sense.

Exercises

You can now use the keywords we have given to create your own prompts for journaling, creating new writing, or the actual reading of the cards.

1. Journaling

Select a card such as the 6 of Pentacles and contemplate the combination of keywords. This would be Beauty (6) and Completion (Pentacles). What is the "beauty of completion"? What comes to mind when you hear that phrase? What feelings does it invoke; positive or negative? What is the best thing about it? What is the worst thing?

2. Create New Writing

To prompt creative writing, we suggest arranging the keywords in different ways to suggest a title for writing, such as with the 6 of Pentacles, "a Complete Beauty" or perhaps "the Completion of Beauty."

---

134   *Ibid,*. 128.

You might also take a pair of cards, and contrast them, such as the 8 of Wands and the 4 of Cups which would be "Triumph of Creation (or Man)" and "Mercy (4) of Mercy (Cups)." If we mash those up a bit, we might write something called "Mercy Squared" or a story about a triumphant man who must show mercy to someone who once did the same for him.

Another prompt is to create poetry or stanzas, epigrams or other pithy statements based on a card or pair of cards. If we took the 9 of Swords and the 3 of Wands, we would have "Foundation of Force" and the "Intelligence of Creation." We can turn this into a couplet:

Before any force is applied to a foundation,
We must know the process of its creation.

This suggests that before we disrupt, undo, or break something down, even in a positive way, we should take a moment to understand how it was created and built in the first place. This will make it far more efficient when we apply ourselves to the task.

3. Apply in a Reading
When you next do a reading, try applying these Kabbalistic keywords to your cards. So, if the outcome card was the 6 of Pentacles again, it would be the "beauty of completion." Take the three-minute tarot template to this phrase and interpret it in terms of a challenge, resource, and lesson. The challenge of the beauty of completion might be that you give in too soon or keep going too long if you are a perfectionist. The resource is that you have a concept in mind of what something will look like when it is complete, so you can concentrate on that as a guide. The lesson is that "whatever is finished is beautiful in its own way" even if there is always work that can be done to make it different or better.

Applying these Kabbalistic keywords or your own associations to the cards through the three components of the three-minute method is the heart of teaching tarot in Tarosophy, as we will see later down the timeline in the concluding chapter of this present book. We owe it to the French poet-kabbalist Eliphas Lévi, as do all the esoteric tarot readers.

The Court Cards

Ever the poet, Lévi gives us a final couplet for the court cards, having already dealt with the majors through the Hebrew letters and the minors through the divine name YHVH on the ten sephiroth of the Tree of Life. He says:

King, Queen, Knight, Esquire [page]
The married pair, the youth, the child, the race;
Thy path by these to Unity retrace. [135]

They are the representatives of the divine forces YHVH, corresponding to the human condition.

Conclusion

Papus and Lévi, along with the earlier Etteilla and the occultist Oswald Wirth, are important nexus points in the evolution of tarot away from cartomancy and into esotericism. The work of creating connections between these systems led to decades of research, albeit often misguided by later standards, translations, and development of tarot culminating in the Order of the Golden Dawn. Whilst it may appear at first glance that such obscure teachings have little relevance to modern-day readings, the structure which was introduced into the tarot through the Golden Dawn was picked up by Pamela Colman Smith and designed into her deck with A. E. Waite. As that deck then becomes the most utilised template for a myriad of decks following in time, the structure of the esotericists is carried unbidden within the tarot through those designs.

The rotund man sitting smugly in front of the nine cups is Falstaff, whom Pamela chose to represent the Golden Dawn *Book T* text of "a good and generous, but sometimes foolish nature" and "self-praise, vanity, conceit, much talking of self." In turn, that text is derived from the nine corresponding to Yesod on the Tree of Life, and the Cups corresponding to the world of Briah. Yesod represents the self-image and Briah the world of creation, hence the "self-praise" where we create our own image of ourselves; the very nature of Falstaff who is told "that thou hast forgotten to demand that truly which thou wouldst truly know." [136]

---

135 *Ibid.*
136 *Henry IV*, part one, act I, scene 2.

So, every card bearing the design of that man on that bench in front of those cups is working only to depict the Kabbalistic correspondence of that card and for no other reason. It is time for us to travel into the magical era that proved so influential to our tarot; let us jump into our time-pod and enter a new golden dawn for the cards.

8

The Magical Years

We must endeavour [once the cipher manuscripts are written up] to spread a complete scheme of initiation.

—Letter from W. W. Westcott to S. L.
MacGregor Mathers, 1887 [137]

27 January, 1893: London, England

We arrive in London on 27 January, 1893, 10:00 am local time. The streets are deep in snow and the buildings obscured by a thick fog. It is exceedingly cold but otherwise dry under a low cloud. It is easy to locate our target, Mr. F. J. Johnson, as he walks excitedly along Cleveland Street and takes the corner into the smaller Clipstone Street. He does not know it, of course, but we know this corner will be dominated by the imposing BT Tower, the "Post Office Tower" as it was originally known when it was completed in 1964.

For now, though, Mr. Johnson has another Tower on his mind—the Tower, which he is studying in the library of the Golden Dawn, now headquartered at 24–25 Clipstone Street. He walks up the stairs and finds the usual small crowd of lady students, whose talk is of many matters, not all of them affairs of the order.

For many, this has become more of a social club, but Johnson is set for study;

---

137   Ellic Howe, *The Magicians of the Golden Dawn* (London, UK: RKP, 1972), 12.

and has loan books to return to the shelves. He takes out "Book T," a handwritten hardback notepad with "LOAN" written in gold on the cover. It has a label inside with Westcott's address on it, should it be lost, heaven forbid.

The Vault lies just behind this study room, a fully illustrated *pastos* of seven sides with elaborate (but crudely drawn) colours and esoteric symbols of the zodiac, planets, and elements. Johnson was initiated in the Vault when it was at Thavies Inn some four years ago, and he has been visiting these new premises regularly—at least once a month—since it was moved in September last year, 1892.

Last month he invoked the Spirit of Jupiter into the temple, and in a vision he had been told to pursue his studies of the "House of God, Struck by Lightning." So here he sits, poring over Mathers notes in *Book T*, trying to make sense of his visions.

Johnson will continue his studies, although with decreasing enthusiasm, for seven years from this time-point, when he will finally resign as the order itself declines from its teaching. But for now, we watch as other order members arrive, and begin to prepare for another adept initiation, one of thirty to be carried out and recorded in the Clipstone Street diary. [138]

Pathworking the Tarot

The Hermetic Order of the Golden Dawn, founded in 1888, initiated a new phase of tarot development with the practice of "rising on the planes" and similar methods variously termed "path-working" and "scrying." These methods are like those now known as "active imagination" or "visualization" in which an image (in this case, a tarot card) is held in the imagination and then we enter into the image as if it were a location to be explored.

We can journey into a card without instruction or follow a "guided visualization" in which we are promoted to carry out certain actions or see specific elements of the landscape. A typical example might be:

You are standing on a path high in the mountains. You can hear the wind about your ears and feel the gusts slightly against your body. As you look up the path you see that it is getting dark. You feel cold but not uncomfortable, as you are wrapped in

---

138   Alex Owen, *The Place of Enchantment* (London, UK: University of Chicago Press, 2004), 72, Marcus Katz, *The Magister, Vol. 0* (Keswick, UK: Forge Press, 2015).

something warm like a cloak. You begin to see a light shining up ahead of you and start to walk slowly and carefully along the rocky path. As you approach the light, you see that it is a lantern held by a cowled figure, the Hermit. He turns to you and says something—what it is that he says to you?

In this working of the Hermit card we allow the participant to hear their own unique message from the Hermit and engage in dialogue with the figure. Some pathworkings can be a matter of twenty minutes, others can take up to an hour or in rare cases even longer.

The purpose of these workings is to develop a deep and profound relationship with the archetype of the card which also aids in everyday readings. When the reader has such a personal experience over time with the images, they become far more than flat pieces of cardboard but living entities in their own right.

As Aleister Crowley writes in the *Book of Thoth*:

Each card is, in a sense, a living being; and its relations with its neighbors [the other cards] are what one might call diplomatic. It is for the student to build these living stones into his living temple. [139]

It is by pathworking that we can take one step in building such a living temple. In this section of our time travellers field manual, we will introduce images from an esoteric deck, the *Tarot of the Secret Dawn*, and give instructions for its exploration. These instructions can then be applied to any deck at your disposal throughout your own journeys.

The Tarot of the Secret Dawn [140]

This deck was re-created from unpublished archive notes discovered in the vaults of a Golden Dawn collection in London. The Adept who originally created this deck was known in the *Order of Stella Matutina* (the Order of the Morning Star) as Frater *Ex Oriente Lux*, "Light from the East."

This Adept of the Amoun Temple of the Golden Dawn offshoot was in fact an English gentleman, born in Ambleside, Cumbria, named Neville Gauntlett Tudor Meakin

---

139   Aleister Crowley, *The Book of Thoth* (York Beach, ME: Samuel Weiser, 1985), 47–48.

140   Text modified from the booklet accompanying the deck.

(c. 1876–1912). He was described by none other than A. E. Waite as an "advanced occultist" and in character as a "man of honour" and "very seriously concerned" with his [esoteric] work. Waite wrote that Meakin had showed him a set of his own tarot images based on the Golden Dawn teachings in 1911.

Meakin was educated in Edinburgh and came from a family line of churchmen including vicars, curates, and deacons. He wrote at least three books, one called *The Court of Sacharissa: A Midsummer Idyll* (1904), and another, *The Enemy's Camp* (described at the time as a "comedy of sunshine") with Hugh Sheringham, to whom he left his estate. He was author of *The Assassins: A Romance of the Crusades*, written in 1902 and dedicated to his mother. The book contains much about the "Order of the East."

It is unfortunate that in 1912, Meakin died suddenly from the effects of tuberculosis. He was aged around 45 and had just returned from a trip to establish relationships between the English occult groups represented by Waite and Felkin (another high-ranking Order member) and German groups. On his trip, he made a visit to Rudolph Steiner; his work appears extremely accomplished.

He had also travelled to Egypt in 1911 on "Bahai business"—and was met with good favor by followers of that religion.

He had been conferred to the high grade of *Adeptus Minor* by Waite in Dr. Robert W. Felkin's temple at Bassett Road in London prior to his ambassadorial duties. At some point, he had held office as the Master of the *Ordo Tabulae Rotundae*, the "Order of the Table Round," an Arthurian-based Rosicrucian group. In fact, he claimed to be in a long line of succession to that group.

Whilst we do not have an exact date for Meakin's creation of his deck, we presume it was in the last few years of his membership of the Amoun Lodge and the original manuscript is bound with a description of a vision in Egypt, recalling Crowley's work in Egypt some years prior in 1904—so we date the deck between 1909 and 1911, likely closer to the later year, just before his death in 1912. This would also date the deck to just following the publication of the Waite-Smith deck.

His notes were typewritten and included hand-drawn symbols for astrological, alchemical, and elemental references. The deck was then designed by the present authors from these notes and realised as a deck by artist Janine Hall.[141]

In all our time travels to date we have not been able to discover an actual original copy of the deck, so we can only surmise how close our re-creation has been to the one Mr. Meakin drew and held.

We will now look at the instructions for travelling into the cards.

Attaining to Spirit Vision

In one of the additional lecture papers that circulated amongst the Order members and functioned as an early forum board for their studies, Florence Farr wrote:

> … placing [the card] before you and gazing at it, until you seem to see into it … you should then deeply sink into the abstract idea of the card … Consider all the symbolism of the tarot Card, then all that is implied by its letters, numbers, and situation and the paths connected therewith.[142]

We will now provide the steps for this journey into the living landscape of the tarot.

1. Visualise the symbol. You can sit in any comfortable position—or lie down—and light a candle and burn suitable incense (see step 6). You may draw the symbol on a card and place it in front of you, and keep opening your eyes before closing them again until the symbol is firmly in your mind.

2. Once you have a strong sense of the symbol, imagine it reducing in size to a small dot in the bottom-left corner of your inner vision.

3. Now create an image of yourself in front of you, facing away from you, so you can see your own back.

---

141 Janine Hall Gallery, www.janinehall.com (Last accessed 6 July, 2016).

142 "An Example of Mode of Attaining to Spirit Vision and What was seen by Two Adepti S.S.D.D. (Florence Farr) and F. (probably Annie Horniman) on November 10th 1892" in *The Golden Dawn Community. Commentaries on the Golden Dawn Flying Rolls* (Dublin, Ireland: Kerubim Press, 2013), 36.

4. When you have a strong sense of your imaginary body (which may be dressed in robes, etc.,) visualizes a strong beam of light from your physical forehead into the back of the head of your imaginary body.

5. When this link is connected, take a deep breath in and as you exhale, will yourself to travel down the beam of light into your other—astral—body. This is usually the step that takes most practice. We cover tricks which can assist this process in our Astral Travel and Visualization class.

6. When you are present in your astral body, allow the sigil to shoot back up right in front of you from the bottom-left corner of your mind's eye. Allow it to vibrate and be soaked with color; get a sense of its texture and even a scent such as earthy soil or patchouli to represent the element of earth.

7. In your astral body, feel your arms parting the symbol like a pair of curtains and enter behind the veil through the rent. You can feel the link of light back to your body out of the back of your astral self. When you wish to return, simply come back through this veil, face it again, and return down the beam of light to your normal state of consciousness.

8. Once you are through into the astral plane behind your chosen symbol, you may explore the landscape you find, meet entities dwelling there, and experience a new reality. We recommend you ask at least two questions of any being you meet:

    a. What can I do in my daily life to manifest the full qualities in balance of this plane?

    b. What can you offer me in this plane to harmonise myself in all worlds?

9. When you have completed your astral journey, return as we suggested in step 7. You should spend no more than an hour in your first journeys at most. It is better to have quality experiences than long,

mediocre ones; the Golden Dawn recommended that one be in a good state before any such exercise, particularly never to go into the astral in a negative state such as anger or resentment. This is because in such a state the flow of energy is reversed and you can be drained by the experience or find overwhelming attachment to certain constructs.

Tips for Dealing with a Wandering Mind

The Golden Dawn also provided useful methods of dealing with the more common challenges that astral travellers encounter in their first journeys. In tracing a symbol in the air in front of you in your journey, you bring the energies and specific qualities associated with that symbol into the astral, which is where the symbol is most powerful.

So if you find that your mind is wandering, draw the symbol of Venus, which is a symbol of unification; if you cannot get clear messages from those you meet in the astral, draw the symbol of Mercury, the symbol of communication. If you require protection, draw a banishing pentagram, and so forth. In the learning of the correspondences of these symbols, the neophyte is also learning the basics of control of the astral plane in addition to other planes, including the material plane of daily activity.

Entering the Astral

You may wish to read this out and record it with pauses, then later listen to it with headphones.

You stand before a stone portal in which hangs a rich and elegant tapestry upon a black rod above the portal. There are three large stones forming an arch above the rod.

You take a moment to look at the tapestry and see that it is of an ancient Egyptian landscape, complete with pyramids, camels, palm trees, and an oasis. You can almost feel the dry heat of the landscape from the tapestry.

You step forward and draw the tapestry aside so that you can step through the portal. When you are ready, take a step forwards.

You find yourself in the desert that was upon the tapestry, only now it is more real. You can feel the heat on your face and body, and your tongue tastes the dry air. Ahead of you is a single large pyramid. Here and there are a few signs of vegetation.

There appears to be a small stream running from the portal towards the pyramid, so you begin to walk along its banks, noticing perhaps lotus blossoms budding in the water and the occasional movement of life deep beneath the surface as the stream widens.

When you arrive at the base of the pyramid you see an open archway leading into a dark tunnel. Above the archway is carved a globe with wings like those of a falcon. You feel a little concerned considering the darkness and must decide whether to enter the tunnel.

As you pass along the tunnel, you can feel seeds breaking beneath your feet, as if crops had been stored here in the past or carried along the tunnel for some other purpose.

The tunnel eventually opens out into a triangular room, with the apex on the other side from where you have entered. In the centre of the room floats a large white egg that appears to be surrounded by flames that do not burn it.

You can feel a strange cold sort of heat against you as you approach the egg in the centre of the triangle.

As you look upon the egg and feel the flames, you notice that the seeds on the floor of this temple sanctum are sprouting to life into all manner of flowers and blooms.

You realise the stream is also entering the sanctum from the tunnel and carrying the flowers out into the desert. It flows both in and out of the pyramid on a magical tide.

After awhile of sensing the work of this place, you turn and walk along the darkness of the tunnel, seeing the desert light ahead of you.

Upon leaving the pyramid, you take a moment to get used to the light and follow the stream back to the portal.

The tapestry appears to have been placed over the portal on the other side. When you are ready, you can pull it to one side and feel yourself returning to the present time and place.

Take a moment to ground yourself after any travel into the cards. It is useful to have a small meal thereafter as a further grounding and return to the body.

The lexicon for the main symbols we have used in this experience is:

- **Egg**: Rebirth, immortality, fertility, aura, receptivity
- **Pentagram**: Life, power, protection, grounding, invoking, banishing
- **Water**: Sustenance, life, promise
- **Triangle**: Trinity, three-in-one
- **Bud**: Hope, innovation, growth
- **Flower**: Spring, female energy
- **Seed**: Fertility, virility, ideas, expectation, cycle of death and rebirth
- **Pyramid**: The work of initiation
- **Winged Globe**: The will, the core of self

You can now look back over the experience as you refer to these correspondences and discern how it was created and how the symbolism is based on a teaching of complex relationships. As every tarot card in every deck is an illustration of combined symbolism, the working of a card and its discrete symbols can be followed in an identical manner. In effect, the illustration is already primed to teach you more than itself.

We next turn to a slightly more advanced method when you have mastered exploring individual cards for a while.

Create Your Own Tarot Time Portals

We can now reveal a hither-to secret method initiates of a magical order have used for some years. In many published works, there are references to pathworking and visualization techniques that draw on a single card, so for example, you might enter into the "Hermit" card for guidance.

However, as the tarot cards are metaphors composed of many symbols, we can construct a simple portal sigil out of a combination of cards.

We first shuffle and draw three cards for a simple timeline reading:

1. What has happened.

2. What is happening.

3. What will happen (if nothing is changed based on 1 and 2).

We can also consult the base card (at the bottom of the deck) if we want a card for:

4. What we can do towards achieving—3) if positive or changing; 3) if negative.

We then chose one key symbol from each of the three cards as we have done in previous books when learning to read tarot by pin-pointing and chaining. [143]

Let us imagine that we have drawn the King of Pentacles, the Queen of Wands, and the 5 of Swords in those three positions.

Whilst we might read those cards as indicating we have been somewhat stubborn in the past, and controlling in the present, and must be careful to avoid argument and trouble in the future, we can also create a portal.

1. **King of Pentacles**—Bull

2. **Queen of Wands**—Sunflower

3. **5 of Swords**—Sea

We then visualize a portal on which a bull's head is illustrated within a large sunflower design above a flat and calm sea. We spend a few minutes concentrating on this emblem and then enter the portal and explore the landscape as we have explored single cards.

We can ask any figures, animals or even inanimate objects that appear as guides within that space to explain and explore the situation we presented to the tarot.

This can be a powerful experience, and whilst there may be verbal and conscious guidance given during the working, there will also be profound unconscious changes keyed by the images.

The legacy of the Golden Dawn provides a major stream from which contemporary tarot still draws into today. It also inspired many other authors and teachers in the decades following its untimely collapse as a functional group.

---

143   See Marcus Katz and Tali Goodwin, *Tarot Face to Face* (Woodbury, MN: Llewellyn, 2012), 4–6.

From Magical Order to Mail Order

The Golden Dawn collapsed after a peak of about twelve years of esoteric innovation, development, and teaching. Whilst this was in part due to the schisms and arguments amongst and between founder members and vocal students, it was also a consequence of these politics. The Order collapsed because it had no time to fulfil its primary purpose: to deliver an initiatory system of teaching, correspondence, and ritual that developed the human condition.

There were many members who began to complain that they were being taught knowledge for the sake of it, without any application, and taking part in rituals whose meaning was empty. This was because they were not being taught properly; the correspondence between the knowledge and the ritual was not being communicated, as the teachers were too busy arguing with each other about the principles of the Order.

The Order collapsed because students were not being properly taught its main secrets and were leaving after years of work, not because a few people were engaged in rivalries.

It is unfortunate that the Order collapsed when it did, for one reason: the postal service.

If it had continued for just a few more years, it would have been able to take advantage of simultaneous revolutions that were just around the corner: the wide-spread availability of motor cars, long-distance telephony, portable typewriters, and the lithograph machine. Together, these revolutionised the world in a post-Victorian "Internet" fashion and brought the rise of improved postal delivery and the mail-order teaching revolution—now called "distance learning."

It was another group which would famously take advantage of these technologies: AMORC, the Ancient Mystical Order *Rosae Crucis* (Rose Cross). This group was founded in 1915 by Harvey Spencer Lewis (1883–1939) and grew rapidly by mass-marketing in print ads, on its own radio service, and by providing a massive correspondence course.

AMORC was not the only group to continue the legacy of the Golden Dawn. Another smaller group, the Brotherhood of Light (the Church of Light since 1932) was founded in 1915 by C. C. Zain, the pseudonym of Elbert Benjamine (1882–1951). [144]

---

144   Christopher Gibson, "The Religion of the Stars: The Hermetic Philosophy of C. C. Zain," *Gnosis* magazine, Winter 1996; Mitch Horowitz, *Occult America* (New York, NY: Bantam, 2009), 217; Godwin, Chanel, and Deveney (eds.), *The Hermetic Brotherhood of Luxor* (York Beach, ME: Samuel Weiser, 1995), 39.

Benjamine had originally been contacted by the founders of the Hermetic Brother-hood of Luxor to rewrite that Order's teachings. However, over forty years he established a huge range of course materials from astrology to alchemy and tarot to weather prediction. The total number of lessons created number over two hundred, and many of them carried detailed exams whose successful passing led to certification.

He also designed a unique deck for the Brotherhood of Light which uses designs based on Ancient Egyptian art and myth. This deck was produced in black and white and is often provided for colouring-in by the earnest student.

C. C. Zain presents an interesting view of how the suits correspond to the tarot. In that he says each suit embodies the Hebrew name of deity: Yod-He-Vau-He; the qualities or states that are "masculine, feminine, union, and the product." They also demonstrate the workings of the Christian doctrine of the Trinity; of one god in three divine persons.

He points out that "in Egypt, (that was heavily influenced by a powerful matriarchal religion and society) Osiris the Father, Isis the Mother, and Horus the Issue were popu-larly worshiped; and in addition there was a fourth deity which included the three others" and that was "the Holy Ghost." Later in history and with the advent of the teachings of Saint Paul, other countries and cultures readily adapted the concept of the Holy Ghost—Father, the Son, and the holy spirit—fully masculine in nature and suitable for Christian patriarchal societies. It soon found favour over then-redundant feminine divinity.

As Christianity marched on, the female was looked upon by priests "as an instrument of evil, a tempting agent of the devil, strictly to be avoided." Women were excised from the church, due to the Adam and Eve story, that portrayed the woman as the temptress that lured man to commit sin, and move away from union in the garden of Eden. C. C. Zain comments that all remaining is the figure of Virgin Isis, (the High Priestess of the tarot), who has from "time immemorial been pictured as a virgin with a crescent Moon in her arms to symbolise the immaculate conception—as the Mother Mary, and venerated." They did however cut her from the Holy Trinity and in her place put the Holy Ghost.

C. C. Zain says that all is not lost of the female influence in religious teachings, how-ever. Their presence is retained in the "common playing cards as in the tarot, she holds her rightful place as Queen, joint ruler with the King." Here the natural balance is still at work, but he goes on to say that this was not the fate for the fourth court.

Zain suggests that the playing cards however miss out the "spirit of rectitude and justice" that still exist in the tarot as the page card.

Origin of the Suits

The symbols used on the playing card suits, that of diamonds, clubs, hearts, scepters, were inspired by the "passing of the seasons."

Diamonds

The season of spring. Zain says the symbology of the diamonds goes back to the common but much valued rose, this symbolism was used in the *Verses of Omar* where the spring is "signalled by the rose." He tells us that the symbol of rose goes back a long way in playing card iconography. Spring, he explains, is "the period of renewed life, and thus the rose, as representing it, in some mystical orders, is the symbol of a renewed life."

Spring brought with it hope and the promise of better times ahead as well as natural resources that were now abundant. Then later when the world became more commercial, these resources became something that could be traded in, and this is where we needed money to do so, the very same money that are the coins that are depicted on the tarot cards. Later in history, when the natural resource of diamonds became sought after and were considered precious, they became more valuable than money itself. C. C. Zain suggest that this is why we now have the suit of diamonds in the tarot.

Clubs

The season of summer. Zain suggests the suit of clubs derives from the trefoil, or three- leaf clover, that came with the advent of summer and he says that the clover "became associated with the heat of summer" and then he says later that from there came an allusion to the heat that is emitted from the process of burning wood (wands) and that "thus the scepters came to be the symbol of summer heat, and are so represented in the tarot." The playing cards of the day still depict the clover, yet still have a connection to the wood of old in that they are called the suit of clubs.

Cups

The season of autumn. Zain suggests that the suit of the cups derives from the drinking of wine that came "from the grape" and from the "seasons of festivities, of dancing and of marriage." The allusion to the emotional state that came from the drinking of wine from a vessel such as a cup, and the cup is still used as a symbol in one of the suits of the tarot. However, the playing cards of today still use the heart to "associate the emotions of joy."

Swords

The season of winter. Zain suggests that the suit of swords derives from the acorn:

> "[From] winter there was a time of dearth and want. To provide for this period when no food could be garnered, it was customary to work hard to gather and hoard a supply sufficient to last until spring. And it was observed that the oak thus provided a food supply which was similarly sorted by the squirrels. Thus, the acorn came to be a symbol of winter."

Later on, this evolved into an association with strife that came from difficult winters because of fighting for limited resources, and this was then associated to "strife among peoples, and came to be depicted by the emblem of strife, the sword." However, an association was made much later by "people who still looked upon the unfruitful season as the cause of their unceasing toil; and to depict this, used the modern emblem of toil, the shovel, or spade as it is still called in present day playing cards."

Zain goes on to correspond these suits to the elements that relate to the seasons as he says the "balmy air of spring is represented by the coins, (airy signs) the fire of summer by scepters, (fiery signs) the bibulous festivities of autumn by cups, (watery signs) and the hardships of winter by swords/acorns (earthy signs)."

The elemental correspondence, however, is not entirely like that of the tarot where we have:

- **Coins/pentacles** = Air (different)

- **Sceptres/wands** = Fire (same as)

- **Cups** = water (same as)
- **Swords/acorns** = earth (different)

Here is a sample of Zain's examination for tarot which is part of the comprehensive compendium of teachings within the original Brotherhood of Light. We have provided the given answers at the back of this present book if you would like to test yourself with these sample questions.

How to Read the Tarot

1. Why should no other than the reader be permitted to handle the tarot cards except when they are being used to give a reading?

2. Why should the cards be only turned over one at a time as read?

3. How much detail can be learnt about the people signified by the Court Arcana turned into a spread.?

4. How is the influence of the life of the client of any person represented in the spread by a Court Arcanum determined?

5. Why is it that any problem is capable of solution by the method of the tarot?

6. What is signified in Arcanum XXI by the winged lingham?

7. To what planet does the Arcanum 0 correspond, and what are the two aspects or influences of this planet as indicated by the common T and the reversed T?

It is time for us to leave the secrets of esoteric tarot for a while and return to a most unlikely artist who was briefly a member of one of the aforementioned magical orders. Her story is one we have told elsewhere but the nexus point she created in tarot will always call us back; her name is Pamela Colman Smith, and we will set our time-dial to meet her in 1909 under the most idyllic of circumstances.

9

The Illustrated Years

It is a gypsy encampment and Edy Craig is its Romany matriarch.

—Vita Sackville West on Smallhythe Cottage [145]

2:30 pm, 12 August, 1909: Tenterden, England

The English air is scented with apple-blossom and barley, lit under a high sun peering through the occasional but polite cloud. We walk up the lane and can already hear the voices of several men, women, and children, punctuating the summer haze.

At Smallhythe cottage in Tenterden, we are in the middle of a fortnight of unbroken sunshine that is uncommon for the country and being enjoyed by many as an endless summer. The red slated roofs of houses bask in the heat, and a second harvest of wheat drifts lazily in the fields. A slight haze hovers over the distant shoreline and the sea is as blue as the skies.

As we walk into the garden to which our visit intends, we see five women in white smocks building a long and impressive trellis, about which are already curled rose bushes and lilies. They are holding up the long, rough-hewn poles and trying them out, some of which still have leaves upon them as they have just been cut. The sunflowers by the wall are standing up like a row of soldiers whilst a young boy plays on his hobby horse in front. He is dressed in a kimono that looks like it is sewn of golden

---

145   Katherine Cockin, *Edith Craig: Dramatic Lives* (London, UK: Cassell, 1997), 52–53.

sun symbols. It was given to his grandmother by the artist Whistler, and is four times bigger than the child.

Across the garden, a dog barks and leaps up joyfully against his owner's legs. "Down, Ben!" the man laughs, "You'll tear my darned trousers!"

Elsewhere in the garden, bails have been set up for an impromptu game of cricket. The young men are letting the children play with good humour, but we can see they are impatient for a proper match. The children are trying to avoid hitting the ball into the pool, where it might get lost in the water lilies and irises. A wooden boat lies half-in the pool with theatre props bundled in it for cleaning; six realistic swords stick up out of the bags.

Ellen Terry is indoors somewhere whilst her daughter, Edy, is sat smoking and talking to a dark-haired artist who is also absently watching the children supposedly under her care. Edy's black cat, Snuffles (Snuffy to his friends) is sat at her feet, watching everyone with a haughty glare subject to his kind. His left paw is held slightly back, always sore since some accident in the barn.

This artist's mind seems more occupied with the music that drifts from the gramophone through the open window, and the easel in front of her, erected in the courtyard between several plant pots, than the children in her care. She is capturing Edy, sat stiffly on a small lion-headed stool, with Snuffles, as an ideal "queen." Edy has managed somehow to hold a sunflower whilst also holding a cigarette in the other hand.

The artist's name is Pamela Colman Smith, and she is painting a big job for little money. [146]

The Abiding Illustration of Tarot

When the theatrical stage artist and storyteller Pamela Colman Smith came to the tarot in 1909, she was presented with a text, likely *Book T*, from which to design seventy-eight cards. She had seen the Sola Busca tarot in the British Museum, perhaps accompanied for a single visit by A. E. Waite, and was aware of the designs required but also aware of the

---

146 The sunflowers and the stool pictured in the Queen of Wands can still be seen at Smallhythe Cottage. Several photographs of Snuffles, the boat, trellis work, and the Smallhythe "gypsy gang" smoking and playing are held in archive. See Marcus Katz and Tali Goodwin, *Secrets of the Waite-Smith Tarot* (Woodbury, MN: Llewellyn, 2015).

time constraints. The text was abstract but laced with possibility so she had to work fast. In fact, she would be almost penniless again by Christmas. So, Pamela took these descriptions previously only seen by initiates within the magical order of the Golden Dawn, and with childlike abandon, transformed them into a pictorial deck driven by storytelling. In doing so, she unknowingly passed the tarot from the Order of the past to the youth who would pick it back up again in the late 1960s through an unlikely holding period where it languished in the pages of women's magazines.

We will first look at several cards Pamela gave a new theatrical twist, artistic choices that went on to influence most decks following in the time-stream. It was not until recent years that these correspondences were re-discovered, so it is again testament to her design that the specific elements of the cards prevailed for so long. In fact, it is only as publishing costs have lessened, technology improved, and the advent of the Internet that independent decks have flourished and more decks have begun to differ from Pamela's template.

2 of Pentacles

It is this card that we visited earlier in our travels to see how it changed through time. We saw that Pamela had painted "False Mercury" inspired by the *Flower Book* by Edward Burne-Jones. The way Pamela illustrated the concept given in *Book T* adds much to its significance in a reading. If we were to receive this card in the past position of a relationship spread, for example, we would know that it signifies deliberate miscommunication rather than the usual meaning of "balancing finances." Although given the magic of tarot, the situation might be a deliberate miscommunication about the finances.

7 of Pentacles

The likely text to which Pamela was working, *Book T*, writes of "promises of success unfulfilled," and more specifically for this card: "a cultivator of land, and yet a loser thereby." Pamela's illustration so cleverly depicts this as a blighted potato plant. The young man looks upon the source of his livelihood and knows that this harvest is not the success that he had hoped.

As we know from history, the famine that struck Ireland in the nineteenth century was caused by the devastation of the potato crops from blight, and it led to starvation and ruin.

Pamela has transported the design from the original concept of the Golden Dawn as a symbolic rose with "buds that do not come to anything" to the practical potato plant. It is apparent even A. E. Waite did not appreciate her design, as he describes the man leaning on a "staff" rather than the potato hoe that Pamela has clearly designed. As Pamela had Bohemian leanings, she was very aware of the social changes that were going on in society. She had surrounded herself with progressive people, one of these being the Irish-born writer, poet, and social commentator W. B. Yeats. She was in tune enough to realise that this was a more accessible and suitable design for the audience of the day.

In depicting this card as the practical potato rather than the mystical rose, Pamela provides us opportunity to ask in a reading, "If your whole crop fails, what are you going do?"

Queen of Wands

It is not only the minor arcana that Pamela took a massive stride in her designs for the deck. In *Book T,* the Queen of Wands is "the Queen of the Throne of Flames" and she embodies "steady rule, great attractive power, power of command, liked notwithstanding. Kind and generous when opposed."

Pamela depicts this energy well in the Waite-Smith Queen of Wands. She places upon the throne her great friend, Edy Craig, daughter of renowned stage actress, Ellen Terry. At the foot of the throne, Pamela replaces the leopard of the Golden Dawn with Snuffles, Edie's black cat. This is very much a humorous depiction, demonstrating personal connections for Pamela at Smallhythe cottage.

In a reading regarding confidence and how best to handle yourself in a social situation, the suggestion would be that the client needs to have a confident outlook and adopt a confident persona. In fact, it would indicate to go totally contrary to social expectations, as did Edy Craig throughout her life.

6 of Cups

Pamela did not just use Shakespeare and the local environment at Smallhythe for her inspiration but also other theatrical references and plays with which she was familiar. The strange figures in the 6 of Cups have long been the subject of speculation, as they are so specific yet without any immediate reference. In *Book T* we have the card as the "Lord of Pleasure," and it speaks of "commencement *of steady increase, gain and pleasure; but commencement only.*"

We see how Pamela portrays the two curious characters in a very sentimental way in her 6 of Cups, seizing upon the gift of the present. The little lady is being presented with a chalice that contains a white star flower by a male character. This image is very like what was used in a stage play, *Nance Oldfield*, the female lead played by Ellen Terry. The storyline of the play centered around an older lady who was an actress (based upon the real-life stage actress Nance Oldfield) who attracts the attentions of a young poet and the complications this entails. The theme being "beguiled by glamour." The Golden Dawn *Book T* speaks of "contention and strife arising from unwarranted self-assertion and vanity" which relates to the young male poet in the play.

If this card presents itself in a relationship reading, it could be warning of the dangers of superficial relationships, and that all is not as it appears. The advice would be to work towards a relationship that offers long-term security, rather than be waylaid by the passion of the moment.

7 of Wands

Book T's description is "the Lord of Valour," and it speaks of "possible victory, depending on the energy and courage exercised; valour, opposition, obstacles and difficulties, yet courage to meet them … victory in small important things; and influence of subordinates."

Pamela expresses the *Lord of Valour* sentiment of the 7 of Wands with a swashbuckling energy in the form of the character Petruchio from Shakespeare's comedy play, *Taming of the Shrew*, specifically act III, scene 2. In that scene, Petruchio is standing his ground in a show of valour and swagger to impress his reluctant bride-to-be and yet make fun of the whole show. If we note the mismatched footwear drawn so clearly on the card, this is written into the scene. It is all part of turning up at the wedding so badly dressed and over-the-top that he can show his influence and control his new bride in the relationship.

Pamela was drawing upon her experience in the world of theatre at the time; the attire of the young man very much resembles that of the stage actor of the time, Oscar Ashe, dressed as Petruchio with the same mismatched footwear. It means that the card also signifies a war of words, fighting to protect your value or to bring someone down.

In a reading about a potential relationship, the advice would be to stand one's ground where a relationship is in doubt. Effort must be spent, however, as the querent may have a battle ahead. He should resort to a war of words and be prepared to give a bit of a performance to attain success. This relationship will certainly be guaranteed to keep him or her on their toes.

9 of Pentacles

In *Book T*, the card is the "Lord of Despair and Cruelty," and yet it speaks of the complete realization of material gain, good, riches; inheritance; covetous; treasuring of goods; and sometimes theft and knavery. The whole interpretation is according to dignity, i.e., the cards surrounding the 9 of Pentacles.

Pamela's 9 of Pentacles shows Rosalind from *As You Like It*, another Shakespeare comedy, particularly as played by Ada Rehan, and with the Snail on the image coming from a speech in Act IV, scene 1:

Ay, of a snail, for though he comes slowly, he carries his house on his head—a better jointure, I think, than you make a woman. Besides, he brings his destiny with him.

Pamela's choice also then stresses the sense of security and self-sufficiency Rosalind embodies in the play, matching *Book T's* "complete realization of material gain."

In readings about love and emotional investment or love and security, this card indicates a need to have your eyes wide open to the practical side of life. To always make sure you have an equal balance of the two, to ensure a happy and prosperous life. If this came up in a reading about finances, this would be advising you to take the safe option; do not take risks. It could suggest investment in property rather than stocks and shares. All this comes from the original text of *Book T* and Pamela's choice of illustration.

The Queen of Swords

Another queen is also based on a character in a play and an actress Pamela would have known well. In *Book T*, the Queen of Swords is the "Queen of the Thrones of Air," described as "a graceful woman with wavy, curling hair, like a Queen seated upon a Throne and crown. Beneath the Throne are grey cumulus clouds. Her general attire is as that of the Queen of Wands, but she wears as a crest a winged child's head. A drawn sword in one hand, and in the other a large, bearded, newly severed head of a man." Her mood is "intensely perceptive, subtle, quick and confident: often preserving, accurate in superficial things, graceful, fond of dancing and balancing."

However, Pamela has not chosen the depiction of a bloody head, but rather decided to paint the Queen of Swords as *Hjördis*, a Viking warrior-woman whose name means "sword goddess."

Pamela's Queen of Swords is depicted in a specific gesture which immediately connects it to the images we have of Ellen Terry playing Hjördis in the play, *The Vikings of Helgeland*, by Henrik Ibsen. She is very much the "graceful woman with wavy, curling hair." She is the "sword goddess" who is quick to respond in movement and thought. However, she can be "accurate in superficial things" in that there could be an obsessive side to her nature and that she can fixate and hold a grudge easily. The card thus signifies a character who is proud and stately and/or suppressed and controlling.

In the play, she is first mentioned as encouraging her husband to war with "scornful words" that hinder peace, perfectly fitting this card's usual readings.

If this card came up in reading about work and career, it could be a warning about becoming too sharp or calculating and the tendency to be overly critical of others in the workplace. It can result in disharmony in the workplace. As we are only too aware, nothing impinges on work productivity more than disharmony in the workplace.

9 of Cups

In the last of this selection of cards we will look at through the work of Pamela Colman Smith, we meet Falstaff in the 9 of Cups. In *Book T*, the card is the complete and perfect realization of pleasure and happiness, almost perfect; "self-praise, vanity, conceit, much talking of self, yet kind and lovable, and may be self-denying therewith. High-minded, not easily satisfied with small and limited ideas. Apt to be maligned through too much self-assumption. A good and generous but sometimes foolish nature."

Pamela's 9 of Cups demonstrates indeed that a picture can speak a thousand words; the character Pamela has portrayed has the look of all these things; he is a man who gives the impression of thinking very highly of himself, he looks like he is confident and he never does anything by half. However, this is his opinion only—his act does not always equate with actual action.

The 9 of Cups is almost certainly Pamela's rendition of Falstaff, a character in three Shakespeare plays: *The Merry Wives of Windsor* and *Henry IV* parts 1 and 2. Theatregoers of the day would have easily recognised the figure as Falstaff. If you asked a Shakespeare scholar in contemporary times to decide which characters the cards represented, they would likely agree—especially if they were aware of the actors and actresses of Pamela's time in addition to the plays themselves.

So, Pamela concentrates on the card as showing over-indulgence, laziness, and a forgetfulness of one's original values. Henry says of Falstaff in *Henry IV*, act I, scene 2:

> Thou art so fat-witted, with drinking of old sack and unbuttoning thee after supper and sleeping upon benches after noon, that thou hast forgotten to demand that truly which thou wouldst truly know.

Analyzing this quote, we can see that there is much that matches the image Pamela conjures in her 9 of Cups; she has drawn Shakespeare's old sack (beer) with the nine cups. Pamela's indulgent-looking gentleman, with his top button loose and casual necktie, is a man who is replete and content with his lot. He sits upon a bench, utterly reminiscent of Falstaff's "unbuttoning thee after supper and sleeping upon benches after noon."

This appearance of this card in relation to a business venture warns against relying too much on what people say they are going to do. The advice would be to only commit to something when you have all the facts and details—*and* to ensure you ask for references to support the claims of an individual. Otherwise, you may find yourself with a business colleague who is all talk and does little work. Mind your expenses too!

Regarding a relationship question, this card warns against becoming involved with somebody who is untrustworthy, only out for a good time. The indication could also be a warning of getting caught up in a rocky relationship that will not bode well for long-term stability.

This card may also indicate a person with an addictive personality. In discovering more about the choices Pamela made to illustrate the card meanings, we find they are increasingly powerful and flexible in our readings.

Three Ages of Interpretation

As we are now more than halfway through our time-travel journey, we can now compare three different periods of reading cards and demonstrate how meaning is layered across time.

Let us imagine that we are performing a simple three-card past/present/future reading and draw:

- **Past**: 7 of Wands

- **Present**: 9 of Cups

- **Future**: 9 of Pentacles

If we were to read this in the time of the Golden Dawn, we would use *Book T* and read it as follows.

Past

7 of Wands: In the past, there has been a situation of where courage has been required. Where we have had a state of "possible victory, depending on the energy and courage exercised, valor, opposition, obstacles, difficulties, yet courage to meet them, quarreling, ignorance, pretence, wrangling, and threatening."

Present

9 of Cups: As we have seen, this is "the Lord of Material Happiness." In the present this is very favorable; the Golden Dawn describes this very beautifully as "complete and perfect realization of pleasure and happiness almost perfect." However, there is a caution against "self-praise, vanity, conceit, much talking of self… too much self-assumption foolish nature." So it could be that in the present the person is resting on their laurels and becoming self-indulgent because of a victory achieved in the past.

Future

9 of Pentacles: The "Lord of Material Gain." In the future, things look good
materially, according to our Golden Dawn reader. There is to be "complete
realization of material gain," but also a warning about "covetousness, treasuring of goods and sometimes theft."

In summary, the Golden Dawn tarot reader would say that this is someone who has strug-
gled against adversity to get where they are but is becoming self-indulgent in their wealth.
This good fortune will continue but again, they could lose it if they keep their vanity.

Next, we will move to Eden Gray (1901–1999), whose work in the late 1960s influenced so many of the authors and teachers who followed that time.

Past

7 of Wands: In the past, there has been "a man holding his own against adver-
saries," there has been "strife, stiff completion is business, war or trade; success against opposition; courage in the face of difficulties." We can see how
this follows the Golden Dawn interpretation.

Present

9 of Cups: We are presented here with "material success, assured future, physical
satisfaction for the subject of the reading. Victory well-being, robust physical
health." Again, this follows the Golden Dawn but is now given a more practical and down-to-earth interpretation.

Future

9 of Pentacles: In the future, there is reassurance, of "plenty in all things," there
is "completion. Material well-being, success, accomplishment, prudence and
safety, solitary enjoyment of all the good things in life." This again is a more
accessible tone to the same interpretation given in the Golden Dawn material.

We see again that the Golden Dawn material was simply being re-presented to a new generation in a more contemporary and practical tone. We now see how Pamela perfectly illustrated this text and thus created a deck that would be the standard design for a century.

Past

7 of Wands: In the past, we see a young man standing up for himself; he is fending off any newcomers who stand in his way. As Petruchio, he is using all his abilities, courage, and wit to put on a performance that will impress the object of his desire. He is a peacock and a showman. This carries the meaning and adds a narrative layer and a psychological profile, opening it up to interpretation by the reader beyond the stark "seven staves" of previous designs.

Present

9 of Cups: If we consider the character of Falstaff, who was once brave but is a type of "fallen hero" we again see how the design of this card not only carries original meanings but adds a layer on top. This is so powerful that for a century even though the world forgot the basis on which Pamela had drawn these images, they still held their place as conveying the meaning.

Future

9 of Pentacles: As the character of Rosalind, who dresses as a man in the play *As You Like It* and is self-sufficient, we are given advice as to how to be proactive through Pamela's design. Rather than the fatalistic designs of the earlier decks, we now have a sense of narrative and therefore choice in Pamela's illustrations.

We could imagine this reading as being an improvisation exercise where an actor must move between playing Petruchio, Falstaff, and Rosalind in a single scene. This would dramatically show the energies and influences the cards are conveying in their passage between past, present, and future.

Having looked at Pamela's designs, we will next return to the practical matter of reading reversals and provide a list of suggested interpretations for reversed tarot cards.

Reversals through Time

A third of tarot readers read reversed cards, a third do not, and the remaining third sometimes do and sometimes do not. So there really is no common rule about using reversals; whichever you choose, you will be on an equal side of the tarot readers consensus.

At the time of Minetta and her book showcasing divination with playing cards, *What the Cards Tell*, she says to avoid confusion "beginners and non-clairvoyants should mark those cards which are the same both ways, as reversed their meanings are changed." [147]

In *The Sacred Tarot* (1967), C. C. Zain writes of reversals when he talks about the "broader significance of the card" in relation to the kings, queens, and youth. He says that if the picture on the card is that of a man, it represents a man when right-side up and a woman when reversed. If the picture is that of a woman, it represents a woman when right-side up and a man when reversed.

He then looks at the majors and the influence the reversal has on the meaning, explaining:

> Some of the cards will be found right end up, and some reversed. But this reversal of ends does not reverse the meaning, as it is sometimes thought. Instead it makes the card somewhat less fortunate than it is when right end up, just as a planet is less fortunate when it receives a bad aspect, or as a sign is less fortunate when its ruler receives an inharmonious aspect. For instance, Saturn can hardly be considered a benefic plane when well-aspected and Arcanum XV is never a good card, even when right end up; but when reversed it is more like Saturn afflicted by a discordant aspect. On the other hand, Jupiter, even when much afflicted, is never very malefic; therefore, Arcanum V, even when reversed can signify very little evil, although it is not so good as right end up. [148]

Eden Grey in *The Tarot Revealed* (1960) says of reversals, when you shuffle the cards thoroughly "some of the cards fall naturally into an upside-down position; therefore, the meaning of the card in reversed position is also given." [149] For example, for the 4 of Swords

---

147   Minetta, 15.

148   C. C. Zain, *The Sacred Tarot* (Los Angeles: Church of Light, 2005), 401.

149   Eden Gray, *The Tarot Revealed* (New York: Signet, 1960), 19.

she gives the interpretation for its upright meaning as "rest from strife, retreat, solitude" whereas the reversed meaning is given as "activity, social unrest."

We will now provide some of our reversed meanings, derived from a survey of hundreds of contemporary readers.

Reversals

Pentacles

Key theme for Pentacles: Resources

Ace of Pentacles: The Seed of Resource
Upright: Wealth
Reversed: Ruin

2 of Pentacles: The Organization of Resource
Upright: Organization
Reversed: Disorganization

3 of Pentacles: The Activating of Resource
Upright: Loyalty
Reversed: Resigning

4 of Pentacles: The Application of Resource
Upright: Selfishness
Reversed: Generosity

5 of Pentacles: The Boundary of Resource
Upright: Loss
Reversed: Fulfilled Expectations

6 of Pentacles: The Use of Resource
Upright: Resources
Reversed: Lack of Resource

7 of Pentacles: The Reorganization of Resource
Upright: Cultivation
Reversed: Barrenness

8 of Pentacles: The Direction of Resource
Upright: Self-Confidence
Reversed: Self-Doubt

9 of Pentacles: The Resting of Resource
Upright: Selfishness
Reversed: Sharing

10 of Pentacles: The Return of Resource
Upright: Good Returns
Reversed: Lack of Return

Page of Pentacles: Resource Channeling
Upright: Starting Work
Reversed: Waste

Knight of Pentacles: Resource Responding
Upright: Capability
Reversed: Incapability

Queen of Pentacles: Resource Connecting
Upright: Nurturing
Reversed: Neglecting

King of Pentacles: Resource Demonstrating
Upright: Obviousness
Reversed: Hiding

Swords

Key Theme for Swords: Expectations

Ace of Swords: The Seed of Expectation
Upright: Movement
Reversed: Fixation

2 of Swords: The Organization of Expectation
Upright: Confusion
Reversed: Clarity

3 of Swords: The Activation of Expectation
Upright: Disappointment
Reversed: Expansion

4 of Swords: The Application of Expectation
Upright: Hiding
Reversed: Truth

5 of Swords: The Boundary of Expectation
Upright: Defeat
Reversed: Winning

6 of Swords: The Utilization of Expectation
Upright: Holiday
Reversed: Work

7 of Swords: The Reorganization of Expectation
Upright: Trespass
Reversed: Integrity

8 of Swords: The Direction of Expectation
Upright: Trust
Reversed: Mistrust

9 of Swords: The Rest of Expectation
Upright: Pessimism
Reversed: Optimism

10 of Swords: *Upright*: Distress
Reversed: Delight

Page of Swords: Expectation Channeling
Upright: Obedience

Knight of Swords: Expectation Responding
Upright: Pursuit
Reversed: Retreat

Queen of Swords: Expectation Connecting
Upright: Acknowledgement
Reversed: Refusing

King of Swords: Expectation Demonstrating
Upright: Deliberation
Reversed: Thoughtlessness

Cups

Key Theme for Cups: Imagination

Ace of Cups: The Seed of Imagination
Upright: Motion
Reversed: Stagnancy

2 of Cups: The Organization of Imagination
Upright: Trust
Reversed: Singleness

3 of Cups: The Activation of Imagination
Upright: Harmony
Reversed: Disharmony

4 of Cups: The Application of Imagination
Upright: Distraction
Reversed: Calling

5 of Cups: The Boundary of Imagination
Upright: Guilt
Reversed: Innocence

6 of Cups: The Utilization of Imagination
Upright: Immaturity
Reversed: Maturity

7 of Cups: The Reorganization of Imagination
Upright: Release
Reversed: Collecting

8 of Cups: The Direction of Imagination
Upright: Attending
Reversed: Absence

9 of Cups: The Rest of Imagination
Upright: Fulfillment
Reversed: Disappointment

10 of Cups: The Return of Imagination
Upright: Ecstasy
Reversed: Heartache

Page of Cups: Imagination Channeling
Upright: Sophistication
Reversed: Primitive

Knight of Cups: Imagination Responding
Upright: Exhibition
Reversed: Recluse

Queen of Cups: Imagination Connecting
Upright: Affection
Reversed: Conceit

King of Cups: Imagination Demonstrating
Upright: Recognition
Reversed: Forgetfulness

Wands

Key Theme for Wands: Ambition

Ace of Wands: The Seed of Ambition
Upright: Advancement
Reversed: Interruption

2 of Wands: The Organization of Ambition
Upright: Planning
Reversed: Ignoring

3 of Wands: The Activation of Ambition
Upright: Building
Reversed: Dismantling

4 of Wands: The Application of Ambition
Upright: Welcoming, appropriate response
Reversed: Loss, Exile

5 of Wands: The Boundary of Ambition
Upright: Disconnection
Reversed: Connection

6 of Wands: The Utilization of Ambition
Upright: Amusement
Reversed: Weariness

7 of Wands: The Reorganization of Ambition
Upright: Exposure
Reversed: Concealment

8 of Wands: The Direction of Ambition
Upright: Management
Reversed: Misdirection

9 of Wands: The Rest of Ambition
Upright: Care
Reversed: Approachability

10 of Wands: The Return of Ambition
Upright: Work
Reversed: Sloth

Page of Wands: Ambition Channeling
Upright: Entrance
Reversed: Retirement

Knight of Wands: Ambition Responding
Upright: Advancement
Reversed: Hesitation

Queen of Wands: Ambition Connecting
Upright: Independence
Reversed: Dependence

King of Wands: Ambition Demonstrating
Upright: Authenticity
Reversed: Falseness

Majors

Key Theme for Majors: Pattern

I: Magician
Upright: Success
Reversed: Failure

II: High Priestess
Upright: Revelation
Reversed: Secrecy

III: Empress
Upright: Cultivation
Reversed: Harm

IV: Emperor
Upright: Endurance
Reversed: Instability

V: Hierophant
Upright: Teaching
Reversed: Learning

VI: Lovers
Upright: Union
Reversed: Separation

VII: Chariot
Upright: Momentum
Reversed: Stop

VIII: Strength
Upright: Action
Reversed: Rest

IX: Hermit
Upright: Solitude
Reversed: Companionship

X: Wheel
Upright: Movement
Reversed: Pause

XI: Justice
Upright: Accuracy
Reversed: Mistake

XII: Hanged Man
Upright: Surrender
Reversed: Struggle

XIII: Death
Upright: Life
Reversed: Stagnation

XIV: Temperance
Upright: Assessment
Reversed: Over-Compensation

XV: Devil
Upright: Withholding
Reversed: Liberation

XVI: Tower
Upright: Acceleration
Reversed: Fall

XVII: Star
Upright: Enlightenment
Reversed: Darkness

XVIII: Moon
Upright: Ignorance
Reversed: Knowledge

XIX: Sun
Upright: Demonstration
Reversed: Concealment

XX: Judgment
Upright: Awakening
Reversed: Sleep

XXI: World
Upright: Beginning
Reversed: Ending

0: Fool
Upright: Frivolity
Reversed: Seriousness

Having looked at the work of Pamela Colman Smith and A. E. Waite in this chapter, we will now travel all the way to Egypt and encounter a totally different type of tarot creator, the notorious Aleister Crowley. Prepare yourself for a riot and let us head to Cairo.

10

The New Aeon

This card is beautiful in a strange, immemorial, moribund manner. It is the card of the Dying God; its importance in the present pack is merely that of the Cenotaph. It says: "If ever things get bad like that again, in the new Dark Ages which appear to threaten, this is the way to put things right. But if things have to be put right, it shows they are very wrong."

—Aleister Crowley on the Hanged Man card, 1944 [150]

Noon, 20 March, 1904: Cairo, Egypt

We stand in the corner of a room, presently unseen, watching a young man who is invoking the ancient Egyptian god of Horus. He is stood with his back to us, holding a sword and speaking his invocation out of a window, against which is a small writing desk. We can see sheets of blank paper, and a small vellum notebook filled with scrawling notes and diagrams. The air is dense with incense smoke—kyphi, rich with frankincense and myrrh yet almost ethereal with lemongrass and wine. It is the world's oldest known recipe for incense, carved in the walls of the most ancient temples. The man is aged twenty-nine and wearing a white robe sewn in gold as well as a turban. His name is Aleister Crowley.

---

150 Aleister Crowley, *The Book of Thoth* (York Beach, ME: Samuel Weiser, 1985), 97.

As his words cascade out into the blazing hot air of Cairo, he begins to shift his whole state of awareness. He has already been promised success on Friday by his god, Horus, who spoke through his wife. The fact that this is their honeymoon has long escaped him; his wife, Rose, has been channelling the gods and he now means to attain samadhi, a Vedic state of ultimate union and bliss.

He has abased himself, made confessions of his sins of ignorance, and pointed his whole mind to transcend time and space. He has already started experimenting with sexual magick but now it is just him, his words and ritual, and a broken string of pearls on the desk.

His words finish, words not spoken in this way for twenty-seven centuries. He then waits, sitting down to take up his pen.

Over his shoulder to us, he says clearly, "I know you are not of this world. Tell me what it is I will write which will prophesy the future and connect me to the divine."

We are startled but not surprised—magick, after all, is the act of transcending time. We look up his Book of the Law[151] on our time pad and begin reading it for him to write down;

1. Had! The manifestation of Nuit.

2. The unveiling of the company of heaven.

3. Every man and every woman is a star.

Awhile later, we complete our reading, and tell Crowley we will return tomorrow and the day following with the other two parts of the book—it is an exhausting process, particularly when we are called across time by such a magician.

The Rituals of the Old Time are Black

Aleister Crowley (1875–1947) was the most infamous magician of his time, and his legacy is still often seen within the headlines of the time where he was dubbed by one newspaper "the wickedest man in the world." However, his life, philosophy, and magic go beyond

---

151   Outside of the scope of this present work, we date the reception of the *Book of the Law* to a slightly different date than later established by Crowley himself, based on unpublished material from Crowley's own 1904 notebook.

a singular headline to encompass the realms of mountain climbing, the foundation of a new magical religion (of sorts), and—of most interest to us—a sublime and complex tarot deck, the Thoth Tarot.

We are about to head into some deep waters in this chapter, so whilst we hope to make everything as accessible as possible, time travellers should be aware that Crowley's work is a lifetime study and that repeated visits may be necessary. [152]

The Thoth tarot deck was designed and executed by Crowley and the artist Lady Frieda Harris between 1938 and 1943 and first published in 1969. To understand it, we first need to understand the concept of Thelema; it is the Greek word for "will," and represented to Crowley a key part of his philosophy and worldview. We will see when we travel backwards in time that Crowley is actually the sixth of many notable Thelemites throughout history, hence why we sometimes in other works refer to his presentation of Thelema to be Thelema v.6.

No doubt Crowley was a Thelemite of some magnitude, and the most recent in popular memory. If we first consider Thelema as a way of life which itself engages life, and not seeks to escape it with distraction, then Crowley certainly engaged life.

At the age of twenty-three, Crowley had already defined himself. He stated that he was a "magus, poet, mountaineer, explorer, big game hunter, chess master, cook." Later in life, he updated his personal résumé to include "poet, novelist, and artist" as well. He also—in an application to design a series of golf courses for St. Andrews (which was turned down)—described his various gaming exploits including his golf handicap of +3, building a golf course on his own estate, and playing chess since the age of four, to the standard where he could play three games simultaneously whilst blindfolded.

When cards came into his gaming, not only had he invented a game called Thelema similar to Fives (a sport played with an Association football), but also three new forms of Patience and a new form of Baccarat.

He was certainly able to put his mind to many pursuits and did so with vigour, as his whole life-story attests. Our favourite of many stories is that he left a troupe of dancing girls stranded in Russia when he himself flitted off to some other country—

---

152   See also Marcus Katz, *Secrets of the Thoth Tarot* (Keswick, UK: Forge Press, 2017).

China, perhaps, or back to Europe. One might not have wished to have been in his irregular and wild company.

However, his taking up of the doctrine of Thelema comes through an interesting lineage, perhaps one that evolved (or devolved) over time, depending on your point of view. When he came to design his tarot deck towards the latter end of his life, he saw it as an opportunity to fully illustrate his teachings, particularly Thelema, sexual magick, alchemy, astrology, and the passing of the great aeons of human history and evolution.

It is vitally important that we appreciate how this simple word—*will*—infuses the deck so much, and that by understanding it as a core concept we can practically use the Thoth deck to provide extremely powerful and proactive readings for ourselves and others.

The origin of the doctrine of Thelema is attributed to an ancient Christian philosopher, Augustine of Hippo (354–430), which may also be surprising to some readers. He wrote in his *Homilies*:

> The deeds of men are only discerned by the root of charity. For many things may be done that have a good appearance, and yet proceed not from the root of charity. For thorns also have flowers: some actions truly seem rough, seem savage; howbeit they are done for discipline at the bidding of charity.
>
> Once for all, then, a short precept is given thee: **Love, and do what thou wilt**: whether thou hold thy peace, through love hold thy peace; whether thou cry out, through love cry out; whether thou correct, through love correct; whether thou spare, through love do thou spare: let the root of love be within, of this root can nothing spring but what is good."
>
> —(Homily VII, paragraph 8)

This philosophy teaches that so long as we find ourselves in the love of the divine, no wrongdoing can follow as a result in our actions. Therefore, it is of paramount importance we attain this grace to avoid sin and wrongdoing.

Crowley recast this doctrine in reverse by stating his fundamental doctrine of Thelema: "Do what thou wilt shall be the whole of the law."

Augustine also points out that discipline can be in the service of charity, which Crowley later re-phrases as his second fundamental doctrine, "Love is the law, love under will."

However, although Crowley was no doubt aware of Augustine, his prime influence for the development of Thelema was François Rabelais (1494–1553). This author, scholar and monk—who is now seen as a Christian Humanist—wrote several satirical books, critiquing the society of the time, the most well-known being *Gargantua and Pantagruel* (c. 1532–c. 1564).

One section of the book describes the Abbey of Thélème, a place where the inhabitants live a life of freedom from social conformity and religious doctrine thus:

All their life was spent not in laws, statutes, or rules, but according to their own free will and pleasure. They rose out of their beds when they thought good; they did eat, drink, labour, sleep, when they had a mind to it and were disposed for it. None did awake them, none did offer to constrain them to eat, drink, nor to do any other thing; for so had Gargantua established it. In all their rule and strictest tie of their order there was but this one clause to be observed, Do What Thou Wilt; because men that are free, well-born, well-bred, and conversant in honest companies, have naturally an instinct and spur that prompteth them unto virtuous actions, and withdraws them from vice, which is called honour. Those same men, when by base subjection and constraint they are brought under and kept down, turn aside from that noble disposition by which they formerly were inclined to virtue, to shake off and break that bond of servitude wherein they are so tyrannously enslaved; for it is agreeable with the nature of man to long after things forbidden and to desire what is denied us.

—François Rabelais, *Gargantua and Pantagruel*

It is this lifestyle, philosophy, and sense of elegant freedom Crowley sought to emulate and promote in his own life. It might be argued, however, that in reality (for example, the abbey he created at Cefalu in Italy), the philosophy was hard to manifest without some form of finance.

Crowley took the Thelemic doctrine of "Do What Thou Wilt" from Rabelais (and Augustine), and others had also adopted it as a lens through which to view the world. Whilst little-known, Walter Besant (brother-in-law of Annie Besant, a prominent author and theosophist) wrote a book styled on Thelema, *The Abbey of Thelema*. Charles Robert Ashbee was another, whose book *The Building of Thelema* is a unique socialist tract promoting the virtues of a Thelemic lifestyle suited to the working man. Ashbee was a fascinating character, influenced in his life by a fellow homosexual, the poet Edward Carpenter (who might also be considered Thelemic). Ashbee was possibly a member of the Order of Chaeronea, a group exploring homosexuality in a time when it was illegal. He was also a major influence in the Arts & Crafts movement.

Our list of Thelemites is:

- **v1**. Augustine of Hippo (354–430), *Homilies*.

- **v2**. François Rabelais (1494–1553).

- **v3**. Sir Francis Dashwood (1708–1781).

- **v4**. Walter Besant (1836–1901), *The Monks of Thelema* (1878).

- **v5**. Charles Robert Ashbee (1863–1942), *The Building of Thelema* (1910).

- **v6**. Aleister Crowley (1875–1947), *The Book of the Law* (1904).

For Crowley, the tarot was an illustration of his philosophy of the "true will," the natural state of a person in finding their own course in life, like the orbit of a star, unique to every individual. We can see this in his cards such as the Hermit or the Star.

He also picked up on the work of Eliphas Lévi, a great influence on his own magical development, in using tarot as a language built from correspondence and as a structure on which to base his own writing. He wrote:

The Tarot is a pictorial representation of the Forces of Nature as conceived by the Ancients according to a conventional symbolism.

We will now look at how we can learn the tarot's structure from Crowley and apply it to our own model of the universe.

The Secret Structure of the Thoth Tarot

At the time of the writing of the *Book of the Law*, Crowley was some forty years ahead of his major work on the tarot, the *Book of Thoth*, designed with Lady Frieda Harris between 1938 and 1943. He was, however, already immersed in the teachings of the Golden Dawn and working on developing the system of correspondences to his own predilections. This development set the backdrop for not only the *Book of the Law* but the Thoth tarot some four decades later. Linking both ends of Crowley's timeline, we can now provide the essential components of his system to examine the Thoth tarot's foundation.

Crowley based his structure of the minor arcana meanings on astrological decans. Thinking of the zodiac as a wheel (360°), each sign takes up thirty degrees of the whole. Decans are ten-degree increments of which there are three for each sign, e.g., Aries 1 (0°–10°), Aries 2 (10°–20°), and Aries 3 (20°–30°). Each decan also has a planetary ruler.

The 2 of Wands for Crowley at that time was not so much based on the "meanings" for that card but rather the combination of Mars in Aries. As Crowley was eclectic, the correspondences to the planets and signs did not just have astrological significance but were connected to a range of biblical, Kabbalistic, hermetic, and alchemical systems, up to and including even the Grail cycle.

Mars, then, would suggest to Crowley an idea of might and warfare, a standard correspondence. However, Aries was applied to the Christian symbol of the lamb, through the connection of Aries being a ram. The combination of Mars in Aries would then suggest the idea of Christ (the Lamb) in his role as the vengeful warrior following the last judgment, i.e., Mars. In this way, Crowley was also able to equate Christ with a form of the ancient Egyptian god Horus—a vengeful solar force.

This use of tarot allowed Crowley to bridge and unify all these systems—magical, religious, philosophical—into a single narrative and personal cosmology.

As we saw in the Golden Dawn's *Book T*, the 2 of Wands was to their system, "Strength, domination, harmony of rule and of justice. Boldness, courage, fierceness, shamelessness, revenge..." so it carries across into Crowley's cosmology in this same sense. By the time of the *Book of Thoth* some three decades later, it remains the Lord of Dominion and represents "the energy of fire; fire in its best and highest form."

Building Your Universe with Tarot

We will now remind ourselves of the slightly earlier teaching of the Golden Dawn who assigned the decans of astrology to the tarot which influenced Crowley in his earliest studies.

We will then see how such a system of correspondences can allow us to create our own model of the universe—a creative cosmology.

THE GOLDEN DAWN ASTROLOGICAL CORRESPONDENCES

- **2 of Wands:** Mars in Aries
- **3 of Wands:** Sun in Aries
- **4 of Wands:** Venus in Aries
- **5 of Wands:** Saturn in Leo
- **6 of Wands:** Jupiter in Leo
- **7 of Wands:** Mars in Leo
- **8 of Wands:** Mercury in Sagittarius
- **9 of Wands:** Moon in Sagittarius
- **10 of Wands:** Saturn in Sagittarius
- **2 of Cups:** Venus in Cancer
- **3 of Cups:** Mercury in Cancer
- **4 of Cups:** Moon in Cancer
- **5 of Cups:** Mars in Scorpio
- **6 of Cups:** Sun in Scorpio
- **7 of Cups:** Venus in Scorpio
- **8 of Cups:** Saturn in Pisces
- **9 of Cups:** Jupiter in Pisces
- **10 of Cups:** Mars in Pisces
- **2 of Swords:** Moon in Libra
- **3 of Swords:** Saturn in Libra

- **4 of Swords**: Jupiter in Libra

- **5 of Swords**: Venus in Aquarius

- **6 of Swords**: Mercury in Aquarius

- **7 of Swords**: Moon in Aquarius

- **8 of Swords**: Jupiter in Gemini

- **9 of Swords**: Mars in Gemini

- **10 of Swords**: Sun in Gemini

- **2 of Pentacles**: Jupiter in Capricorn

- **3 of Pentacles**: Mars in Capricorn

- **4 of Pentacles**: Sun in Capricorn

- **5 of Pentacles**: Mercury in Taurus

- **6 of Pentacles**: Moon in Taurus

- **7 of Pentacles**: Saturn in Taurus

- **8 of Pentacles**: Sun in Virgo

- **9 of Pentacles**: Venus in Virgo

- **10 of Pentacles**: Mercury in Virgo

Now that we have these correspondences for the minor cards, we can provide the keywords and associations from Crowley's earliest notes on the tarot by reverse-engineering his writings of the time.

First, the overall theme of the suits in Crowley's mind at the time was:

- **Wands**: God/religion

- **Cups**: Grail/temple

- **Swords**: War

- **Pentacles**: Earth

We should remember where we are in the time-stream at this point, in 1904, a decade prior to the First World War. There is a substantial amount of prophetic writing in Crowley's notes, correspondences, and the *Book of the Law* itself on protracted periods of war and terror in the future. These warnings and intimations of social change were to have a huge impact on Crowley's life as they repeatedly came to pass.

We now give the keywords for the planets based on Crowley's original writings on the tarot:

- **Sun**: Triumph, resurrection, temple of the Grail, rule

- **Mercury**: The mind, reason, persecution, affliction

- **Venus**: Babylon

- **Moon**: Imagination, the blood of the saints

- **Mars**: Wrath, war, fire/flame

- **Jupiter**: The father, lust, wisdom

- **Saturn**: Ending, rest, repose, terror

And now the correspondences and themes of the signs of the zodiac. In these cases, although they are sometimes simply the description of the sign, in Crowley's mind they take on a wider significance. When he talks about Taurus as "earth" he means the whole planet throughout time. It is in these correspondences that Crowley places his blend of other systems, such as the sign of Cancer being the charioteer (through its correspondence to the Chariot card in the Major Arcana) that bears the Grail; Leo being the "Beast" of the Apocalypse in the Bible; and Gemini being the twin-warrior forms of Horus, the ancient Egyptian deity. It is a heady mix:

- **Aries**: The Lamb, Christ, Son of God, the Bride of the Lamb

- **Taurus**: Earth

- **Gemini**: Twins, dual force, two wands of power

- **Cancer**: Chariot, charioteer

- **Leo**: The beast

- **Virgo**: The virgin

- **Libra**: Balance

- **Scorpio**: The great dragon

- **Sagittarius**: The rainbow

- **Capricorn**: The goat

- **Aquarius**: Purification

- **Pisces**: The night, darkness of the temple, shadow

We can now see that any card can produce a piece of mythic narrative from the combination of these correspondences.

We can unlock the 10 of Swords, for example, by first looking up its zodiacal correspondence, which we see is the Sun (triumph) in Gemini (twins). We then take the keywords for that correspondence and merge it with the keywords of Crowley's Aeonic correspondence, in this case Kingdom/Earth (10, Malkuth) and War (Swords).

When we put these two together we might get "war upon the earth" and "the twins triumphant."

We can see how this tarot system influenced—and indeed is likely the secret structure of—the *Book of the Law* in which Crowley was to write as he reached the final lines of the book, "Hail! ye twin warriors about the pillars of the world! for your time is nigh at hand." [III.71] [153]

There are additional concepts that Crowley brought into his tarot, based on a mapping of the Tree of Life through the lens of ancient Egyptian initiatory myth.

He saw the cards arrayed from ten at the bottom, corresponding to the area of the "Abomination of Desolation," arising through the nines to the fours through the "Chambers

---

153   The *Book of the Law* was written on three sets of papers each marked 1 through 22, the number of
         cards in the Major Arcana.

of the Pylon" to the "Temple of The Abyss" marking the division from the lower (higher numbered) cards to the threes, twos, and aces, which dwell in the upper part of the Tree where the "City of Pyramids" may be found.

If we take the 3 of Pentacles, we get the correspondence of Mars in Capricorn and the keywords of "wrath" and "goat." The energy is very earthy and angry but when applied, becomes very constructive and capable of breaking through any limitations or constraints.

When Crowley wrote about this card thirty years later, he writes:

It is ruled by Mars in Capricornus; he is exalted in that sign, and therefore at his best. His energy is constructive, like that of a builder or engineer. [154]

He goes on to say:

The pyramid (on the card image) is situated in the great Sea of Binah in the Night of Time… the sides of the pyramid have a strong reddish tint, showing the influence of Mars. [155]

Perhaps these enigmatic quotes will now appear a bit more relatable, as we can now consider them with the structure on which they were built in mind.

Exercise: Build Your Own Cartomantic Cosmology

Create your own list of the signs of the zodiac and the planets as we have given, and against each of them write down your own keywords and themes from your experience. If possible, make these mythic or based on your own philosophy or religious outlook.

As an example, you might be a pagan or druid and correspond Virgo to Diana, the moon goddess. Similarly, you might correspond the Sun to Apollo, her brother. The 8 of Pentacles is "Sun in Virgo," so you could create a line of verse such as: "In learning the language of the land (Diana), we may come to natural prophesy (Apollo)."

If you work with alchemy, the planet Saturn might correspond to the base metal lead, and the sign Leo to the corrosive power of sulphur and all it represents in your life. We

---

154 Aleister Crowley, *The Book of Thoth* (York Beach, ME: Samuel Weiser, 1985), 213.
155 *Ibid.*

would then see that the 5 of Wands, Saturn in Leo, might be phrased, "There is Necessary Chaos when Lead is Corroded by Sulphur."

As you work through the cards, you can go back and refine cards to create a consistent feel to all the verses, and you may tweak your keywords as you go along. There is no "right answer" to this exercise, and the creation of a personal cosmology structured on the tarot is an evolutionary experience; you may often come back and with new insight, re-write parts of your narrative. You can also design your own tarot deck based on your work.

The Ranks Renamed

Aleister Crowley took the names of the Court Cards and slightly altered them, based on his Golden Dawn lessons, enough to cause a lot of confusion in later readers. Here is how we remember them:

> "A Thoth Knight is a King, a Prince is a Knight, a Princess is a Page, but a Queen is always a Queen."

The Natural Landscape of the Court Cards

One of the many gems hidden in the depths of the *Book of Thoth* is a table of the natural elements of the Court Cards according to their elemental qualities. This is called by Crowley "Triplicities of the Zodiac" and can be summarised in the table below:

Court Card	Element (of)	Element	Correspondence
Knight (King) of Wands	Fire	Fire	Lightning
Prince (Knight) of Wands	Air	Fire	Sun
Queen of Wands	Water	Fire	Rainbow
Knight (King) of Cups	Fire	Water	Rain, Springs
Prince (Knight) of Cups	Air	Water	Sea
Queen of Cups	Water	Water	Pool
Knight (King) of Swords	Fire	Air	Wind

Court Card	Element (of)	Element	Correspondence
Prince (Knight) of Swords	Air	Air	Clouds
Queen of Swords	Water	Air	Vibrations, Resonances, Echoes, Ripples
Knight (King) of Disks (Pentacles)	Fire	Earth	Mountains, Gravity
Prince (Knight) of Disks (Pentacles)	Air	Earth	Plains, long-lasting life
Queen of Disks (Pentacles)	Water	Earth	Fields, supporting life

Crowley uses as the basis of this system the concept that the cardinal sign of each element represents its birth, the Kerubic sign its life, and its mutable sign the passing over of the element into its ideal, archetype, or spirit. The princesses (pages) here represent the spirit of the element, not yet formed. This develops the Golden Dawn system and is built on the same issue regarding making a correspondence of sixteen court cards to twelve zodiacal signs. The pages or princesses are removed from the correspondence by (in effect) making a nominal correspondence to "spirit" or the "nascent" (unborn or unformed) aspect of the elements.

Method: Creating a Landscape of Change

In this method, we take Crowley's elemental correspondences and apply them to a situation we want to change. It is quite often the case that to change a situation, we must do something differently than we have done; in doing so, we become a different person. Whilst we may all be every aspect of the whole court at times, it is often difficult to step out of our usual nature and become a totally different person.

We will use the twelve court cards (minus the pages or princesses) in this method to lay out a landscape of change.

1. Select the court cards from your deck—a Thoth tarot deck is ideal, but any deck will suffice; the Druidcraft deck has excellent landscapes built into the Court cards and the Mythic Tarot has a good foundation in the astrological correspondences for the courts.

2. Take out the four pages (or princesses) of the sixteen court cards.

3. Take the remaining twelve cards and shuffle whilst considering your question or situation. This method is ideal for situations with questions such as "What should I do that is different to change this situation for the better?"

4. Complete your shuffle and select out two cards, placing them face-up, one card above the other card; that is, the second card above the first.

5. Consult the table and read out (or write down) the word(s) in the right-hand column in the following way; "[first word] ABOVE [second word]."

As an example, if we had the Queen of Cups above the Prince (Knight) of Wands this would be "the pool above the sun."

6. Contemplate the landscape and weather combination as a solution to your situation. It may suggest how you should act or how you should prepare.

If it makes more sense, you can instead use the word "beneath," so the Prince (Knight) of Swords and the Knight (King of Wands) beneath would be "the lightning beneath the clouds."

As an example, in the "lightning beneath the clouds" we might adopt a strategy of presenting a lot of confusion but underneath striking selected goals quickly and powerfully. If we were looking at the first example, "the pool above the sun," we might want to drink from that pool before the sun dries it out; i.e., take immediate advantage of an opportunity that might suddenly be withdrawn.

You might also see that this is a neat way of making the court cards function as a mini I-Ching reading, which is another divination system in which Crowley also had expertise.

The Vast Aeons of Time

Crowley perceived that time passed through great aeons, equivalent but not identical to the "Zodiacal Ages" of Pisces, Aquarius, etc. We have also met this idea in the first era of tarot, through Comte de Mellet. Crowley also developed this idea from several sources, including his own religious upbringing and the teaching of the Golden Dawn. He also worked from Eliphas Lévi, who followed a teaching based on the ages of the Father, Son, and Holy Spirit (or Nettle, Rose, and Lily) first codified by Joachim of Fiore (c. 1135–1202). In Crowley's cosmology and illustrated throughout the Thoth Tarot, we see the passing of the Age of Osiris and the new Age of Horus of which Crowley (of course) was the chief prophet.

The old aeon (age) of Osiris was characterised by a singular father-god, a central myth of death and resurrection, and a time of institutions and organisations. The new Aeon of Horus is to be a time of rebellion, individualism, and the practice of true will by every person not as anarchy but as a hard-won duty. These aeons last approximately two thousand years, and Crowley saw 1904 as the commencement or ushering in of the Aeon of Horus; leading in part to his rebellious tarot.

We see this most explicitly in one of the renamed major arcana, Judgment, which Crowley has renamed the "Aeon." At the back of the *Book of Thoth*, Crowley conveniently hid some advice about divination, before going on to give some "general characters of the Trumps as they appear in use" (i.e., divinatory meanings). Before we look at his divinatory meaning for the Aeon, here is his advice about divination:

> It is quite impossible to obtain satisfactory results from this [the Opening of the Key Spread] or any other system of divination unless the Art is perfectly required. It is the most sensitive, difficult and perilous branch of Magick. [156]

It is surprising to read that the same Aleister Crowley who attempted an ascent of K2 (the most perilous mountain in the world) and was told if he were not messing with the dangerous demons of the *Goetia* then *they* were certainly messing with him, *and* who experimented with tantric magick long before it became vogue, considers that a tarot reading is the most perilous branch of magick.

Divination is a sensitive art in that it must never replace "will" or "agency" in our lives; a reading is not an excuse or confirmation of a bad decision, nor should it ever compel us fully into any act alone. Whilst the oracular moment is sacrosanct, our common sense and other evidence must always be weighed in the balance. Therefore, divination is difficult and perhaps perilous.

---

156   Crowley, *Book of Thoth*, 253.

Here is the divinatory meaning for the Aeon card: "Final decision in respect of the past, new current in respect of the future; always represents the taking of a definite step." His poem for the card is:

Be every Act an Act of Love and Worship,
Be every Act the Fiat of a God.
Be every Act a Source of Radiant Glory.

The Aeon card is about every act. In every moment, we are acting. We are making one decision, one movement after another. Crowley's philosophy of Thelema asks us to consider where those acts are leading us and whether they are congruent towards a singular aim. The appearance of this card in a reading challenges us to ask every decision, connection, and action: "Are you with me or against me?"

We must also ask why Crowley changed some of the names of the cards and their fundamental design deviated from what had gone before. It is in the Aeon card we get this explanation from him. He firstly says, "In this card it has been necessary to depart completely from the tradition of the cards to carry on that tradition." [157] He then says later, "this new tarot may therefore be regard as a series of illustrations to the Book of the Law; the doctrine of that Book is everywhere implicit." [158]

The Aeon card illustrates the Stele of Revealing, a central icon of Crowley's experience at the time he received the Book of the Law. This wooden funeral plaque, originally labelled 666 when Crowley saw it, features the ancient Egyptian deities of Nuit, the sky goddess whom we see arched over the card, and Hadit, the winged globe we see pictured in the centre of the card. Out of them arises the god Horus in two forms, pictured as the enthroned warrior and the silent child.

When using this deck, it is a good idea to be able to utilise the deities in the cards as symbolic within the situation of the querent. We can point to these deities and read what is the overarching and supporting Nuit of the decision—what will nurture it? What is the fiery core of it (the Hadit)? And how will the long-term plan and the short-term passion marry together to create a new entity, Horus? Finally, how will that Horus be both expressed and protected in equal measures?

---

157   Crowley, *Book of Thoth*, 115.
158   *Ibid.*, 116.

Having briefly looked at how the Aeon is seen within the Thoth tarot, we will conclude with a practical reading method using the Thoth tarot or any other similar deck which expresses the primacy of Will and proactive decision making.

Exercise: How to Be Prudent in Your Planning

We take for this method just one card as the inspiration for the spread. This is using the tarot to design and explore itself, a common method used in our following chapter on Tarosophy. We will use the 8 of Disks, a card entitled "Prudence."

Crowley says of Prudence, "there is a sort of strength in doing nothing at all." [159]

We are not sure that Crowley himself understood that dictum, given his own lifestyle, but it is certainly the one he puts forward for this card. He goes further to describe the atmosphere of the card:

> One thinks of Queen Victoria's time, of a man who is 'something in the city' rolling up to town with Albert the Good advertised by his watch-chain and frock-coat; on the surface he is very affable, but he is nobody's fool. [160]

He says this card is "intelligence lovingly applied to material matters" (8 = *Hod*, the *Sephirah* of intellect, in *Assiah*, the material world). It has the sense of investment as well as engineering.

We can really drill down into this card and then use it in a reading. Each of the fruits of the Tree on the card can be considered one of the eight components of **Prudence** in terms of philosophy:

- **Memoria**—Accurate memory; that is, a memory that is true to reality.
- **Intelligentia**—Understanding of first principles.
- **Docilitas**—The kind of open-mindedness that recognises the true variety of things and situations to be experienced, and does not cage itself in any presumption of deceptive knowledge; the ability to make use of the experience and authority of others to make prudent decisions.

---

159   Crowley, *Book of Thoth*, 184.
160   *Ibid.*, 185.

- **Shrewdness or quick-wittedness** (*solertia*)—Sizing up a situation on one's own quickly.

- **Discursive reasoning** (*ratio*)—Research and compare alternative possibilities.

- **Foresight** (*providentia*)—The capacity to estimate whether an action will lead to the realization of our goal.

- **Circumspection**—Ability to take all relevant circumstances into account.

- **Caution**—Risk mitigation.

If we create a spread with eight positions based on the card and its correspondence to these eight components of prudence, we might suggest these positions:

30. Prudence Spread.

1. **Memory**: What situation or resource in the past can be applied to this present situation?

2. **Intelligence**: What is the smartest way to consider this situation?

3. **Response**: What is the best response to what is happening now?

4. **Immediate Action**: What is the best new action or decision to take immediately?

5. **Alternatives**: What should I consider as an alternative if I need to change this plan?

6. **Likely Outcome**: What is the likely outcome?

7. **Missing Information**: What is the most important thing I am missing in my planning?

8. **Risk**: What is the risk against which I must weigh the outcome?

This spread is very useful for adding caution to your planning and throwing up any realistic questions about your expectations. It is extremely powerful when used with the brutally honest Thoth tarot or similar esoteric decks that have dynamic designs or accompanying interpretations.

This method of using a single card to design a spread can be applied to any card or deck for specific situations; if you had a deeply spiritual and abstract question to which you really needed a grounded answer you might take an ethereal deck such as the Nigel Jackson Rumi Tarot and remove the 3 of Pentacles. This card represents a very stable (3) grounding (Pentacles) in a spiritual deck.

When we look at that card, we see that it has a quote from Rumi reading "God opens the door of knowledge to the bee so that it builds a house of honey."

The design of the card features a sun, a bee, and a hive set in a frame of three coins.

We might design a spread from this image with three positions:

1. **The Sun**: What is the illumination that seeks expression in my situation?

2. **The Bee**: What work must I accomplish to realise that illumination?

3. **The Hive**: What must I build to know my work is realised?

In this manner, we can use our deck of cards as a portable divinatory companion capable of not only answering our questions, but guiding us to ask the right questions in the first place.

Aleister Crowley and his deck would come to be written in cartomantic history in addition to influencing the flower power age, the new age, and likely many ages we have not yet visited in the future. However, he was certainly not the only occultist, magician or mystic to take the tarot in deeper directions. Let us jump next to Los Angeles, two decades before the hippy generation, and see how the tarot was already carrying messages of spiritual revolution.

11

Spiritual Tarot

The life of the mystic belongs to the divine degree, and it would be difficult to say that it is attainable in the life of the world; but some of its joys and consolations—as indeed its trials and searching—are not outside our daily ways.

—A.E. Waite, *Words from a Masonic Mystic* (pp. 129–30)

26 August, 1944: Los Angeles, USA

A dark-haired woman in her early thirties walks into a small living room and takes her seat as around her more people arrive to listen to the spiritual lecture about to take place in this incongruous space. She is restless and under duress; her sister, Rosalie, has persuaded her attendance to learn about tarot. Whilst Rosalie is a gifted and ardent clairvoyant and psychic, Anne, her sister, is not, and knows nothing about the tarot other than it is a fortune-telling parlour trick.

She leans over to Rosalie and complains about the hard, wooden chair and asks why they had taken a streetcar to get here, at their expense. She is just about to raise another complaint when the speaker (also the house's owner) enters. She is shocked to find that her whole body is struck with an almost electrical force; she even begins to shake. She feels an overwhelming recognition of the man made even more astonishing when this stranger strides across the short space to her and throws his arms around her. He is saying how happy he is to see her again, and how very long it has been since they last met. She feels both recognition and confusion at the same time; he seems to think she has been here before but it is her first time, surely.

After greeting several other students, the man begins his lecture. As he picks up a large image of one of the tarot cards, she groans inwardly. She had thought this man to have some presence, some inescapable power or spirituality, and yet here he is about to start convincing her about some fortune-telling bunkum.

He holds up the card image, the numbered fifth tarot card of the major arcana and begins to speak: "The Hierophant corresponds to the Hebrew letter *Vau*, the nail. It is the perfect symbol for the Will of the Divine which is joined as if by a nail to our own Will. The Will is a small point but a beginning; it is a coming forth in a search for itself; a hunger; and a desire; and a longing. Out of that longing comes purpose and the fixing of your boundaries, but the Hierophant is the teaching of that divine boundary and the revelation of its mystery..."

As he continues, Anne is transported by his words into an astonishing, glorious, and joyous place within herself. Time is forgotten. She feels swept into a new world of wisdom and wonder. Indeed, she sits there, the hard chair long forgotten beneath her. She turns round and even sees us there in the room, observing everything. In the background, the man continues and it now seems as if he is talking to us...

"And when thou hast reached this goal of conscious unity illustrated by the Hierophant tarot card, what shall be a day, or a month, or a year, or a lifetime, or a hundred lifetimes? Time ceaseth for those who come to this." [161]

For a moment, we too are caught by his words and awareness. He is Paul Foster Case, and the woman looking at us is Anne Davies, and between them both they will develop the teachings of a new mystery school, from the ashes of the Golden Dawn, the Builders of the Adytum.

---

161   Paul Foster Case quotes re-worded from *A Book of Tokens: Meditations on the Tarot*, and the event was recalled by Anne Davies and re-printed in full by Paul A. Clark, *Paul Foster Case: His Life and Works* (Covina, CA: Fraternity of Hidden Light, 2013), 96–100.

The Cube of Space

As with C. C. Zain and others, Case took the teachings of previous esoteric groups and developed them; modifying, adding, or removing subjects as he saw fit to his own philosophy. Case reworked a lot of the astrology of the Golden Dawn, developed much of the tarot teaching, and removed all references to Enochian magic, which he considered to be harmful to most students.

Case was initiated into the Hermetic Order of the Golden Dawn in the USA, but with much more information then becoming available to the public on all matters, both esoteric and historical, he could take those teachings and make them far more consistent and accessible.

His brief and succinct work, *22 Tokens,* is a major development in meditation work on the tarot correspondences with kabbalah. A further contribution to the esoteric tarot was his introduction of the Cube of Space, a three-dimensional version of tarot correspondences based on the *Sepher Yetzirah,* one of the earliest written texts on the Kabbalah. This has since been touched upon by other teachers such as Gareth Knight and R. J. Stewart. [162] It has also been more recently described in detail by Kevin Townley and David Allen Hulse.

The Cube of Space is built by arranging the Hebrew letters into their directions in space according to the correspondences of the *Sepher Yetzirah.* As the twenty-two Hebrew letters fall into three categories, it makes it more obvious as to their allocations to space:

- **Three mother letters:** Three interior dimensions (vertical, horizontal, diagonal).

- **Seven double letters:** Centre of cube and six faces.

- **Twelve single letters:** Twelve edges of cube on the outside frame.

These are directly derived from the *Sepher Yetzirah.* For example, the section "Seven Double Letters" point out seven localities: Above, Below, East, West, North, South, and the Palace of Holiness in the midst of them sustaining all things. [163]

---

162 Gareth Knight, *Experience of the Inner Worlds* (Cheltenham, UK: Skylight Press, 2010).

163 W. W. Westcott (trans.), *Sepher Yetzirah* (Lynnwood, WA: Holmes Publishing Group, 1996), 20.

We then take the correspondences of the twenty-two Hebrew letters to the twenty-two tarot cards and "wallpaper" the edges, faces, and corners of our cube with the cards. We take the Golden Dawn system of correspondences for this section, but you can also try the Waite-Trinick model as an alternative.

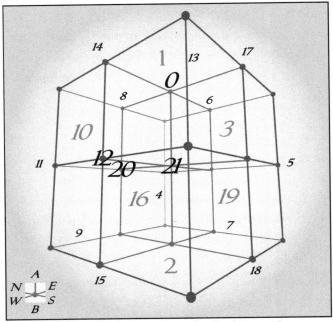

31. Cube of Space by authors after Paul Foster Case,
The Tarot, A Key to the Wisdom of the Ages, 1947.

Why would we do this rather complex yet intriguing process?

- The Cube of Space serves us as a meditation model and a representation of these twenty-two powerful archetypes in many dynamic relationships.

- It provides a container for other models that can be mapped onto the cube to provoke new insight.

- It gives us a portable tarot temple in which we might conduct ritual, evocation, dream-work, astral journeys, or other magical work.

We will now give several avenues for time travellers to explore this trans-dimensional object.

1. As Above/So Below

If we close our eyes, we can imagine that we are in a cubic temple with two great pillars to either side of us. The floor is decorated with the image of the High Priestess and the Ceiling is similarly decorated with an illustration of the Magician.

When we look down we imagine that we are reaching through the veil of the Priestess into the very deepest mysteries of the underworld. We see the pomegranate on the veil of the Waite-Smith tarot, giving us a symbol of the nature of the underworld.

When we look up to the ceiling, we imagine that we are reaching up to the very heavens and celestial realms through the nature of the Magician. We adopt the position of the Magician at the altar of the four elements and sense how this might connect what is above to what is also below.

This type of method is known as **creative** (or **guided**) **visualisation**.

2. With the Wheel at Our Back

On arising and standing up in the morning, we imagine that the Wheel is behind us as a turbine or spinning vortex. In front of us is the Empress, signifying nature in all its constant unfoldment. As we walk through our day, we sense the Wheel behind us and Nature opening in front of us. It is likely that not only will this exercise open awareness to the cycles of time, repetitions, and habits, it may also offer new insight into the manner of our accomplishments.

This type of method is known as a **constant practice**.

3. The View from the Sun Tower

For five minutes at the start and end of each day, we face East (or an open window) and visualise the Sun on our right side and the Tower on our left. We build up the presence of these two powerful images in our imagination by first concentrating on sizes, shapes, and then colours. Sense the sphere of the sun and its golden glow, and the strike of the lightning to your left with the sound of crashing masonry. Begin to feel yourself held between these two forces—the expansiveness of the sun and the constant churning change of the

Tower. Hold this position for five minutes as you find a subtle point of equilibrium between the two energies. Repeat this exercise daily for a week and journal how it encourages new behaviour towards positive change in your life.

The tarot time traveller can now perform variations of these three exercises with different sets of cards on the cube of space, in effect using it as a tarot hologram overlaid on your life.

This type of method is known as a **regular observation**.

4. The Portal of Four

As you begin to fall asleep at night, visualise a square door or portal about which are four tarot cards; at the top of the portal is the Lovers card, to the right is the Hierophant, at the bottom is the Chariot, and to the left is the Emperor.

I used to imagine the cards were in medium-sized card holders around the door or more recently, on display screens like in a conference center to tell you what meeting is being held within a room. The bottom card would always be a design on the portal door itself, at the base of the door.

You can alternatively make these more simplified for easy recall by creating your dream portal with a small border, about which each of the four sides contains just one symbol or the color of the appropriate card. In this case, you could have the symbol of a pair of trees running along the top of the border (Lovers), crossed keys running down the right (Hierophant), a pair of sphinxes along the bottom border (Chariot) and an orb with a cross atop it repeated up the left border (Emperor).

Just before you fall asleep, you can imagine that you feel yourself being gently drawn into the portal (it might have a veil or mist within it), and get a sense that there is a landscape beyond it.

Record your dreams each morning and repeat this exercise every night with no expectation so that you are not impatient or frustrated. If you awake with just a feeling or fragments of a dream, write these down as they will promote further recall in following nights.

You might also experiment with turning the cube around so that whilst the four edges are the same cards, they are in different locations on the door. So if you rotated the cube once to the right, the Emperor would be at the top of the door, and the other three cards moved one position clockwise. This is sometimes like turning a combination lock that opens different vistas beyond the portal.

This type of method is known as **dream work**.

5. The Path of Initiation

Take time in your journal to contemplate and record chains of meaning between the cards as you trace any route around the space of the Cube. These will suggest stories, teachings and meanings regarding the path of initiation—or willed change in your life. The more that you are aware of these combinations, the more that you will begin to see them acted out at every level in your life and those around you. This will provide further depth for your readings, particularly if you switch to majors-only readings whilst you are following this method of study.

As an example, we might trace a route starting with the Magician above and then heading towards the Sun on another face of the cube. This will take us over the edge of the cube to which corresponds the Star card. We will then reach the Moon on the next edge and cross the next face of the cube where the High Priestess sits, eventually arriving on the opposite edge where we meet the Hermit.

So the Magician's Journey in this particular route is one of awareness (the Sun). We aim to use magick to increase our awareness of the true nature of the World (which is at the centre of the cube). In doing so, we must discover our true will (the Star), the bright core that is our own inner Sun and the beacon of navigation that takes us into our engagement with the world. As we follow that Star, we come to the path of the Moon and face the illusion of the apparent world which is our own reflection of the light. When we seek the Sun, first we must meet the Moon. We then must go deep within ourselves to connect to our innermost and mysterious self, the High Priestess. It is she who is the veil through which "no man hath ever seen," and she who connects us to the divine. When we acknowledge her secret, we pass it on and become our own Self, the Hermit, who holds the Star in his lantern and shines as a beacon of self-acceptance, self-knowledge, and self-sufficiency. We set off on the path of magick and have at last become magick ourselves.

That's just one example of how we might chain the meanings of the cards together to elucidate or evoke both mysteries and practical matters. You can also use keywords from this time traveller manual and place them instead on the faces, edges, and dimensions of the cube to discover many hidden combinations and patterns. In doing so, you will rapidly increase your card-reading abilities.

This type of method is known as **permutation**.

You can now repeat any of these five methods for any side, orientation, or faces of the cube of space giving you a realm of possible combinations and approaches to explore this model of the universe. You might also choose to explore one pattern or combination of cards through all five methods.

You may be surprised that although here illustrated by tarot correspondences and not by Hebrew letters, these methods and the structure of the cube would not be unfamiliar to the earliest Kabbalists or their contemporary counterparts. There are eddies and swirls in the time-stream; it is not a straight line. In fact, we will take a brief side-trip now in time.

Moreton, 15 January, 1936

A reporter for the *Gloucestershire Echo* is stood in front of a large colourful mural decorating the wall of the out-patient's ward of the newly refurbished Moreton-in-Marsh cottage hospital. The mural is painted on beaver-board and is 6½' by 5½'. We can see he is looking for the right words to describe the art, and we sympathise with his predicament in part. He will later that day write up his notes and the *Echo* will publish that the artwork is:

> …a masterly piece of work an ultra-modern representation of health. [It] contains two figures—a man and a woman—bathing at a well. The completed effort is symbolic of the waters of health, sunshine, the health and strength of outdoor life. [164]

He does not realise that Miss Colquhoun of Chelsea, the local painter commissioned for this piece and two other further works for the hospital is not only a surrealist painter but a member of many esoteric groups for which she has a lifetime fascination.

---

164   http://www.ithellcolquhoun.co.uk/decorations_for_the_hospital.htm (Last accessed 28 June, 2016). Also the *Gloucestershire Echo*—Thursday 16 January 1936 in the British Newspaper Archive.

The art he is looking at is none other than a huge depiction of the Temperance card and the Star card, pouring forth their energies into the hospital ward.

Here is a hand-drawn version of the cube of space by Ithell Colquhoun (1906–1988) who worked with the cube and further developed her ideas in drawings of a four-dimensional cube called a *tesseract*.

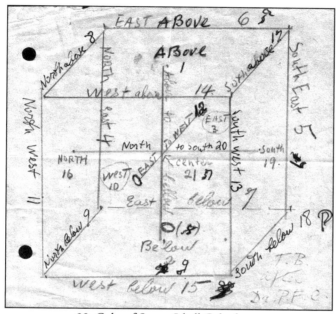

32. Cube of Space, Ithell Colquhoun
(1906–1988), undated, (private collection).

She also painted a surrealist version of the tarot, creating a full deck based on the Golden Dawn and Thoth cards more than the Waite-Smith designs. She wrote that she aimed to "render the essence of each card by the non-figurative means of pure colour, applied automatically, in the manner of the psycho morphological movement in surrealism." [165]

The deck was first exhibited in 1977 and published in a limited edition by Adam McLean. [166]

---

165   www.ithellcolquhoun.co.uk/taro.htm (Last accessed 28 June, 2016).

166   www.alchemywebsite.com/tarot/art_tarot19.html (Last accessed 28 June, 2016).

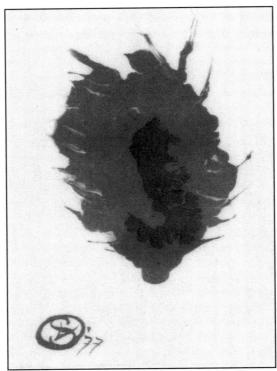

33. III. The Lord of Sorrow Tarot Card, Ithell
Colquhoun, published 1977 (private collection).

A Meditation Method

Following her initial meeting with Paul Foster Case, Anne Davies went on to become
Prolocutor General of the Builders of the Adytum following Case's death in 1954. It was
a role she maintained until her own death in 1975. She was to write much more upon the
tarot, including *Inspirational Thoughts on the Tarot* which includes her poetry.

On 25 March, 1962, she gave one of her regular Sunday services and spoke on the real
meaning of meditation, which concludes with a method of meditation of interest to the
tarot traveller.

She said that "when you work with the Tarot Keys at home, remember that each of
them is stimulating your ability to care more." When we care, she suggested, and when
we are interested, we reach for an answer, we enquire; we *meditate*. So, this is the secret

of meditation—to cast a question we care about to the world. In effect, it is also a living divination.

Davies encouraged us to cast our question at a tree, a bird, a person, making our day "an emotional quest." To do this with tarot we can ask a question of the tarot and draw a single card. We then make enquiry of that card to everything we see during the day until our question is fully answered. We ask the traffic queue, "What are you telling me about my card?" We ask the way water spills out of a knocked cup, "What are you telling me about my card?" We ask until the world has divined the depth of our enquiry.

Davies leaves us with this promise: "Cast it to everything you see. You will eventually find that meditation is a part of you every moment of life and you will attain something more staggering than you could ever have imagined."[167]

Later in the time-stream we will see this form of living divination arise in the practices of *Tarosophy*.

Following now is another major arcana layout for spiritual contemplation.

Jewels of the Wise

"One gem from many facets blazes fire,
One Light paints sacred scenes of stained-glass hue;
To just One Truth do many faiths aspire—
There is One Way, but many paths thereto"
—Jewels of the Wise, 1974

The practice of laying out cards into layouts or patterns for study is found throughout the esoteric era of tarot and is often dismissed by practical card readers as unnecessary complication or abstract philosophy. However, such layouts can train the reader to perceive important threads, themes, connections, and storylines through the cards (usually the major arcana) and then apply that depth to everyday readings. It is like seeing a multi-layered jigsaw that can make a different and complete picture in each separate layout; one picture is of "how change works," another is "how a person's life is a heroic journey," yet another is "how men and women relate together," and so on.

---

167 *The Lantern*, Vol. 8, No. 4, Summer 2007 (California: BOTA), 15.

When we then perform a reading, and one or more major arcana appear, we see these as fragments of one or more of these big pictures; as we should, as they are images of archetypal or universal patterns. We can then weave these as powerful stories as they play out in the querent's life, or our own life, knowing them to be part of many bigger pictures.

In the late sixties is an example of these layouts from the Holy Order of Mans: *Mysterion* (mystery), *Agape* (divine love), *Nous* (knowledge), and *Sophia* (wisdom).

This group, founded in the San Francisco Bay area in 1968 by ex-engineer Earl Wilbur Blighton (1904–1974) mingled Christian teaching with New Age thought and would have a turbulent history ahead of itself.

This history involves a fire-bombing, negative publicity, and personal politics following Blighton's death in 1974. There are still splinter groups and versions of the Order surviving today.

The original Holy Order of Mans taught esoteric principles (inspired by AMORC) alongside its version of "Christian Yoga" teaching and in 1974 published *Jewels of the Wise*, a book on tarot which features Christ on the cover in front of a pyramid and between two pillars.

Whilst the main body of the book deals with an interpretation of the major arcana, we instead turn to the back of the text and reveal an interesting card layout. The Order taught that tarot was not for divination but for self-discovery and meditation, and it represented a path of initiation, and depicts the workings of mind and soul on the Way of Enlightenment.

The cards used for illustration in *Jewels* was a redrawn black-and-white version of the Waite-Smith by way of AMORC with several curious or innovative design features such as the musical notes on the veil behind the High Priestess. They also touched briefly on the Cube of Space model, simplified from the original taught within AMORC previously seen in this chapter.

This layout was also referred to as a tarot tableau; recall the word "tableau" also used by Lenormand readers for the layout of thirty-six Lenormand cards.

34. Holy Order of Mans Layout.
Llewellyn's Classic Tarot by Moore and Smith, 2014.

The Fool or Spirit is setting off on his journey from right to left, ultimately manifesting in the World, providing a descent narrative of the Soul. The return path or ascent narrative is also given in the journey of the World back to the Fool, left to right across the layout.

The use of correspondences can also deepen our appreciation of hidden patterns and structures within the relationships of the cards. We can see that the Hebrew letter *aleph* corresponding to the Fool means "Ox" and that the Lamed or "Ox-Goad" corresponds to

Justice. The element of Air (associated with the pure spirit) corresponds to the Fool and to Gemini, which corresponds to the Lovers. The Hebrew letter *zayin* which corresponds to the Lovers means "Sword," which is shown on the Justice card. So, the Fool is goaded on his inevitable journey whilst the Sword falls and closes the gate of the heavenly Garden of Eden behind him. It is this weaving of correspondences and layers that allows us to tell a story merging Christian teaching and New Age teaching or initiatory myths played out in religious parable.

We will now look at the separate columns as showing separate elements of the same theme.

Vertical Column One

The first column of the Magician, Lovers, Justice, and the Tower shows aspects of thought and how we speak our truth. It illustrates the progression of an original thought to its effect upon the world, whether that word is the original *logos* that created the universe or a simple thought that something in one's own life needs to change.

Magician

This figure conjures up ideas (corresponding to Mercury) and presents options on the table; as the Charlatan or Trickster whose first illustration was with gambling cups on the table. He is the master of Will and choice from the first principle of thought.

The Lovers

Under the corresponding sign of Gemini, this illustration brings thoughts together, shows their comparison and assimilation to the first act of free will. It is the realization of choice and to some extent, the intuition as the thought becomes more conscious in awareness. The Holy Order of Mans taught very insistently that we have two selves, the unconscious and the conscious.

The practice of these layouts will soon make your inner belief systems and stories more explicit and obvious. This is a useful initiatory practice as it will help consolidate your beliefs and values into a whole; increasingly creating a more congruent, comprehensive, and consistent sense of self.

Justice

The next card clearly presides over the whole process of making decisions, the enactment and application of the values we hold and our beliefs. It is our own law, our own constraints, balances and checks, and our own boundaries. It is through this filter that our thought must be processed; it is our own self-checking and internal control system. This may or may not accord with the social structure of our own time or place, leading to an imbalance.

The Tower

The final card in this sequence is the result of the application of our thought; it is the making of change in the world of matter and manifestation. There is no going back once the word has been spoken or the thought turned into action. A new reality is created and it always breaks down whatever was in place before—it is the true secret of time travel in that change is time in motion.

We could potentially see these four cards in each column as the four worlds of kabbalah, from the highest principle of *Atziluth* (emanation), through *Briah* (creation) and *Yetzirah* (formation) to *Assiah* (action). If we can see such subtle interconnections as the Tower being the lowest arc of the Magician, or the Lovers and Justice as a pair in this sequence and all the other permutations, we begin to make our readings more profoundly connected to the bigger patterns of the universe, played out in everyday life. In effect, this is the Kabbalistic practice of "permutation," usually done with the Hebrew letters, but here done with their corresponding illustrations in the tarot deck.

Vertical Column Two

The *Jewels of the Wise* describes this column in a cursory fashion as "various functions of the alchemical water." In their work on alchemy, they define this water more specifically:

> "Alchemical Water is the Life-Power in its aspect of substance, or the principle of embodiment." [168]

---

168   http://www.holyorderofmans.org/Book%20of%20Alchemy/Alchemy-9.htm (Last accessed 28 June, 2016).

It is a symbol of the structure or matter of the universe, from which all things are born and created. It is the feminine womb and matrix of manifestation; it is form in comparison to force.

The cards illustrating this column are the High Priestess, the Chariot, the Hanged Man, and the Star.

High Priestess

The veil of Isis no man has removed, this represents the inner secrets of matter and the hidden work of the spirit prior to manifestation. In a personal sense, it is the deepest well of our inner state—things hidden to us that can only be intuited or sensed as mystery.

The Chariot

As our inner nature or the inner nature of the world comes into being, it is first presented as duality, a difference; a "this" and "that"; a "self" and "other." It is then harnessed into creativity and from this duality all things arise, including notions of good and evil.

The Hanged Man

This card corresponds with the Hebrew letter *Mem* which means "water" so is the core of this sequence. It is the suspension of spirit in matter, shown more clearly in the original Golden Dawn illustration (also picked up by the Waite-Trinick Tarot) and the presence of the divine in the world. At a personal level, it is the sense of connection we feel when we live our values consistently and are truly authentic.

The Star

On a universal scale, this is the final manifestation of the metaphorical point of light hidden by the High Priestess, and the will of the divine shining forth in the universe. In ourselves it is the delicate balancing of our conflicting and multifaceted nature towards one ideal against one sense of self. The Star is one of many stars, but all shine in one universe. The Star pours forth the "alchemical water" on both water and land—the process of manifestation through duality.

If we should now receive both the Star and the High Priestess in a reading, we might be reminded of their places in this layout (or another such layout) and apply them more powerfully as a connected pair, knowing their relationship in this context. A relatively mundane reading for a workplace-related question could then be elevated into a discussion of the person's deepest feelings, their own dualities, and their potential conflict within the workplace situation.

Vertical Column Three

This column is "devoted to growth and change, primarily in the area of the subconscious."[169] As we have previously mentioned, the Holy Order of Mans taught very strongly the idea of the conscious and unconscious selves. In this column, we may see more in this context.

The Empress

She is indeed the subconscious realm, our natural and primitive self, and the nurturer; the place where we give birth to new ideas and ambitions. On a wider scale, she is the wild, the unknown, the unbounded place where the conscious mind has not yet come to dwell.

Strength

At the next level down, we begin to connect to the simplest part of ourselves, we start the process of embracing the animal side of our self and wrestle with its primal instinct. All change is of this nature, a constant battle of desire.

Death

The process of change brings about transformation as symbolised by this card. It is one thing being turned into another by our ongoing march within existence. In terms of the conscious and unconscious, it is the fear of death manifest by our sense of self against its dissolution into the unconscious underworld.

Moon

At a base level, the facing of our fears is illustrated here; it is demons and our own madness; the borderlands between the rational and conscious self and the irrational unconscious. The Empress manifests them in our dreams and lights our journey through the moon into the wild places of the soul.

---

169 Anon, *Jewels of the Wise* (San Francisco, CA: Epiphany Press, 1979) 197.

In this column, we see the power of tarot to reflect and illuminate our very deepest existential concerns from the fear of death to the sense of self. Whether we are reading for the simplest relationship situation or a profound spiritual crisis, all the cards can go where we need them to go.

Vertical Column Four

We now begin to reach earthier concerns as we move across the journey of the Fool from right to left in this layout. The whole layout is a descent or progression from left to right and from top to bottom. So, the highest card in this context is the Magician, the ultimate Will or Word, and the lowest is Judgment, the final realization of spirit in matter and the call to its return home back through the process.

This column is said to show "different degrees of accomplishment."

The Emperor

We begin with insight, order, control and a constitution of our ambition. The Emperor is the onlooker who has vision and from this comes all accomplishment; the ability to see what is not yet present and act to bring it into manifestation.

The Hermit

At the summit of attainment, the Hermit is open to the divine influence and allows it to pass through him without hindrance. He is one with the path in his wisdom and has accomplished the journey to reach this singular point. He illustrates the purity of action in service.

Temperance

As the illustration of the alchemical fire in which we are truly tempered, this card shows what can be accomplished by enduring the journey of trial and tribulation. It is the card of patience and long-term work, a persistent will to work on oneself. In this column, we can also see clearly the journey back up the hierarchy from the Sun (below) of awareness through the work of Temperance, the path of the Hermit, and arriving at the throne of the Emperor.

The Sun

At the base of this column of accomplishment we have the card illustrating the child-like innocence of pure awareness. It is the self-knowledge and sacrifice that begins all true accomplishment. As it is said, "therefore, my beloved brethren, be ye steadfast, unmoveable, always abounding in the work of the Lord, forasmuch as ye know that your labour is not in vain in the Lord" (1 Corinthians 15:58).

Vertical Column Five

In this final column, it is written that it "shows a series of triplicities" which is an interesting observation on the designs of these cards: the Hierophant, Wheel of Fortune, Devil, and Judgment. We might also suggest that these cards are more about the way in which choice and free will takes place in the world, given the descent narrative of the overall layout.

The Hierophant

In the literal meaning of the word *hierophantos*, this card is an interface between one world and another, one who reveals sacred mysteries. In a cosmic sense, this illustrates the way in which the entire universe can be taken as an exemplar or demonstration of the divine structure. In our everyday world, the Hierophant shows the trinity that arises when we consider our options, choices, and consult others beyond ourselves. If we only have one choice, we are a slave; if we have two, we are in a dilemma. It is only when we have three options do we begin to have freedom.

The Wheel of Fortune

Here we have fate in its usual sense: the up and down of life and chance and/or fortune. However, it is also the cyclic principle in evolution, the testing of something through repetition, and the spiral process of initiation in time. Here our choices have consequences that we must allow to teach us until we attain the position of the centre of the Wheel. In a mystical sense, the Wheel is also the unity of all things, leaving only the Devil and Judgment below it.

The Devil

At almost the very base of the last column, it is perhaps no surprise to see the Devil in this place. As the symbol and illustration of ignorance, attachment, and even evil, the Devil appears here as the rawest and basic instrument of matter. It is both the first and the final temptation on the journey between spirit and matter, and the card indicates the responsibility that free will bestows upon us.

Judgment

As we have already suggested, here is the final resting place of spirit and yet also the start of its return to its rightful estate. It is the tomb and the calling forth to the divine realm for those who can hear it and rise to its invitation. We are reminded in this card of the opening of the *Chemical Wedding of Christian Rosenkreutz*, when an angel blows a trumpet on Easter Day outside the titular character's house and delivers an invitation to a great wedding. This wedding is the journey of unification which this layout illustrates, as we rise from our sleep and return to the Garden indicated by the Lovers and the Fool who is ever present in the World.

As with any layout, we can look at other patterns such as diagonals, pairs, and in this case, the rows across the square to provoke our thinking. If we took the pairs at each end of the rows, for example, it would be the following:

- **Row One:** The Magician and the Hierophant

- **Row Two:** The Lovers and the Wheel

- **Row Three:** Justice and the Devil

- **Row Four:** The Tower and Judgment

What concepts might these pairs represent, and how would they work as four levels of the same sort of concepts? As we explore layouts, we study not only the cards but ourselves as well:

"We have not told everything about each Key, because no one can. You have to find much of it yourself, and it cannot all become clear the first time around. But this material should provide an accurate and fruitful beginning to encourage the dawning Sun of Reality." [170]

---

170   *Ibid.*, 1.

Christian Tarot and a Card a Day

We will now take a moment to consider the Christian origins of the tarot images. In our time travels, we have come to see how the tarot deck is very much a product of a Christian society and mindset, constantly being re-tuned to individual and collective cosmologies. It is what Tali calls a "blank bible" onto which any philosophy can be projected—and there are few tools, if any, that really serve this singular purpose.

In fact, the whole idea of a "card of the day" where a tarot student is encouraged to take one card for study each day, is no different from the earliest use of cards as morality teaching. In 1718, Augsburg, Germany, we find morality cards being used as a "card of the day." Decks like these were called *Geistliche Karten*, "a motto for the day," and each card contained text listing a playing card (such as the 7 of Spades) and a spiritual musing designed to promote virtuous behaviour.

Each card text began with *Heut*, "today" and continued with a homily to guide the reader towards moral fortitude—and provide preparation to meet your maker. As an example, card 8 (*Hertz* 8) contains the verse:

Today … imagine death, you have to die, death is certain and will come soon, do not know today or tomorrow or whether he waits longer. Prepare soon, take the ladder of Christ and climb up to virtue. To achieve this mercy say a Lord's Prayer and an Ave Maria for the soul that does not regard death and doesn't prepare enough for it. [171]

It perhaps suggests a good way to use tarot through this method, where each card provides a homily to contemplate during the day. An example might be the 6 of Swords:

Today … imagine travel in all its meanings; that every movement you make is traveling from one state to another as well as through space. Consider too that all whom you meet this day are fellow travellers each on their own journey in addition to their companionship on your journey. Say this day, "I am travelling and I know not to where."

---

171 Translations by Peter Endebrock, taken from http://www.wopc.co.uk/germany/geistliche (Last accessed 1 July, 2016).

It would be a good journal exercise to create a homily for every card and contemplate them all over a period of seventy-eight days.

When we examine this spiritual or deeper aspect of tarot, in addition to our trip to 1909 and the work of A. E. Waite and Pamela Colman Smith, we should also take a brief hop to the life of an author whose work was published anonymously and posthumously. The work remains one of the hidden gems of tarot.

The book *Meditations on the Tarot* was first published in English in 1984, and to those of us around at the time it was a major revelation. A dense tome on the major arcana, each card was described and developed over at least twenty-five tightly written pages, drawing on sources as diverse as Nietzsche to Buddha.

The author was later revealed to be Valentin Tomberg (1900–1973). He was Estonian-Russian and engaged with Theosophy and Anthroposophy, later converting to Roman Catholicism. His life would make a novel as he was active in the Dutch resistance, gained a PhD, and translated Russian for the BBC during the cold war. Perhaps somewhat incongruously to this vibrant patchwork of life, he died on holiday in Majorca.

We have summarised a brief selection of the concepts to which Tomberg associated each of the major arcana in his work. We will then look at how these might be used in a reading for spiritual rather than mundane affairs.

1. **The Magician:** Creativity, capability, working without lust of result, active relaxation, mindfulness, suspending disbelief, spontaneity.

2. **The High Priestess:** Knowledge, knowing, awareness, divine channel/medium, epiphany, intuition, receptivity.

3. **The Empress:** Sacred magic, belief, miraculous, regeneration, transcendence, generation, fecundity.

4. **The Emperor:** Authority, divine power, omniscient, (all seeing), emissary.

5. **The Pope:** Benediction, blessing, teacher, poverty, inner emptiness, promulgation.

6. **The Lovers**: Union, chastity, return, soul mate, reciprocation, compatibility, temptation.

7. **The Chariot**: Autocratic, controlling, manipulative, resistance, self-sufficient, self-standing, initiative, individuation, self-actualization.

8. **Justice**: Mediation (Law), cause, effect and retribution, prove/refute, evidence, rationale, appraisal.

9. **The Hermit**: Detachment, objectivity, impartiality, observer created universe, silence, space, solitude, contemplation, inactive, neutrality, knowledge, heart wisdom.

10. **The Wheel of Fortune**: Evolution, cycles, movement, spiral, repetition, commencement, retrograde, rest, fate, lessons, rotation, eternity, reincarnation, spinning, destiny.

11. **Force**: Grace, co-operation, natural, if there is no resistance there will be no obstacle, unity, reconciliation, concordance, fusion, alliances.

12. **The Hanged Man**: Suspension, gravity, opposition, faith, tolerance, limbo state, half world, liminal.

13. **Death**: Withdrawal, forgetfulness, sleep, loss, disappearance, relinquishment, withdrawal.

14. **Temperance**: Inspiration, intuition, liberation, miracle, ambiguity, duality, letting go, discipline, focus.

15. **Devil**: Counter-inspiration, generation, slavery, projection of inner demons, intoxication of the will, temptation, prosecution.

16. **The Tower of Destruction**: Construction, struggle with the body, desire, sense of self against the divine, evolution. Non-specialisation.

17. **The Star**: Growth, the magical link (between consciousness and action), woman, the flow of life.

18. **The Moon**: Retrograde movement, retreat, absurdity, diminution, magical enchantment.

19. **The Sun**: Intuition, intelligence, spontaneous wisdom of the heart, pure vision.

20. **Judgment**: Accountability, sensibility, intuitive, cognition, critique, judgmental, resurrection, restoration, awakening, rebirth, reincarnation, accountability, realization, heightened awareness, rationale, sensitivity.

21. **The Fool**: Folly, induction, initiation, aspiration, inspiration, seeking.

22. **The World**: Creative act, movement, change, show and tell, learn by example, materialization, cycles, rhythms, design.

Tomberg most importantly to our time travelling preoccupation discusses the "meaning" of the cards and the problems inherent with interpretation. His thoughts on this are worth quoting in full as he looks at the Chariot card:

Let us now return to the Arcanum, "The Chariot", whose tradition meaning is "victory, triumph, success":

> This meaning is derived naturally from the bearing of the personage (the charioteer) and presents no difficulty. (J. Maxwell, *Le Tarot*, Paris, 1933, p. 87)

Now, there is all the same a difficulty that it presents, namely that of answering the question: Does this Card signify a warning or an ideal, or rather both at once?

I am inclined to see in all the Arcana of the Tarot simultaneously both warning and aims to be attained—at least, this is what I have learnt through forty years of study and meditation on the tarot. [172]

When we see each of the major arcana as a warning and an aim, we can lay out a spread in the form of a cross with four positions.

---

172   Anon, *Meditations on the Tarot* (Longmead, UK: Element Books, 1991), 164.

1. Warning

2. Aim

3 + 4. Balance

35. 4-Card Cross Spread.
Llewellyn's Classic Tarot by Moore and Smith, 2014.

So, if we laid out the Chariot as a warning, the Moon as an aim, and the Hermit and Judgment as our balancing cards, we might say:

There is a warning not to become too full of oneself and manipulate others to meet your own aims. Your aim should rather be to retreat from activity and reflect on the absurdity of your ambitions before continuing. This will require a significant amount of detachment [Hermit] combined with a proper sense of responsibility to your actions and their consequences [Judgment].

The reading of the major arcana in a higher or spiritual manner allows us to use the tool of the tarot in a deep and profound manner, as a constant guide to our inner life and outer action. If we take the symbol of the cross as a symbol of both balance and sacrifice, we can lay out our cards in this way to make of ourselves a living example of our own personal spirituality.

Christian Tarot

Whilst there is really no such thing as a Christian tarot, we have seen during our tarot time travel that the cards are compellingly based in Christian culture, both in acceptance of that culture (the Lovers in the Garden of Eden and the Devil) and its rejection as seen in the fortune-telling books. As society becomes more inclusive and even permissive, we will later see a return to the religious interpretation of the cards through theosophy and other worldviews.

However, the interpretation of the deck of cards as a Christian cosmology can be traced back to tracts such as *The New Game at Cards*, or *A Pack of Cards Changed into a Perpetual Almanack*. This is also known as the Soldiers Tale and here we use a version printed in Stirling, Scotland, in the 1800s.

The tract takes the form of a dialogue between a nobleman and his servant, or sometimes a soldier. Having been caught with a deck of cards, the speaker (the rogue) makes an impassioned defence that the cards as being entirely a Christian prayer-book. As he says, because he is "no scholar," "My Lord, if you call these cards, I do not; neither do I use them as such." This is a response that many tarot readers might still find themselves giving when people presume to know how we use the cards.

Here is the reasoning for the cards providing, first, an almanac. In this, we have a 52-card pack.

- **Four suits** = Quarters of the year
- **Thirteen cards in each suit** = Weeks in a quarter = Lunations in a year
- **Twelve court cards** = Months of the year = Signs of zodiac
- **Fifty-two cards in pack** = Weeks in year
- **Total number of pips** = Days in a year

The reasoning concludes that by having this reminder, we can count then the number of spots (pips) in the deck, coming to 365, then multiply by 24 and then by 60 to calculate the exact number of hours and minutes in a year.

We can see here how the structure of the pack has been turned into a temporal device using the deck's structure and design as correspondence to the way in which we measure time.

Our narrator then goes on to demonstrate to his accuser that "I sometimes convert cards into a Prayer Book." The accuser relents a little and gives him space to continue, as the almanac's method has impressed him.

Here is the reasoning for the cards providing a prayer book.

- **Four suits** = Four principle religions; Christianity, Judaism, Mahometanism [sic] (Islam), and Paganism.

- **Twelve court cards** = Twelve patriarchs = Tribes = Apostles = Articles of faith

- **King and queen** = Allegiance to Royalty

- **Ten** = Cities destroyed in the plains of Sodom and Gomorrah = Plagues = Commandments

- **Nine** = Hierarchies = Muses = Noble Orders

- **Eight** = Beatitudes = Altitudes = Persons saved in Noah's Ark = People resurrected in scriptures

- **Seven** = Administering spirits before throne of God = Seals of Book of Life = Angels with veils = Liberal arts and sciences = Wonders of world = Planets = Days of week

- **Six** = Petitions in Lord's Prayer = Days of working week

- **Five** = Senses

- **Four** = Death, Judgment, Heaven and Hell = Theological virtues = Evangelists = Seasons

- **Three** = Trinity = Days Jonas in belly of whale = Hours Saviour hung on cross = Days in tomb

- **Two** = Testaments, Old and New = Law and gospel = Virtue and vice

- **Ace** = One Lord and God = One faith = One truth = One baptism = One master

In this manner, we can see that whilst it is of a popular and uncertain source, the system of making correspondences can bridge any system.

Conclusion

As we move through time, we see the tarot returned to its playing card origins in the surprising manner of a morality game, as were many original card decks. Cards have always been used as a portable book, a game, and a teaching device and tarot is no exception to this tradition. Artists and philosophers, esotericists and poets have all taken to the tarot as a sequential piece of art on which to write a spiritual narrative. These meanings are applicable to everyday readings when they provide the "big picture" of the situations we read on the most mundane level. The time travelling tarot reader can provide more profound and productive readings when they are aware of these higher levels of meaning for the cards.

Now, as we start to come to the end of our present jaunts through time, we will push further ahead into the moment now—and look at what might be considered cutting-edge in tarot.

12

Tarosophy

Now that we have seen these greasy pieces of cardboard become a museum of old masters, a theatre of tragedy, a library of poems and novels, the silent brooding over down-to-earth words bound to come up along the way, following the arcane pictures, we can attempt to soar higher, to peal forth winged words, perhaps heard in some theatre balcony, where their resonance transforms moth-eaten sets on a creaking stage into palaces and battle-fields.

—Italo Calvino, *The Castle of Crossed Destinies* [173]

The Present Moment: Here

Our time-pod returns you now to the present moment, holding this book as your guide to travels both past and future, literally in your hands. We have visited here just a few of the selected moments that took tarot in unexpected directions; perhaps the world's greatest gift carried through time by the most unlikely of people. We have watched how people spent their own time creating and developing the art and methods of cartomancy, and now it is our turn—and yours. As you leave the time-pod for now, consider the future, which we have not yet visited.

---

173   Italo Calvino, *The Castle of Crossed Destinies* (London: Harcourt Brace, 1997), 113.

Shuffle your cards—tarot, Lenormand, oracle, or playing cards—and feel them connected to the whole of this history we have travelled together. Place three cards down.

What do they tell you about your future with the tarot?

In this penultimate chapter, we travel no further in time than today and look at contemporary methods of tarot reading developed from *Tarosophy*, our term for the living wisdom of tarot. It is a way of working with tarot that encourages us to engage with life, not escape it using techniques that employ tarot to initiate change in our lives.[174]

These techniques include "gated spreads," chains of specifically designed spreads that take the real-life action divined by one spread into the question directed to the next spread. You cannot follow a gated spread without making changes in your life, as the next spread will not make sense without the result of the change being presented to it, hence the term.

We have seen throughout our time travels how the very first meanings were applied to dream symbols by the nature of the objects, animals, and events within the dream. These meanings were applied to the events of the time, so whilst a flock of birds might have signified a good hunt to our earliest ancestors, to an Edwardian gentleman the same symbol would have meant idle chatter and gossip in the park, and to us in the present might mean freedom of self-expression.

None of these meanings are any truer than the others; all derive from the divinatory core of birds in flight having the nature of noisy freedom … and perhaps in the beginning, the nature of food or an approaching winter.

Over time these signs, portents, and symbols in the real world became symbols in dream and in language, for example Sirius rising on the horizon, a star that heralded the flood of the Nile. Such symbols were elevated in consciousness and became divine. As we evolved, they turned into systems that could be found in the entrails of animals, the shape of the clouds, or the way shells or sticks fell on the ground when cast with appropriate ritual. More time passed, and the symbols were also seen in the bottom of sherbet cups and coffee and tea cups, providing a convenient way of divining to everyone, not just the shamans, priestesses, priests, and oracles.

---

174 See Marcus Katz, *Tarosophy* (Keswick, UK: Forge Press, 2016).

Time continued to pass; selections of these symbols were categorised, formulated, and pasted into fortune books at a time when such fortune-telling arts were falling by the wayside in a grand renaissance of human civilisation.

The symbols found their way to print onto cards, a far more accessible and portable way of manufacturing and selling them as products for teaching...as well as gambling. Along the way, their meanings were being taken (recovered all the way back from their source in our primitive life and dreams) from the fortune books and applied directly to the very cards often used to navigate the books.

In this way—as we have seen throughout our time travel—playing cards (including tarot) became divinatory tools and were then adopted by esotericists who projected their own systems through history, linking a chain of meaning from the very earliest religions to the present day.

Yet for all the enthusiastic and mistaken notions of their history, the cards remain an incredible link in the same manner we might suggest alchemical symbols reveal our inner psyche. The cards are tools, a blank bible upon which we write our own stories—and those stories have not changed in their core since the beginning of history.

We continue our search for meaning in life throughout time, with the cards at our side. Now it is up to us to write the next chapters beyond this one—for there is no final chapter in the cards; we can shuffle them and start anew at any time.

As we close this present work, we will first look at how tarot tells us about its own future, allowing the cards to speak for themselves. We have learnt in our travels through time that tarot is a language—now let us listen to what the twenty-two major arcana would say about their own future. Then we will provide a range of cutting-edge Tarosophy techniques for you to take tarot into your own future.

Tarot Tells Its Own Future

If the major arcana cards could speak, what would they suggest about the future of tarot?

1. **Magician:** It will be more magical: And as more is revealed more will be concealed. The Law of the Trickster's Table is that the ball under the cup was in the hand of the one moving the cups.

2. **High Priestess:** It will be more spiritual. And it will take its place again between the pillars. The Law of the Scroll is that what is written in the future will always look the same as what was written in the past until you change your tool of writing.

3. **Empress:** It will become alive. And it will unfold in ways which only she imagines. The law of the Robe of Water is that what is on the surface is shaped by what is deepest. We must learn to hold our breath, then, and leave our shorelines far behind.

4. **Emperor:** It will be more influential. And it will shape more decisions even as it resists its own regulation. The Law of the Throne is that those who take it are not alone in sitting in their own blood.

5. **Hierophant:** It will become more traditional. And it will recover its dignity from its own roots. The Law of Revelation is that it is only the Resurrection of the Forgotten.

6. **Lovers:** It will be more popular. And it will become surfeit of its own choices. The Law of the Lovers is that you cannot have something without there being something else.

7. **Chariot:** It will head in new directions. And as it becomes drawn by the few, it will be driven by the many. The Law of the Reins it that when you pull, you are no longer in charge.

8. **Strength:** It will be resisted. And even as it struggles to retain its shape, it will create that shape. The Law of the Lion is that we become that which we fight.

9. **Hermit:** It will become more individual. And we will each own our own possibilities. The Law of the Lamp is that you have created everything before you even recognised it. Technology will allow for everyone to have their own unique deck which is unlike any other and can be changed instantly.

10. **Wheel**: It will change the way we see time. And the way we see time will change tarot. The Law of the Sphinx is that the riddle is its own answer.

11. **Justice**: It will become accessible to all. And new channels for its manifestation will be found between the pillars. There will be no singular deck, style, or approach favored above any other—all will be found and considered equal in the balance.

12. **Hanged Man**: It will rise in its value. And in ways we cannot yet imagine its value will be a place-holder in culture, society, and our psyche. There will always be a necessity for divination and tarot, to remind us of that from which we depend.

13. **Death**: It will transform itself as a language. And there will be new ways of inscribing and designing the tarot which will be almost unrecognizable to us today. Yet these will be obvious developments each arising from the other.

14. **Temperance**: It will be more integrated. And people will use it more regularly and engage with it in new ways to create projects, make decisions, and guide themselves daily. The rise of apps is merely the first part of this development.

15. **Devil**: It will be abused. And people will be concerned about its use, in the same way that people might be concerned about addiction to computer games or other distractions.

16. **Tower**: It will re-invent itself. And the way we talk about it will change, with new words to describe how the cards interact with each other, their names and meanings, and the way they offer advice—all these things will accelerate their change.

17. **Star**: It will go with us into space. And as we develop as a species, it will continue to guide us even in the far darkness of the heavens.

18. **Moon**: It will become more psychological. And it will be used as an adjunct to insight and personal development long after personal development is called something else.

19. **Sun**: It will become even more open and expansive. And even as it rises and falls several times in celebrity and popular culture, it will cycle round each time in a new way, lighting our future.

20. **Judgment**: It will provide a calling. And for many it will be a calling for life as a career, passion, or interest—a constant companion from cradle to grave.

21. **World**: It will become global. And in doing so it will provide a common language that is as unique as every person. It will reflect our common heritage, our common inheritance whilst at the same time celebrating our diversity and independent will.

In short, tarot has only just begun.

We will now look at a selection of contemporary and innovative methods of using tarot that may inspire you to experiment further and develop your own uses of this time-transcending tool.

Long-Term Prediction with the Major Arcana

You can use the predictions we have made above for your own situations by simply doing a reading with the twenty-two major arcana, and asking for a long-term prediction. Select one card and apply it to your own question.

So if you asked, "What is the long-term prediction for my relationships over my life?" and received the Sun card, it would be a positive prediction. It would suggest your relationships will become more expansive and open to more people in your life, rather than living in the future with fewer contacts, family, and friends. You can apply any global meaning as we have given in the list above to your own life or the life of a long-term project or situation.

Having made these predictions from the major arcana themselves, let us look to more practical key phrases of the minor arcana for use in contemporary readings. In modern or clickbait parlance, here are "just two words you need know to master every card—and you won't believe number four!"

The Tarosophy Lexicon

WANDS

1. Own it

2. See it

3. Start it

4. Befriend it

5. Fight it

6. Ride it

7. Stand it

8. Move it

9. Master it

10. Carry it

CUPS

1. Give it

2. Share it

3. Celebrate it

4. Ignore it

5. Lose it

6. Remember it

7. Imagine it

8. Leave it

9. Enjoy it

10. Recognise it

SWORDS

1. Cut it

2. Balance it

3. Split it

4. Hide it

5. Settle it

6. Transport it

7. Watch it

8. Free it

9. Mourn it

10. Stick it

PENTACLES

1. Offer it

2. Juggle it

3. Build it

4. Save it

5. Invest it

6. Distribute it

7. Abandon it

8. Work it

9. Own it

10. Protect it

These simple key phrases can be used to perform a one or two card reading with a deck of just the forty minor arcana (four suits, ace to 10). These methods are unique to Tarosophy and are called **split-deck** methods. They were developed from the work of Papus, whom we met in an earlier chapter.

Shuffle the split-deck of forty cards whilst considering your question and then select the top and bottom card of the pack, inserting the keyword pairs for both cards into the oracular construct like this:

OK, it's time to [keyword pair of top card] but not [keyword pair of bottom card].

If I asked: "In these changing economic times, how should I consider my own finances?" and received the card at the top as the 6 of Swords and the card at the bottom the 7 of Cups, I would get:

6 of Swords: Transport it

7 of Cups: Imagine it

And this would produce the oracular sentence:

"OK, it's time to transport it but not imagine it."

I need to move my finances into something else and not imagine that the current times will not impact on my security. This is a downright practical reading with serious advice.

Before we look at the court cards, having looked at the major and minor cards in this contemporary light, we will address an issue that many modern students face, that of connecting their cards.

Connecting Cards

Many new students of tarot tell us they have most difficulty connecting cards together so that they can speak to another person about what the cards are telling them about the situation. In this little variation of one of our Tarosophy skill-teaching games, practice will help your story-telling flow.

Card Connecting

Shuffle and take three cards out from your whole deck.

For the first, write or think of one action shown or suggested by the card, e.g., dancing.

For the second, select a situation in life it suggests, e.g., the home, the workplace, friends, and so on.

For the third, think of a state of mind or emotion the card depicts, e.g., separation. Then put the three together in a sentence as follows...

"I see you [or "myself"] in these cards [action] in the situation of [situation], resulting in [state of mind]."

Now take three more cards and repeat the same process to come up with another action, situation, and state. Place those three words into the following sentence...

"So, these cards show us that you [or "I"] should [action] to bring about [situation] and gain [state of mind]."

If I selected 2 of Pentacles, 8 of Pentacles, and 4 of Cups, I might say:

"I see myself in these cards **juggling** in the **workplace**, resulting in a feeling of **boredom**."

Then if I selected for my second sentence, the Hermit, 6 of Swords, and Page of Cups:

"So, I should take **time to myself** to bring about **travel** and gain a **new enthusiasm**."

This is both a practice and a way of reading a six-card reading to describe and advise upon any question. The more you practice this, the more variations you will produce until it becomes very easy to speak your own voice and tell a more elaborate story from your cards.

We will now add the court cards into our toolkit so we can work with a full deck of possibilities.

Defusing a Bomb with Court Cards

Whilst our other books have dealt with different ways of reading court cards and we have given a three-minute method in the Orientation chapter at the start of this present book, now we can add a very contemporary way of practising court cards.

When practising with court cards, first take the core of the question to an extreme by turning it into a dramatic movie scene requiring a resolution.

So, if the question is about facing a deadline, turn it into defusing a bomb. The more dramatic and over-the-top the better; we really want to take the core of the question into a scene that is outside of itself. The bomb should be a huge bomb capable of blowing up the entire planet.

As another example, if the real question was "is X the right partner for me?", we might ask instead, "Is X the notorious time-travelling serial killer that has been hunted by special agents for centuries?" We can risk making the situation outlandish or even ridiculous, that is part of the technique.

We would then shuffle a split-deck made of the sixteen court cards only and select two cards.

In this example, rather than try and work out the answer to the original question, which some students find difficult with court cards only, ask instead about the over-dramatic version:

If these two court cards were special time-travel agents, how would it work out if Mr. Normal is the serial killer or not? How would they work together?

Or in the former example question, "How would they work together to defuse that bomb?"

We can even wonder about their back story, whether these two court cards are best friends, or a good cop/bad cop type relationship, or uneasy partners like in a buddy movie.

We can also use just one card, although we find two-card draws are somewhat easier. A question about a work project with a one-card draw from the court cards would become

"We have a month before global disaster, what does this court card invent that no one has considered to save the day?"

Always make the scenario ludicrously extreme. That's the first trick with the technique, then there is a twist.

The twist is that you simply produce the strange scenario from your original situation or question, then you create the solution with the court cards as characters in a B movie film ... then you simply forget about it and wait a few days.

In this cutting-edge technique, you have already processed the answer unconsciously by "chunking it up" to an extreme; the actual solution to your question should arrive naturally and suddenly in your conscious mind after a just few days. It may also come to you on awakening, in a weird episode of synchronicity, or in a dream—it is quite a magical technique.

This Neuro-Linguistic Programming (NLP)-based practice will also help you whenever court cards come up in a reading or any spread as you will have unconsciously sorted and filtered their application to a wide range of situations. [175] NLP is a modern approach to human behaviour and the way we represent the world, which often concentrates of how language serves as a code for the way we process our experience. It can be used in tarot to model and teach elegant communication methods but more importantly it can be used to treat tarot as a language. This allows us to go beyond the usual box of tarot and use it in novel ways for powerful readings.

We will now take another NLP-based approach to the court cards and in this next case, see how they can be used to deal with a question about a past situation, in learning for the future. It sometimes surprises us that in the same way that we only consult a doctor when we are ill, or take a car to the garage when it is broken down, often we mainly read tarot for the future. As real-life time travellers, we have a lot of past that can provide useful lessons for our present and immediate future, and tarot can read for the past as much as it can read for the future.

---

175   See Marcus Katz, *NLP Magick* (Keswick, UK: Forge Press, 2017).

Court Card Advice

A way of getting quick and frank advice from the court cards by NLP, before doing something you might regret or to learn from something in the past which you could have done better—or might have done—or will do—or should do … is to consider what we call "modal operators of necessity" in the sixteen court cards. This phrase sounds complex but is something we do all the time; use words such as could, should, might, may, and would, etc.

We all know the difference between someone saying, "Can you open the window?" versus "You must open the window." These words give the scale of need to a sentence, be it a definite demand or a casual enquiry. There are some people who are just one court card and use just one word all the time; we must all know someone like that. Or perhaps we *might* all know someone like that. We *should* know someone who does that, surely?

Here are the modal operators for the court cards.

- **Pages**: Might do … Might not do [reversed]…

- **Knights**: Should do … Should not do [reversed]…

- **Queens**: Would do … Would not do [reversed]…

- **Kings**: Can do … Cannot do [reversed]…

We then take the suits and consider them as meta-programs. These are aspects of NLP that model different types of fundamental behaviour in people. Again, it is a complex phrase that refers to something we all know about—one simple example is a can-do person instead of a naysayer. There are some people who think big and some people who see details. These are examples of different types of meta-programs or more simply, ways we go about looking at the world.

Here is a selection of meta-programs for the suits.

- **Pentacles**: Short-Term/Long Term [Reversed]

- **Swords**: Little Steps/Big Steps [Reversed]

- **Cups**: For Yourself/For Others [Reversed]

- **Wands**: Towards Something/Away from Something [Reversed]

We now put these together to look at what we can learn when we ask two court cards about a situation we regret or might be about to regret. We will get their most straightforward advice as they will be true to their own personality in what they say.

NLP Court Card Method

Take the sixteen court cards. Ask their advice. Shuffle. Select one card.

Read it according to the rules above. We will call this sentence X. So, if we had the Page of Pentacles, this would be "might do" (Page) and "short-term" (Pentacles). This suggests we might make do with a short-term solution.

Turn the deck so the cards are reversed, repeat, and select one card reversed.

Read it according to the rules above. This is sentence Y.

So, if we then had the Queen of Swords reversed this would be "would do" (Queen) and "big steps" (swords reversed). This reads as "would do big steps." We can see this makes sense as the Queen of Swords upright is someone who decisively (must or should) cuts down to the point, so reversed it is suggesting we should perhaps be more laid back and look at bigger steps.

Now place the two sentences together into one sentence, i.e., You would do X [and/but/if/so...] you cannot do Y.

Use your intuition and common-sense to construct the sentence towards a positive outcome and use a linking word (e.g., *and, if, but, when, so, then*) as may be appropriate. If alternate linking words fit, use your intuition as to which one is correct for the question. This is part of the art of the method rather than the science of constructing the sentences.

In the example given above, we have the Page of Pentacles and the Queen of Swords reversed.

As we have seen, these are "might do short-term" and "would do big steps."

We put those together in a sentence: "You might always try and take short-term actions, but you would have to go and do bigger steps instead."

This tells us bluntly that we are fooling ourselves in life by taking big projects on but pretending we are just doing little things; this is a strategy that is not good for long-term health and one day may trip us up completely. The court cards do not provide a "solution" as such, they just "tell it as it is" which is often enough to shock us into different behaviour.

As another example, I might consider a question and draw the Page of Cups + the Knight of Wands reversed.

The result: "You might do it for yourself [but] you should not do it away from something."

I might want to do it for myself, but I should not do it in blind and immediate response to someone else doing something I don't like.

Try this method and see what frank advice the court cards hold for your situation and life. As you practice this method, you will find yourself also more proficient in reading the court cards within general spreads.

We will now move on to other reading methods and first practice using the whole deck to learn an essential quality of each card; what it provides in the deck and what impact it has in the world. This allows us to quickly and easily read every card as a reversal.

A third of tarot readers often read reversals, a third usually do not read reversals, and a third sometimes do and sometimes do not read reversals. This response has been consistent in every survey we have run over two decades, so you can see there is no "rule" or common practice in reading cards upside-down other than it is up to you.

Brings and Leaves (Reversals)

In this practice method, we take a card out of the deck.

We then consider how it both brings its nature into the world, and what it also leaves. We use the sentence structure "It brings ... but it leaves ...."

Here are some examples:

- **10 of Swords**: It brings a stop to all those plans but it leaves no room for doubt.

- **Queen of Cups**: She brings depth but leaves insecurity.

- **Hermit**: He brings peace of mind but leaves loneliness.

- **6 of Swords**: It brings movement but leaves ripples.

When you can do this easily for every card you will realise that you can read them reversed by using the "leaves" as an alternate way of reading the impact of a reversed card.

So, if you had a reading containing the Queen of Cups and the Hermit both reversed, these would indicate that there is emotional insecurity resulting in loneliness going on within the situation. The two things that these cards "leave" in their reversed role.

And that is all there is to it; you can now read the entire deck reversed with this simple trick.

We will now look at performing a one-card reading with just the major arcana, another aspect of reading often considered difficult when applied to a mundane question. When we take a contemporary view of tarot as a language, the method can become simple.

How to Do a One-Card Major-Only Reading for Mundane Questions

The problem many new readers have with the major arcana is they believe these cards are big picture things; archetypes, huge effect, and literal majors. Books tend to reinforce the idea, equating majors to the gods and goddesses, and other higher planes or concepts.

So, what happens when we try and apply these big players to a mundane question such as "Should I buy a new car or repair my current car?" The trick is to get to the cartomantic core of the major card by asking about its function, not its symbolism.

To do this we ask one question of the card; "What does it *do* for me?"

To make it even easier, you can simply fill in the blank word at the end of this sentence …

The [major card] makes … [your word here]

Here are our examples for the majors. It is important that you also ascribe your own functions and words to the cards which will make them even easier to use.

- **The Fool** makes fun

- **The Magician** makes magic

- **The High Priestess** makes mystery

- **The Empress** makes plenty

- **The Emperor** makes tracks

- **The Hierophant** makes tradition

- **The Lovers** makes union

- **The Chariot** makes tracks

- **Strength** makes endurance

- **The Hermit** makes his way

- **The Wheel** makes movement/revolution

- **Justice** makes laws

- **The Hanged Man** makes sacrifice

- **Death** makes transformation

- **Temperance** makes tolerance

- **The Devil** makes mischief

- **The Tower** makes change

- **The Star** makes clarity

- **The Moon** makes reflection

- **The Sun** makes will

- **Judgment** makes awareness

- **The World** makes evolution

In completing that simple sentence, you automatically, naturally, quickly, and easily communicate with the archetype, tune into it, condense everything you have learnt about the card, and discover the core of it—the *function*.

The function of the archetype illustrated by the Magician is to carry "magick" in the world and our relationship to it. The function of the archetype that is illustrated by the Tower is to hold all notions, concepts, and examples of "sudden change" or shock.

Now that we have created this simple sentence, we can apply it straight to any mundane question by asking:

What **action** would **make** the same thing as **the card**?

If I pulled the Magician, I would have to ask: What action (buying a new car or keeping my current car) would also **make magick**?

To me, making magick is about changing things at the very least, so that function would be served by buying a new car. The fact that Mercury corresponds to the Magician backs that up, but is not necessary to know.

If I got the Devil card for the same question, I would realise that keeping my current car would be quite mischievous, rather than buying something brand new and obvious. The fact that the Devil has chains and signifies something we are attached to is useful but not necessary to know.

For you, it might be the other way around, but this method is about your relationship to the universe through the archetypes, so you go with whatever words you have set and your interpretation.

Go through the majors first and write down what each one *makes*, as we have given above: "this [card] **makes** ... [your word]." Then having fixed your answers, think of a question, pull a card from the majors only, and choose the action that will also function to make the same thing—you will have your answer. This simple method will also help you practice for when major arcana turn up in a general spread for other mundane matters.

Whilst we are dealing with majors, there is one major card that often causes issues in readings and for new students, so we will briefly consider the Death card and then move on to other methods of reading from the whole deck.

How the Time Traveller Deals with Death

When we consider the Death card in any reading, over time we have learnt to deliver it in terms of its role as "transformation" in the functions of the majors, as we have seen in the previous exercise.

Tarot readers often talk about the card as "transformation" but what is that really? It comes from two Latin phrases, *trans-* and *form* respectively, meaning "across" and "shape."

So, it means to change something from one shape to another, to change its appearance or structure without changing what it is.

A simple example is when water transforms from a liquid to a gas when we boil it—it is still the same molecules, just in a different state.

So, the card is saying that wherever it appears in the spread is **where** we need to change the shape of things; not add something or take it away, but work with what we have (even if it is not a lot).

The Death card is saying you can only change things around, there is nothing new to come or anything of which you should get rid.

When we consider Death in the time-related parts of a reading, in the past position of a spread, Death tells us that we must change the shape of our memories. We cannot add anything into the past nor take anything away. In a practical sense, we should perhaps make some memories bigger than others by recalling them as more important and positive.

However, it is that we think about the past, we must change the shape of it. As another example, stretching a bad memory further back or bringing a good memory from childhood closer towards us. We can massively change that landscape, even if we cannot add or remove anything from what has already happened.

In the future position, Death tells us that we might want to stop trying to find something new and simply start to re-arrange what we have already. In a practical sense, it is making changes in the workplace without looking (yet) for a new job, or similarly in a relationship. Whatever we want in the future, the card is telling us that before we go there, we should transform what we already have now. And perhaps strangely, it's often that new opportunities present themselves in the future when we simply reorganise the present.

In the present position, Death tells us that we are already being changed, but because it is not dramatic like the Tower or subtle like the High Priestess, we probably will not see it yet. It tells us in the present that we are changing the shape of our relationship to everything, and this is always inevitable and always happening, so if anything, we should let it happen.

In a practical sense, Death in the present is a card that tells us to notice what is the same but different and in doing so, realise how far we have come . . . and how far we might yet go.

We will now take a moment, having dealt with Death, to align ourselves to the elements of the tarot before moving on through a selection of Tarosophy methods for relationship readings.

A Brief Interlude Method to Align your Life to the Elements

This is a simple balancing exercise for times when you feel out of alignment with your own time-stream.

Take your tarot deck and lay out the four aces face-up to four quarters of your table.

Take the sixteen court cards in your hands face down. Put to one side the twenty-two majors and forty minors.

Consider your life as it is now and say this, very deliberately, whilst also shuffling the court cards:

- **The Ace of Wands** is my Will in this World, the fire I bring from above, chosen for me and me alone.

- **The Ace of Cups** is my Love in this World, the water of grace I draw from the depths, given to me and me alone.

- **The Ace of Swords** is my Vision of this world, a mirror, a blade, an edge for my use alone.

- **The Ace of Pentacles** is my Body of this world, the earth of my soul I manifest, as me and me alone.

Place the shuffled sixteen court cards in a small pile and place them in the centre of the four aces, face down.

Take a moment, then turn the pile of sixteen court cards face up to discover the bottom card, saying:

And this is who I need to be right now to balance these elements.

Consult the various interpretations of the court cards given throughout this present book to discover what sort of qualities you need activation through action in your life right now, to bring yourself back to the centre of the circle.

A Tarosophy Relationship Pattern Method

This method is ideal for a quick reading for new or stagnant relationships, or when the reader/querent is wondering why certain patterns of relationship are repeated.

In this method, we use the deck itself to configure the spread required, as it is considered its own language. So, if we want to look at the basis of a relationship, we use the first three cards of the suit of cups—ace, 2, and 3—as the basis of our spread. The deck can be used in this way as an infinitely configurable spread generator for any situation the time traveller may experience.

1. Take your Ace of Cups, 2 of Cups, and 3 of Cups out of your deck. Place them in a triangle, with the Ace of Cups at the top, the 2 of Cups to your left and the 3 of Cups to your right.

You can also simply write or imagine the three cup cards used as the layout and then use the entire deck including those cards, but I prefer to extract those energies as the template and then read from the remaining deck.

2. Shuffle the remaining deck, considering your relationships or those of your querent/client.

3. Lay out a card, placing it above the Ace of Cups, straight, saying, "This is where your passion is rooted."

4. Lay out a card, placing it diagonally 45 degrees, tilted to the right, next to the 2 of Cups on the left, saying "This is how your passion passes into relationship with individuals."

5. Lay out a third card, placing it diagonally 45 degrees, tilted to the left, next to the 3 of Cups on the right, saying, "This is how your relationship to individuals passes into groups of friends, and communities, the workplace, etc."

You can also read the three cards in relationship to each other, showing how the relationship to individuals compares to groups, etc.

Intermediate Variation

A very powerful and profound addition can be to place the 10 of Cups in the middle of the triangle at the beginning, and then lay out the three cards as above, and place a fourth card on top of the 10 of Cups in the centre of the triangle, saying finally, "And this is how your relationship to everyone and everything was formed by your family upbringing."

Advanced Variation

You can also place another round of cards at right angles to the diagonals, building a star layout. The next round of cards at right angles are "This is how you block these relationships [within yourself, with individuals, with groups]," then the next round, which are placed again at diagonals, are "This is how you can incorporate and make use of these challenges to improve your relationships [within yourself, with individuals, with groups]."

His and Hers Method

For general relationship readings, a quick method is to shuffle your deck, split it roughly into two piles (one for each person), shuffle each pile whilst thinking of each partner and then take the top card from both decks.

Place these two cards to the left and right with a gap between them.

This tells you what is going on for each person in the relationship on the surface.

A court card indicates the personality traits the person is expressing in the relationship, a minor card shows the situation the person tends to provoke or encounter in the relationship, and a major card reveals the archetypal pattern that is playing out through that person in the relationship.

Put the two remaining piles together again, shuffle, and select the top and bottom cards, placing them between the two separate cards in a column.

The top card tells you what can be aimed for in the relationship between the two, and the bottom card what resources can be drawn upon to achieve that aim. Nice, quick, and simple.

Intermediate Version

You can also split the deck into the majors, minors, and court cards, split those three piles into two each and then pull one card from each for each partner, showing the three facets of the relationship from either side (i.e. a court, minor, and major for each partner).

Then put the remaining cards from the three piles together and draw a resource and aim card after shuffling for the relationship.

We will now look at two reading methods that are specifically time-based; in this case, for performance at the new moon and once a year at the summer solstice.

New Moon Method

This method is suitable for when you seek to open an opportunity and do something different in your life. The new moon is a good time to do so and this method is specifically attuned to this time of the lunar month.

You will just need three cards and a few minutes on the night of the eve of the new moon, and a few minutes on the day of the new moon.

You will also need to do something in your life, as Tarosophy is "tarot to engage life, not escape it."

The Method

Sit at your usual place of tarot reading, altar, or a regular table. Ideally, this should be just before you go to bed. Visualise a black circle (or draw one or use something that is a black circle) and imagine it contains all possibilities.

See it on your table and imagine that tomorrow an "eye" will open during the day and let something new through into your life.

Shuffle your tarot deck and lay out one card to the left of the circle and one card to the right, both face-up.

The left card shows something you need to face in your life or come to better terms with that has been hidden.

The right card shows something that you need to look out for tomorrow as a way of doing something about the left card. It shows how you must nail down the situation or hook it into your life.

Look at the two cards together until they have something simple to tell you that makes sense.

When you have that, for example, "You are holding back too much (Chariot) and should look for a moment when you are doing too much (10 of Wands)," draw the next card out of the deck but place it **face down** in the centre of the circle.

Leave the reading as it is and go to sleep.

The following morning, on the new moon day, turn up that middle card and it will tell you what **to say today** when that situation arises that helps you face what has been hidden.

In this way, we create a new opportunity in our lives to make a significant change, on a new moon day (or night) which supports such transformative work.

It might be in our example that we turn up the Hermit card and that tells us that we must say **"I need time to myself."**

So, we would look out that day for a moment when we feel as if we are carrying too much (10 of Wands) and then say out loud, "Hey! I need a time out from this, leave me alone for a bit" and that will lock into our need to face the Chariot challenge in our lives.

Most of all, it creates a new opportunity that will open all sorts of things that will follow it.

You may also discover that this simple change in your life acts out over twenty-eight days before coming to a new state, with the full moon.

Advanced tarot time travellers will see that this simple method is constructed of the Hebrew letter corresponding to the Moon, QOPH, spelt in full as Qoph + Vau + Peh. These three letters in turn provide the transformation's operating steps.

Travel Through Dark Times

Take your deck and consider the darkest times of your day, your week, your month, your year, and your life. Shuffle whilst contemplating how utterly hopeless each of those moments seemed at the time. Consider if you are performing this spread on the winter solstice day itself, how it is indeed the shortest and darkest day of the year.

When you are ready, turn your deck face up and carefully go through the cards in order until you find the **Sun** card. Remove it as well as the two cards either side of it. Place them in front of you.

Now shuffle the rest of the deck and ponder if those two cards either side of the Sun are the hidden light you can now gain. Where might be the darkness in which they are to be discovered?

Turn the deck face up again and this time search for the **World** card. The sun and the earth are powerfully straining at this time of year, so we look for the darkness in the World card (it also corresponds to Saturn, for those of an astrological nature). Take the World card and the two cards either side of it, and place them below the Sun and its pair of cards.

Read the card to the left of the Sun and the left of the earth together as "This light is discovered in this darkness." Do the same for the cards to the right, above, and below.

36. Summer Solstice Spread.
Llewellyn's Classic Tarot by Moore and Smith, 2014.

For example, if I had the Queen of Wands and the Tower above and below on the left, that could be read as: "The light of my inner compassion comes from the darkness of shock and sudden change." On the right-hand side, if I had the 6 of Swords above and the 2 of Wands below, I would read: "The light of my self-sufficiency and forward-thinking comes from the darkness of everything that I did not accomplish…yet."

You can make powerful affirmations for yourself using this method, ready for the year until the next solstice.

We will now conclude our chapter on modern methods with two simple but elegant ways to use the tarot for yourself and in time travel.

Your Tarot Superpower

What does the tarot tell us about our superpowers? Try this one-moment method and you may be surprised to discover a secret to your skills.

Consider something you do very well or something other people say you are skilled at.

It can be anything from knitting to looking after people, from party-planning to keeping things tidy. It can be any skill, no matter how big or small. You should do it well enough that it is common knowledge to others.

Consider it and ask, "What is the essential secret to this skill?"

Take a deck, shuffle, and pull a card.

Let us say we ask about our skill, high productivity, i.e., doing many tasks at once and accomplishing a lot of things simultaneously. What is the essential secret to this skill?

We get a major arcana card, the Empress; a card of creativity and enjoyment, of nature and pregnancy. So, the essential secret to doing a lot, is to do what you enjoy, what is creative, and what nourishes yourself and others. In effect, do what is most natural—the Empress.

Once you know the secret of your own superpower, you can repeat this exercise for anyone else who has a desirable quality and discover the secret of *their* success for yourself.

Tarot Time Travelling

Every so often, spend a moment and strongly imagine that you can send a message back in time one year to yourself that includes anything you need to know to avoid any serious mistakes. Visualise this with concentration in whatever way feels right to you. We imagine it as casting a stream of blue light through a swirling time-tunnel. When you have done this, draw three cards from your tarot deck to immediately receive the message from your future self a year ahead of you. The more regularly you practice this powerful method, the more you will know where you are going in life and get there.

Conclusion

As we reach the end of this selection of contemporary and cutting-edge methods for tarot, we would like to remind all readers that they should never build doors out of the keys. Do not make tarot difficult for yourself. If you are stuck, ask the tarot, if you are confused, ask the tarot—learn to listen, and it will teach you everything you need to know.

Here is what they might say about the concerns that some readers think could hold them back, starting with the Magician to the World, and what the Fool answers at the end.

- I don't have the skill.

- I don't have intuition.

- I don't have experience.

- I have no power.

- I don't know the rules.

- I don't love tarot enough.

- I don't go far enough.

- I am frightened.

- I am alone.

- It goes around and around in my head.

- I am unbalanced.

- I can't read reversals.

- I'm scared of the Death card.

- The spirits do not talk to me.

- People think it's the work of the devil.

- I keep learning, but then it all falls apart.

- I'm hopeless.

- I am not deep enough.

- I am not bright enough.

- Everyone will judge me.

- I'm not as good as/like everyone else.

"You know what?" says the Fool, "I don't care. Just read your tarot. They are the keys to your freedom, not the locked doors."

13

Time Travel Guide

The true Tarot is symbolism; it speaks no other language and offers no other signs. Given the inward meaning of its emblems, they do become a kind of alphabet which is capable of indefinite combinations and makes true sense in all.

—A.E. Waite, *Pictorial Key to the Tarot*

In this final chapter, we will briefly summarise several of the key concepts we have discovered in our travels across time and provide a closing selection of methods for the tarot time traveller. Our journey has been bumpy, and we have rapidly made our way across time, so we should take a moment to take stock and recover before going on our way.

Cartomantic Correspondence

As we have seen, there have been different systems for reading cards, whether playing cards, tarot, Lenormand, or any variety of pictures on cardboard. In appendix 2 we have provided a list of correspondences between the Lenormand card inserts and tarot cards so we can see what happens when we compare and contrast systems. This is called correspondence.

The 7 of Pentacles corresponds to the 7 of Diamonds according to the system we most commonly use of making such correspondences, what we would call a cartomantic map. The seven of one system corresponds directly to the seven in the other. We have four suits in each, so we make a one-to-one correspondence between them. In this case, we chose to correspond the diamonds of playing cards to the pentacles of the tarot.

When we now look at the original meaning given to the 7 of Diamonds (see earlier section on Flamstead & Partridge), we see that it was a negative card for men, bringing "crosses" one would have "cause to fear." In Flamstead & Partridge it goes on to say that for women, it is the opposite, that they have no need to fear "crosses, of a straw" perhaps an allusion to the straw cross of Brigid. Later, this card as a Master Card in the Square of Sevens, is a "card of good omen," particularly in commercial ventures, which is the same in several other authors, alluding to the card as one of "money" even if just a small amount—or a pet or child.

This card is used as the insert of the Birds card (card 12) in Lenormand, which traditionally refers to "happiness" and messages (or later, chatter and gossip), of "joyful tidings." So, it is not a like-for-like correspondence; generally, the *cartomantic core* of the card is "good."

If we further correspond this to the Tarot, we have the Golden Dawn version of the 7 of Pentacles, which is "success, unfulfilled" and illustrated later by Pamela Colman Smith as an Irish farmer leaning on his hoe gazing disconsolately at his ruined potato crop. It is not such a completely "good" card; it does remind us of an earlier meaning in coffee cards for the Birds, which was that there would be love, but it might come to nothing if it was just ruled by passion, and not common sense, we would guess.

In conclusion, we can see that the 7 of Diamonds, the 7 of Pentacles, and the Birds card all hold unique positions within their own systems, and only casually correspond between each other—leading us to question whether any card has any single and true meaning across all systems.

What Does a Card Mean?

In all our travels through time, one question has returned again and again: what does it *mean* that a card has a *meaning*? What does a playing card, tarot card, or Lenormand card mean? How can it mean more than one thing? Which meaning is right, or better than the others?

We have seen how a meaning gravitates to a consensus over time, and then settles as a stable meaning for a period before being shifted again slightly in its orbit. We saw earlier in this book how the 2 of Pentacles had a very clear meaning of "miscommunication" prior to Pamela Colman Smith's depiction of it as "false mercury." As people were then not provided the key to this metaphor, they took a visual cue from the overwhelming symbol in the illustration; that of "juggling" and then applied it to money and work, the correspondence of the pentacles being "juggled." Over time, the card has been shifted away from its earlier cartomantic core.

Other cards have had different journeys of their meaning; their family tree can be traced to a major branching-off point from Eden Gray's books, for example, which were a major influence on the authors and teachers arising in the following decade. These meanings then became canon until they were re-interpreted in contemporary language which was more attuned to the increasingly technological-generation.

Finally, some cards have only recently become more associated with specific meanings that have slightly changed from earlier meanings because of a popular website called Learn Tarot that appears to have been abandoned but left up for many years. As such, it has been (and remains) prey on "passive income entrepreneurs" and others who have largely built their own tarot sites from the "inspiration" of that original site. In turn, those meanings and in some cases exact phrases have been copied and pasted regularly across social media, memes, viral images, and attained popular consciousness.

So, what does any card actually *mean*?

The answer is that the card means *nothing*; what it points to is what matters, and what each card points us towards is a specific point in the fabric of the universe from which all patterns and predictions arise.

Imagine that the universe, or at least, our relationship to it through our senses, has a structure as notable as gravity or inertia, as present and certain in our every day that we know not to drop an object because it will fall. Let your imagination stretch to contemplate that.this structure is *atemporal*, somehow not just arranged in space but across time. It is a structure that connects past, present, and future together in a way that we have not yet discovered.

Imagine that in the same way we have classified colors or numbers, shapes and animals, this deep time-structure can be best modelled by seventy-eight interrelated points of core meanings, in four different layers with ten points in each layer, and two sets of sixteen and twenty-two shells of meaning.

Imagine that it is the equivalent of quantum scientists discovering patterns of ten, twenty-two, and six plus four in their models, as did the Kabbalists when they looked at the Universe—because we are all looking at the same single thing.

We can then suggest that from these seventy-eight points arise all experience, all events, and all patterns and connections across time. The points can be given labels, each slightly different from another such as "the point from which all sudden change emerges, no matter when and where, or at what level"; "the point from which things start to work together but are not yet fully organised, whether that be countries or brain cells, a chemical reaction or a project team"; and so on.

Every meaning we assign to those points is because that meaning is more suited to one point than another, and yet just in seventy-eight points we can categorise everything.

Let us remember Eliphas Lévi:

> So arranged, the Tarot is a veritable oracle, and replies to all possible questions with more precision and infallibility than the Android of Albertus Magnus. An imprisoned person with no other book than the Tarot, if he knew how to use it, could in a few years acquire universal knowledge, and would be able to speak on all subjects with unequalled learning and inexhaustible eloquence. [176]

So, the Tower arises as an illustration of the point referring to all sudden change but is never the only or singular illustration, symbol, or example of such change. Neither does it mean only sudden change but everything else closer to sudden-change-type of patterns in all time than closer to "the point at which things start to work together..." which would

---

176   Eliphas Lévi, *The Ritual of Transcendental Magic* (London, UK: Rider & Company, 1995), 480.

be closer to the 5 of Wands. The seventy-eight cards of Tarot are each a "strange attractor" to which *meaning* approaches but never finally reaches. [177]

At last we come to the great secret of this book, and of the tarot.

It is the tarot who is the real time traveller, not us. We are part of its journey more than it is part of ours, and we all arise from the same seventy-eight points of the time-matrix.

What is Interpretation?

Having advanced a notion of tarot as a time traveller, how do we then speak with it? It is identical in this regard to our unconscious which does not recognise linear time, nor conscious filters, and is deeper than language, so both speak in symbolism and metaphor. We speak to it by interpreting its language as we would do any other language. The word "interpretation" comes from the Latin *interpretari*, to explain or translate. In conducting a card-reading, we are thus acting as an agent to explain the cards' symbols and translate these into the context of the sitter's life.

It is the *translation* which is the important trick; again, the word comes from Latin and means "to move across." In a reading, we are *moving* the fields of meaning attracted to each card (or to which each card is attracted or an attractor) *across* time and space into the context of other arising situations—the question being asked of the cards. There is no more magic than the fact that everything is connected at a deep level, and our lives and the tarot reading itself are all emerging simultaneously across time from that singular nature.

The Role of Intuition

Tarot readers are often aware of the importance of intuition in their readings, but the idea can be confused with guesswork or any immediate and simple response to images. It is the case that we can only intuit something about which we have knowledge. A car mechanic can intuitively know what is wrong with a car but not about a heart in the middle

---

177   In the mathematical field of dynamical systems (sometimes referred to in part as "chaos theory"), an attractor is a set of numerical values toward which a system tends to evolve. It is "strange" when it has a fractal nature.

of surgery; we would hope the surgeon can also be intuitive in that case, as well as having knowledge and experience.

Intuition arises from knowledge and experience (often, lots of experience), but unless it commences with sound knowledge, it is little more than casual guessing. It is therefore important for the traveller in time to learn at least one system or another as a touchstone, as we have suggested, within which intuition may be developed.

There are many methods of exercising, recognising, and building intuition, tarot reading, journaling, dream working. Several of the methods we have provided in this current guide are designed to strengthen intuition. [178]

The Importance of the Question

We have seen over time how language has changed for questions and yet the basic questions remain the same. Here are several situations and questions placed before the ancient oracle of Dodona:

Geris asks Zeus concerning a wife, whether it is better for him to take one.

Heracleidas asks Zeus and Dione … whether there will be any offspring from his wife Aigle.

Cleotas asks Zeus and Dione whether it is better and profitable for him to keep sheep.

Thrasyboulos asks by sacrificing to and appeasing which god will he become healthier in his eyes? [179]

Further along the timeline we see that in 1934, the reader of *Woman's Own* magazine loves to consider the lives of others. She (almost certainly a she) has an interest in the problems of others as no doubt they are problems shared by many, including herself. Before settling down to read about fortune-telling, she reads the regular problem page in the magazine, aptly called "Life and You." This column has the tagline "Don't let troubles and worries get you down." There is a suggestion to "talk them over with Mrs. Eyles instead and get her advice and help."

---

178   The development of intuition is outside of the scope of this present book, but the reader might consider the Facebook group, Tarosophy Psychic Development.

179   Quoted in Marcus Katz, *Tarosophy* (Keswick, UK: Forge Press, 2016), 103–104.

The problem page was not a modern invention; it was invented in 1691 by a troubled adulterer, John Dunton. Our Agony Aunt Mrs. Eyles ("bestselling novelist, socialist, journalist") is then mentioned as the first agony aunt of *Woman's Own* magazine and sold as "a woman who understands."[180]

We have seen that people's problems and how they dealt with them have changed due to cultural shifts. There was a notable class division in England in 1934; some people lived in big houses and others just worked in them. So "Mrs. Eyles" is asked questions about working in service. However, the questions asked of an Agony Aunt or across a tarot table at the time are basically no different than those asked of readers today. People have always been concerned about their relationships, confidence, and work.

The Role and Responsibility of the Reader & the Querent

When people ask questions of a tarot reader, there is a responsibility of sorts upon the reader to read the cards—it is their contract. Whether the client expects anything seriously or otherwise, the reader must read the cards and communicate an interpretation as best as they are able—which is our profession. The transaction between the reader and client is one of different responsibilities; the reader is responsible for reading the cards. The client is responsible for their actions resulting from the reading. This is much the same for readers of Agony Aunt advice:

> Readers, they point out, aren't mindless automata. "You can expound and lay down the law to your heart's content," says Raeburn. "Nobody will take on board what doesn't serve them—except a fool or a masochist—and I haven't met many of either." Ironside agrees. "No one takes advice to the letter—they mix it up with their own feelings, a bit of advice from friends, a bit from family. They are not a gang of dummies waiting to be dictated to.[181]

---

180 Langhamer, 15.

181 The Guardian, "A Brief History of Agony Aunts" (Nov 2009), http://www.theguardian.com /lifeandstyle/2009/nov/13/agony-aunts (Last accessed 4 June, 2016).

The skills needed for a tarot reader are much the same as an Agony Aunt, and perhaps share much in common with other professions that care for the human condition. [182] Here are several of the skills and resources required of the contemporary reader, if we were to advertise it as any other job or career:

- Excellent communication skills.

- Good people person.

- Wide range of real-world experience.

- Aware of the range of issues facing real people from relationship situations to psychological concerns.

- Very adaptable.

- Knowledge and access of professional agencies and support organizations to which to potentially refer clients.

- Trained in a range of decks, methods, and spreads suitable for most questions.

- Very flexible in terms of working conditions, hours, and recompense.

- Comfortable working with initially skeptical, concerned, or negative clients.

- Able to draw boundaries.

Having briefly summarised what might be called our mechanics, operating conditions, and conduct out in the wild, we will now conclude with a selection of advanced methods for the ardent tarot time traveller. These methods are for personal orientation in life or the life of those whom accompany us in the journey.

182　The "Standards of conduct, performance & ethics for Professional Tarot Readers" promoted by the Tarosophy Tarot Association was written with assistance from several advisors in the Nursing and Care professions, along with those working with vulnerable adults. This was to ensure that the widest coverage and responsibility was promoted with awareness of legal and social issues arising from offering readings in an unregulated profession, in addition to legal, contractual, advertising, and other business regulations.

Time Travel Spreads

The tarot time traveller is encouraged to learn these several advanced spreads to navigate their journey. It is possible to get lost or slip out of time altogether, and our tarot provides a tool to locate our exact location and orient ourselves to the present moment. We can also use tarot to provide a compass for the past and future.

Let us first consider how we see time itself. We do not have actual clocks in our head although we are aware of the passing of time. We do not really know what time is other than a concept. The British astronomer Arthur Eddington (1882–1944) described time as a process that only goes one way, "time's arrow." [183]

Our first spread considers time as an asymmetric (one-way) channel where *cause* leads to *effect* through correlation. That is, when we drop a glass of wine, the glass shatters and the wine spreads across the floor—it never goes back the other way. The effect of the wine stain was caused by our dropping the glass, not the other way around. In our habitual perceptual state, this is the way the world works.

The Arrow of Time Spread

In this method, we look at the causes and consequences (effects) of an event that has led to a present situation. We then continue looking at how the arrow of time is likely to continue … with a twist that at any point we can change its direction by making different decisions.

This method is ideal for situations that feel out-of-control or very uncertain and can bring much-needed clarity and a sense of control or connectedness.

Prepare a table or floor space for your cards, as this spread develops into a large space.

Shuffle the deck and when ready, take the top card out and place it in the centre of the space.

This is your temporal significator—a card that denotes the present moment in time.

Now take the bottom card from the deck and place it to the far left of the space available.

---

183   Arthur Eddington, *The Nature of the Physical World*, 1928, at https://archive.org/details /natureofphysical00eddi (Last accessed 4 June, 2016).

This is your *time root*—a card that illustrates the main moment when the present situation was set in motion, twisted from its course, or took a direction other than you would wish in the present.

Now take the next top card from the deck and place it to the far right of the space.

This is the *Time Target* or card which signifies the future point of your ambition or desire. If this target is undesirable, i.e., a negative card for your situation, we will navigate elsewhere in this method, otherwise it is your target.

Stand near to the temporal significator and look back to the time root card. Then turn to look at your target.

If your target is desirable, select one card and place it down in front of you in the direction of the target. This indicates your next action. Decide on the action required.

If your target was undesirable, select one card and place it down towards your time root card and read it as indicating what you should learn from the past before continuing. Then, if you heed this lesson, turn towards the initial target card and place a new card in your future path slightly at an angle away from the initial target. This will indicate the action to take on a slightly new path.

Once you have taken the action required, return to your layout and stand beyond the action card and look again at your target card.

Repeat the process of selecting out a past and/or future card, deciding an action, and then returning to the layout over time.

If you need the space between times, simply make a note of the cards and their positions (a photo on a smartphone suffices) and return them to their places each time you perform the reading.

At any point if the actions appear to move you away from your target card, create a new direction from that action card at a new angle, using the action card as a "past" card from which to learn.

In this way, you will follow an ever-changing arrow through time towards your destiny.

The next method uses a fixed spatial representation of time to offer another means of orientating our course in life through time and the tarot.

The Hall of the Moon

In ancient China, farming was often carried out in a 3 x 3 grid, forming a pattern of nine squares. This pattern or template became a common layout for architecture, particularly in sacred temples and was known as the "Hall of the Moon." [184]

The pattern was also called *ming tang,* "bright hall," and it became a template for living arrangements whereby a space was divided into nine squares. As the year progressed, one could spend one month in a room where the light was better, then two months in each of the corner room (which has two sides), and so on around the house.

We have taken this universal pattern for the time travellers equivalent of a "year spread." As ever, our time traveller has a charged-up version of the usual spread.

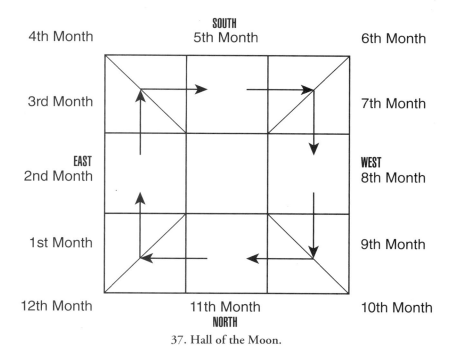

37. Hall of the Moon.

Shuffle your whole deck and consider the year ahead.

---

184   Nigel Pennick, *Secret Games of the Gods* (York Beach, ME: Samuel Weiser, 1997), 132.

Select a time-period from which you will draw your keywords and interpretations, for example, you may wish to select a Golden Dawn era list if you are working magically, or from the Agony Aunt age if you want a more domestic reading.

Lay out the first card in position 1, which is month one, January, if you are doing this for a new year.

Go around the temple and lay out a card in position 2, two cards in position 3 (a corner), one in position 4, two in position 5, one in 6, two in 7, and one in 8.

You should have twelve cards laid out, each of which relates to one month.

Make a note of how these cards might describe the month ahead, and as you go around the temple, create a story for the year by linking the cards together in a sequence.

Next pair together the corner cards, so read together pairs in positions 1, 3, 5, and 7. These are the "corners of the year" and illustrate how you might better keep to your most ideal position during the year.

Now read the four cards in positions 2, 4, 6, and 8. These are the four directions of the temple (east to north) and provide a standard direction or compass for any situation that arises this year.

Finally, lay a thirteenth card in the centre of the square. This is the "axis of heaven," and it indicates how you might best retain your centre in the year ahead.

If your axis for the year is major arcana, it indicates a repeating life lesson that can be resolved during the year; if minor arcana, it tells of a situation that might arise which will be challenging and must be overcome; if a court card, it suggests the type of person you will learn to become more like during the time ahead.

Advanced Variation

If you would like to explore this powerful method even more deeply, you can look at the card (or cards for the corners) that are opposite for each card (or cards) and this will tell you what you need to sacrifice or let go in the month.

So, the sacrifice which will help you pass month 2 best (position 2) is indicated by month 8, which is position 6. The sacrifice for months 3 and 4 (considered a pair) is indicated by months 9–10 together, i.e., positions 3 and 7 at opposite corners.

Our final two methods to close this present book return us to Kabbalah and tarot, although you do not need to know any Kabbalah to use the methods. The first method allows us to discover the appropriate response to significant moments in our own timeline.

The Tree of Life Locator

Take your deck, and consider a situation in your life about which you seek a Kabbalistic and spiritual perspective to guide your response.

Split the deck into three decks: 22 majors, 56 minors, and 16 court cards.

Step 1. Courts: What is actually happening?

Take the court cards and shuffle. Ask, "To which world does this situation actually call me?"

Take out one court card and consult its rank:

- **King:** This situation is coming from the highest world and requires contemplation ...

- **Queen:** This situation is coming from the creative world and requires me to create ...

- **Knight:** This situation is coming from the formative world and requires me to organise ...

- **Page:** This situation is coming from the world of action and requires me to act ...

"with regard to [consult suit of the court card drawn] ... "

- **Wands:** My ambition
- **Cups:** My feelings
- **Swords:** My thoughts and plans
- **Pentacles:** My behaviour

I pull the Queen of Pentacles, who says, "This situation requires you to create [new] behaviour." This is a situation that doesn't require contemplation, planning, or organisation, but actual behaviour and creativity. In this case, it refers to writing new material—not discussing it or thinking—just writing. So, that's what I should do—I was tempted to respond in a situation by a longer-term plan, but the time for that may be later; this reading makes me do stuff instead.

In using this method, you will soon start to dynamically and experientially appreciate the Tree of Life model of the four worlds, and the elements, as they are modelled by the court cards. This brings Kabbalah into your everyday activity through the map of tarot.

Step 2. Minors: What is the actual problem?

Take the deck of minors and shuffle, asking, "What is the state of this situation?"

Select one Minor card and consult its number:

1. This situation has only just started and ...

2. This situation is full of energy and ...

3. This situation is starting to get stuck in a pattern and ...

4. This situation is getting out of control and ...

5. This situation is getting constrained and ...

6. This situation is being balanced and ...

7. This situation is going around in circles and ...

8. This situation is being focused and ...

9. This situation is establishing a foundation for something and ...

10. This situation is finished and ...

Then consult the suit of the minor card and add ...

- **Wands:** is consuming everything.

- **Swords:** is dividing everything.

- **Cups:** is splashing over everyone.

- **Pentacles:** is costing.

EXAMPLE

I draw the 3 of Cups, so put together that this situation is getting stuck in a pattern and splashing over everyone. That makes sense for my question, although it brings my attention more to that it is becoming a pattern, and affecting others—so I need to change my behaviour, which is what people respond to, as indicated by the first card. At least I can see that there is no "cost" in this situation, which was a concern. This method also tells us a lot by excluding the other states and situations, alleviating false concerns.

This part of the method teaches you how to use the ten Sephiroth in the four worlds via the correspondences of the elements in a real application. You are seeing here how the ten Sephiroth flow into creation, from the source (aces) to the manifest world (tens). In each of those states are the four worlds again, as the pure divine source flashes down the Tree into the world as we experience it.

Step 3. Majors: In what activity is the resolution?

The majors are attributed to the twenty-two "paths" between the ten Sephiroth, so in effect arise from the activity between them. This is a perfect mapping because it allows us to use them to see what two Sephiroth (aspects of the universe) we really need to balance, resolve, sort, merge, or whatever we have been advised by the previous two parts of this method.

Take your twenty-two majors. Shuffle them and ask using the words from the previous two-card draw, "What activity will bring the most divine outcome to this situation [use your words here from the previous two cards]." In my example of the 3 of Cups, it would be "What activity will bring the most divine outcome to this situation requiring me to create new behaviour after being stuck in a pattern that spilled over and affected everyone?"

For reference, we have given each major card the numbers of the Sephiroth (e.g., 5–6 is Geburah and Tiphareth) so intermediate students can see which two Sephiroth are being worked with by the corresponding tarot card on the path between them.

Consult the card:

0. [1–2] Do something new, novel, totally unexpected. But do it with a leap of faith.

1. [1–3] Get everything together, out where everyone can see it. Expose.

2. [1–6] Withdraw, find your own centre and source. Remind yourself what the point is.

3. [2–3] Weigh up and balance what you are putting in and what you are getting out. That's it.

4. [2–6] Look at one particular matter on which to focus all your energy and effort. Do that.

5. [2–4] Other people can give you advice to expand from where you are. You need help.

6. [3–6] Only associate and work with things that are harmonious. Make choices.

7. [3–5] Use a set plan to rein in what is happening. Stick to the rules. Drive safe.

8. [4–5] This is a card of perfect reconciliation. There is only one working solution. Find it. No blurry lines or grey areas allowed.

9. [4–6] As you expand, you must keep everything in balance. Take some time off and away from it. Don't get dragged down below.

10. [4–7] There is an obvious pattern here, again. Do something that changes it. Anything. Take a chance.

11. [5–6] It is up to you—the power is with you. Make the best decision you can, no one else can.

12. [5–8] You are being asked to raise the stakes. Take a step up, don't hang around.

13. [6–7] Transform. Everything changes. You must accept the fact and go with it now. You've done it before; you'll do it again. Do it now.

14. [6–9] Everything needs to be in the mix—include everything and everyone, no matter how difficult.

15. [6–8] You must be the bad guy to get what you want, in holding people to their word. Don't allow others to hide in the shadows, stick to what was agreed.

16. [7–8] There is no simple resolution; let it all fall where it may and get ready to rebuild.

17. [7–9] Sticking to what is important, keep that vision, even through change. Wait for a while and then continue.

18. [7–10] Go back over it and repeat. Repeat again, keep on going on.

19. [8–9] Clarity is what will resolve this situation once and for all, even if it burns someone.

20. [8–10] Make a decision, shake things up a bit, and call on others to change. You are the one who knocks!

21. [9–10] Resolution comes from completing everything, take on nothing new, close the doors, and get everything tidied up once and for all. It is almost done.

EXAMPLE

I pull the Hermit, so (unsurprisingly) I am advised that I need to take a break from being dragged into the situation that the previous cards told me is splashing over others, requiring new behaviour. Given the third card, my course of action is obviously now to get away, not to engage—but to take time to create new things. That is the course of action I choose, thanks to this method.

Also notice (according to kabbalah) that the advice also counsels and suggests *not* doing the opposite, as that is likely the temptation. As an example, if you had the Magician, you may have tended to try and resolve the situation by keeping secrets, hiding things, not calling someone out on their behaviour.

Although it is not necessary, the more you learn kabbalah too, the more powerful this method will prove. We will now finish with another kabbalah spread, requiring no knowledge of kabbalah.

Kabbalah Middle Pillar Spread

Take a question and choose a suit corresponding to it:

- If it is about material things, resources, money, or health: Pentacles

- If about clarity, education, logic, decisions, learning: Swords

- If emotional, relationship, or family matters: Cups

- If about ambition, will, values, importance, lifestyle, the big picture, self-development, or spirituality: Wands

Whichever suit you have now decided covers the question, take the Ace + 6 + 9 + 10 of that suit out of your deck.

Example

If it were a job or employment question about resources, you would take the Ace of Pentacles + 6 of Pentacles + 9 of Pentacles + 10 of Pentacles.

Lay them out as illustrated in the example: a vertical column, ace at the top, 10 at the bottom.

38. Middle Pillar Spread.
Llewellyn's Classic Tarot by Moore and Smith, 2014.

What you have done is created an illustration of the central pillar of the Tree of Life in the most appropriate of the four Kabbalistic worlds concerning your question. But you do not necessarily need to know that for the spread.

Look now at the pictures on those cards.

They will tell you:

- **Ace:** The crown of your situation. Where it comes from. The absolute thing you really need to get from this question.

- **Six:** The beauty of the situation. Where you can find balance in it, where it will all make sense and hold together.

- **Nine:** The foundation of the situation. Where in that world—of money, of love, of ambition, of decision—you can find stability and get it fixed.

- **Ten:** The kingdom of the situation. How you can act, what you can do, where the activity must concentrate to manifest and complete it.

Take a moment to look at how those four cards illustrate those things. If you are using Waite-Smith, a variant, or Thoth, et al., you should see those lessons illustrated to some extent.

Other decks may have surprising things to say in their illustration of those numbers.

Now for the Kabbalistic magick ... take a breath, shuffle the rest of the deck and lay out a card on each of those four positions, so one card on top of the Ace, one on top of the 6, one on the 9, and one card on the 10.

Those cards can now be read as the universe telling you how to align yourself to those four essential creative steps: the card on the Ace will show you what to aim for, the card on the 6 how to balance, the card on the 9 how to stabilise, and the card on the 10 how to act and manifest.

All four cards will work together because you are reading them to the most powerful map of all creation—even if you don't know any kabbalah!

Back to the Future

You may recall a long time ago when you started this book, in the first chapter, we gave you a method of aligning or illustrating your life through the tarot cards in reverse sequence. This was to demonstrate that the major arcana act as a time map of any creative process, including your own life at present.

Having become expert tarot time travellers, we can now simply reverse the method to plot a new course for our own future.

Take the twenty-two major arcana and place them in sequence from the Magician to the World. We do not use the Fool, who represents our own awareness and is beyond time. Take twenty-one small pieces of paper and write on each one the corresponding event for the card that you matched in your past.

In our example is *birth in San Francisco* as the World card and *the move to a bigger house* in childhood as Judgment, and so forth. On each piece of paper also write a word or phrase for the specific challenge, resource, and lesson that event introduced into your life. This is your living tarot correspondence to the cards.

Now take an overview of your history and consider where you want to go from now into the future. Look at the first card, the Magician, and whatever challenge, resource, and lesson this provides to you in life. Match that to the first step of your future.

Continue through the cards until you reach the World, which should match the completion and success of your ambition or goal. Every stage and every card should reflect your past into your future, because our future is only an extension of our past—as you will see when you look back at your life from every moment.

The cards have now illustrated that journey in time for you, and we have come full circle.

The Tarot Wayfarer

We have seen throughout this journey that the tarot is not only an illustrated map but is also a language. It is a language that transcends time and offers a universal key to the mysteries of life. It is much more…it is the very place in which that language is spoken. Tarot is a space of exploration and revelation, a landscape of our relationship to the divine. As such we can build not a temple nor a church for its worship but a living workshop for its practice. This place already exists and was constructed at the same time as this book was being created.

There is indeed a world of tarot beyond this world, and it is called *Arkatia*. In that realm can be discovered further mysteries and magic for all those who seek to become a Tarot Wayfarer. We now invite you into that world to continue your unlocking of the infinite gates of tarot. Even in Arkatia, there we are. [185]

Conclusion

We will leave our travels in time at this point in the time stream. In doing so, we encourage your further wayfaring with your deck of cards, whether it be playing cards, tarot, Lenormand, an oracle deck, or other cartomantic device. We will take a final moment to add to your time-log these words of praise for the tarot from Eliphas Lévi, whom we have seen as such an important nexus in our journey. He knew that tarot was a time travel device and a philosophical machine:

> Such are the twenty-two keys of the Tarot, which explain all its numbers. Thus, the juggler, or key of the unities, explains the four aces with their quadruple progressive signification in the three worlds and in the first principle. So also the ace of deniers or of the circle is the soul of the world; the ace of swords is militant intelligence; the ace of cups is loving intelligence; the ace of clubs is creative intelligence; they are also the principles of motion, progress, fecundity, and power. Each number, multiplied by a key, gives another number, which, explained in turn by the keys, completes the philosophical and religious revelation contained in each sign. Now, each of the fifty-six cards can be multiplied in turn by the twenty-two keys; a series of combinations thus results, giving all the most astonishing conclusions of revelation and of light. It is a truly philosophical machine, which keeps the mind from going astray while leaving its initiative and liberty; it is mathematics applied to the absolute, the alliance of the positive and the ideal, a lottery of thoughts as exact as numbers, perhaps the simplest and grandest conception of human genius. [186]

---

185 Experience the Tarot Wayfarer at www.tarotwayfarer.com.

186 Eliphas Lévi, *The Ritual of Transcendental Magic* (London, UK: Rider & Company, 1995), 479.

Afterword

Coming events cast their shadows before.

—Minetta, *What the Cards Tell*

Whilst in the final stages of completing this book, we were suddenly faced with several unexpected challenges. It really did seem like something was working against us to get this work finished by the deadline. As the deadline approached, we became somewhat dispirited and began to lose all confidence in the concept of the book and the ambition of going through time to meet all the great tarot readers of the past.

We were completely lost and struggling with the whole project, with just one week remaining before the deadline. It was the same time as the EU Referendum in the UK, so the whole world also seemed askew that week; wherever we looked was confusion and turbulence. There was even more turbulence to come in the political world, and we were also feeling the bowing wave of that future flowing back into the present.

After a horrible lack of another night's sleep, the umpteenth in a row, I (Marcus) got up to prepare for another onslaught of social media woe, and found my name tagged by Veronica Chamberlain, one of the tarot readers in our *Tarot Professionals* group of 22,000+ members on Facebook. [187] She wanted to share a dream she had recalled from

---

187   The Tarot Professionals Facebook group is now 29,000+ people at the time of final writing and available at https://www.facebook.com/groups/tarotprofessionals/.

that night, which was so powerful she had written it out on her mobile phone before even getting out of bed.

Here is her dream, slightly edited for this book:

What a dream I had. I dreamt I was on a ghost train with Marcus Katz and he was giving me a tarot lesson. I don't remember the cards he had out on the table and I know it was a gated spread. Three other people were at the table. For some reason the time was set back in the 1920s and everyone had these fabulous clothes on and hats on. I dreamt the train went to many stops through time and I was invited into all the hidden parlours of old Tarot Readers. All the cards and decks were fabulous! The readers told interesting stories and threw some wild parties.

I also dreamt we were being stalked by some haters at some of the stops and Marcus kept saying, "They never go away and try not to pay attention to them."

In one part of the dream I wanted to go to the 1920s Tarot Library across a field that was covered in manure! I saw a short-cut to get to the library except it had a gate that stated, "Only Very Good Readers May Enter. Others Are Strictly Prohibited!"

So, I climbed over the gate and entered the library. This led me to a basement where the walls were covered in gold. A male guide in a fur coat showed me all the writings on the wall and said they held the secrets. Then I was led to an older crone-figure who was sitting at a desk. She had a pen and a huge book. The crone asked me, "Do you know any Very Good Tarot Readers?" I started listing the names of very good tarot readers.

The old crone gave me a penetrating gaze and then I then realised what she meant and I said confidently, "My name is Veronica Chamberlain and I am a very good Tarot Reader!"

The woman smiled and wrote my name in the book and said, "Now you must do the work you're supposed to do!"

Then I woke up. Holy!

We immediately asked Veronica if we could use this dream in our book, without her knowing anything about the subject or theme of it—no one knew anything about the time travel concept at that stage other than ourselves, our spouses, and the publishing team at Llewellyn.

The dream and its utterly clear connection to this book as well as its timing and direct communication to us was transformative. We picked up our laptops, cleared the desks again, got out our piles of cards and set to hard work for days on end to complete this book with a new passion.

We believe that it was a clear message that the tarot readers throughout time want to continue to inspire every reader through their work. The message to us all is a simple one: if you can cross the field of manure, you get to call yourself a Very Good Tarot Reader.

If you like, for completing this book and journey with us, you can also now register your own name in Veronica's Book of Very Good Tarot Readers at www.tarottimetraveller.com.

You can discover more of the obviously very-connected Veronica on her site:

https://www.facebook.com/TarotandV

Now go do the work you are supposed to do.

—Marcus & Tali, 4 July, 2016, and 21 December, 2016
  The Lake District, England

Answers to the Exam Questions [188]

1. The reason that no other reader should be permitted to handle the tarot cards except when they are being used to give a reading is "because the more the tarot reader handles the cards the better, for this allows the cards to become impregnated with their magnetism and they are able to respond to the subtle thought vibrations of his unconscious mind. But the magnetism and thought emanations of others tend to impair this responsiveness through mixing the influences."

5. The cards should only be turned over one at a time as read so that the reader looks at it individually and "notes any impressions that he receives in connection with its usual divinatory significance as he states them to the client." Additionally, if all the cards are turned over before the reader starts, the mind spontaneously wanders over the spread and this detracts from the ability to draw correct conclusions from the card under consideration.

8. The detail that can be learnt about the people signified by the Court Arcana are the type of individual they are: their sex, male or female, as "[i]f the picture of the card is that of a man, it represents a man when right way up, and represents a woman when reversed. If the picture is

---

188   These answers are paraphrased from the original tarot booklets by C. C. Zain.

that of a woman, it represents a woman when it is the right way up, and represents a man when reversed. Then the suit alone represents one of the four general temperaments."

10. The life of a client is represented by a Court Arcanum through the "brief description and key phrase and the description of their astrological sign in relation to the card will give full detail of their characteristics; personal appearance, allegorical story and their spiritual possibilities."

14. The reason that any problem is capable of solution by the method of the tarot is because "everything which exists has an astrological correspondence which is also associated with a tarot card, therefore, by selecting the proper factors, any physical or occult problem may be solved by the use of the tarot."

15. The winged lingham signifies the permanent union of soul mates and their ascension into the angelic world.

21. The Arcanum 0 corresponds to the planet Pluto and the two aspects or influences of this planet as indicated by the common T and the reversed T are having the energy directed upwards, the crossbar resting below on the earth, and thus indicating that the thoughts, emotions, and actions are directed exclusively towards spiritual endeavour.

Appendix 1: Card Meanings

Major Arcana Keywords

We have attempted to narrow the keywords down to one single keyword but in some cases have provided several to remind and prompt time travellers that the cards are *multivalent*, carrying many possible meanings and avenues for interpretation.

We have also recorded seventy-eight videos discussing how these keywords were derived and apply to readings in terms of relationship, finance, spiritual, and career questions that are available to members of the Tarosophy Tarot Association. [189]

World

Resource: Education, experience

Challenge: Power

Lesson: Connection, networking

Judgment

Resource: Calling, vocation

Challenge: Humility, exposure

Lesson: Impartiality, surrender

---

[189]   Join the Tarot Association at www.tarotassociation.net.

Sun

Resource: Vitality

Challenge: Receptivity, authenticity

Lesson: Openness, naturalness

Moon

Resource: Intuition

Challenge: Sensitivity

Lesson: Grounding

Star

Resource: Vision, plan

Challenge: Doubt

Lesson: Action

Temperance

Resource: Endurance

Challenge: Blending, compatibility

Lesson: Patience

Hanged Man

Resource: Perspective

Challenge: Grasp, maintenance, hanging on

Lesson: Principle, conviction, values

Devil

Resource: Discipline

Challenge: Temptation

Lesson: Responsibility, accountability

Tower

Resource: Amplification, acceleration

Challenge: Stability

Lesson: Shock

Death

Resource: Renewal

Challenge: Fear

Lesson: Faith

Wheel

Resource: Change

Challenge: Finding a centre

Lesson: Life

Justice

Resource: Balance

Challenge: Inequality

Lesson: Order

Lovers

Resource: Divine oneness, union, choice

Challenge: Self, choice

Lesson: Relationships

Emperor

Resource: Governance, management, control

Challenge: Power

Lesson: What to control and what to let go

Hermit

Resource: Introspection

Challenge: Distraction

Lesson: Focus or self-control/discipline

Chariot

Resource: Focus

Challenge: Outcome (working without lust of result)

Lesson: Participation and dedication

Strength

Resource: Strength, ego, face

Challenge: Right relationship

Lesson: Mercy

Hierophant

Resource: Tradition, legacy, inheritance

Challenge: Authority, rebellion, challenge

Lesson: Belief, place of rules, structure

Empress

Resource: Abundance

Challenge: Laziness

Lesson: Natural progression

High Priestess

Resource: Intuition, receptivity

Challenge: Stillness, openness

Lesson: Emptiness, vessel

Magician

Resource: Capability

Challenge: Application

Lesson: Success

Fool

Resource: Freedom

Challenge: Experience

Lesson: Life

Court Card Keywords

Page of Pentacles

Resource: Steadfastness

Challenge: Consistency

Lesson: Commitment

Page of Swords

Resource: Observation

Challenge: Forthrightness

Lesson: Communication

Page of Cups

Resource: Spontaneity

Challenge: Ownership (of emotions)

Lesson: Liberation

Page of Wands

Resource: Enthusiasm

Challenge: Realisation

Lesson: Passion

Knight of Pentacles

Resource: Experience

Challenge: Complacency

Lesson: Persistence

Knight of Swords

Resource: Intelligence

Challenge: Cruelty

Lesson: Equality

Knight of Cups

Resource: Faithfulness

Challenge: Temptation

Lesson: Duty, allegiance

Knight of Wands

Resource: Ambition

Challenge: Distraction

Lesson: Contingency, preparation

Queen of Pentacles

Resource: Security

Challenge: Loss

Lesson: Diversification

Queen of Swords

Resource: Rationality

Challenge: Obsession, manipulation

Lesson: Consequence

Queen of Cups

Resource: Intuition

Challenge: Ego

Lesson: Humility

Queen of Wands

Resource: Independence

Challenge: Cynicism

Lesson: Worth, sufficiency

King of Pentacles

Resource: Practicality, talent

Challenge: Risk

Lesson: Moderation

King of Swords

Resource: Logic

Challenge: Emotion

Lesson: Control

King of Cups

Resource: Vision

Challenge: Possessiveness

Lesson: Detachment

King of Wands

Resource: Empowerment

Challenge: Tyranny

Lesson: Power

Minor Arcana Keywords

10 of Pentacles

Resource: Legacy, established wealth

Challenge: Greed, comfort

Lesson: Security

10 of Swords

Resource: Surety

Challenge: Novelty

Lesson: Flexibility

10 of Cups

Resource: Family

Challenge: Remembrance

Lesson: Gratitude, celebration, recognition

10 of Wands

Resource: Determination

Challenge: Stubbornness

Lesson: Delegation

9 of Pentacles

Resource: Security

Challenge: Independence

Lesson: Complacency

9 of Swords

Resource: Introspection

Challenge: Perspective

Lesson: Acceptance

9 of Cups

Resource: Satisfaction

Challenge: Self-indulgence

Lesson: Service

9 of Wands

Resource: Boundaries

Challenge: Paranoia

Lesson: Trusting experience

8 of Pentacles

Resource: Diligence

Challenge: Burnout

Lesson: Work

8 of Swords

Resource: Self-withdrawal

Challenge: Responsibility

Lesson: Autonomy

8 of Cups

Resource: Changes

Challenge: Moving on

Lesson: Vision

8 of Wands

Resource: Momentum

Challenge: Stalling, lack of motivation

Lesson: Spontaneity, action, responsiveness

7 of Pentacles

Resource: Investment

Challenge: Investment (again)

Lesson: Investment (yes, *again*)

7 of Swords

Resource: Guile

Challenge: Observation

Lesson: Ethics

7 of Cups

Resource: Imagination

Challenge: Confusion

Lesson: Alchemy

7 of Wands

Resource: Training

Challenge: Confidence

Lesson: Strategy

6 of Pentacles

Resource: Charity

Challenge: Balance

Lesson: No idle choices

6 of Swords

Resource: Foresight, knowing your destination

Challenge: Uncertainty

Lesson: Navigation

6 of Cups

Resource: Sentiment

Challenge: Acting your age

Lesson: Maturity

6 of Wands

Resource: Success

Challenge: Hubris

Lesson: Completion

5 of Pentacles

Resource: Faith

Challenge: Despair

Lesson: Service

5 of Swords

Resource: Responsiveness

Challenge: Conscience

Lesson: Authenticity

5 of Cups

Resource: Loss

Challenge: Regret

Lesson: Time, inevitability

5 of Wands

Resource: Teamwork

Challenge: Ego

Lesson: Coordination

4 of Pentacles

Resource: Maintenance

Challenge: Timing

Lesson: Planning

4 of Swords

Resource: Rest

Challenge: Excessive work, over-extension

Lesson: Mental energy

4 of Cups

Resource: Choice

Challenge: Indecision

Lesson: Decisiveness

4 of Wands

Resource: Invitation

Challenge: Acceptance

Lesson: Society

3 of Pentacles

Resource: Planning

Challenge: Impatience

Lesson: Work

3 of Swords

Resource: Separation

Challenge: Attachment

Lesson: Decisiveness

3 of Cups

Resource: Sharing

Challenge: Division

Lesson: Devotion

3 of Wands

Resource: Initiation

Challenge: Originality

Lesson: Commitment

2 of Pentacles

Resource: Balance

Challenge: Perspective

Lesson: Mindfulness

2 of Swords

Resource: Self-control

Challenge: Poise

Lesson: Balance, consideration

2 of Cups

Resource: Alliance

Challenge: Disagreement

Lesson: Empathy, understanding

2 of Wands

Resource: Vision

Challenge: Action

Lesson: Extension

Ace of Pentacles

Resource: Abundance

Challenge: Scarcity

Lesson: Wealth

Ace of Swords

Resource: Clarity, novelty, uniqueness

Challenge: Fixation

Lesson: Expectation

Ace of Cups

Resource: Inspiration

Challenge: Stagnancy

Lesson: Flow

Ace of Wands

Resource: Ambition

Challenge: Interruption

Lesson: Will

Appendix 2: Tarot Time Convertor

Tarot Pip	Tarot Suit	Playing Card	Lenormand	Coffee Cards
9	Cups	9 of Hearts	1. Rider/Messenger	Roads
6	Pentacles	6 of Diamonds	2. The Clover Leaf	Ring
10	Swords	10 of Spades	3. The Ship	Leaf of Clover
King	Cups	King of Hearts	4. The House	Anchor
7	Cups	7 of Hearts	5. The Tree	Serpent
King	Wands	King of Clubs	6. The Clouds	Letter
Queen	Wands	Queen of Clubs	7. The Snake	Coffin
9	Pentacles	9 of Diamonds	8. The Coffin	Star
Queen	Swords	Queen of Spades	9. The Bouquet	Dog
Knight	Pentacles	Jack of Diamonds	10. The Scythe	Lily
Knight	Wands	Jack of Clubs	11. The Rod/Whip	Cross
7	Pentacles	7 of Diamonds	12. The Birds/Owls	Clouds
Knight	Swords	Jack of Spades	13. The Child/Little Girl	Sun
9	Wands	9 of Clubs	14. The Fox	Moon
10	Wands	10 of Clubs	15. The Bear	Mountains

Tarot Pip	Tarot Suit	Playing Card	Lenormand	Coffee Cards
6	Cups	6 of Hearts	16. The Stars	Tree
Queen	Cups	Queen of Hearts	17. The Stork	Child
10	Cups	10 of Hearts	18. The Dog	Woman
6	Swords	6 of Spades	19. The Tower	Pedestrian (Man)
8	Swords	8 of Spades	20. The Garden	Rider
8	Wands	8 of Clubs	21. The Mountain	Mouse
Queen	Pentacles	Queen of Diamonds	22. The Ways	Rod
7	Wands	7 of Clubs	23. The Mice	Rose/Carnation/Flower
Knight	Cups	Jack of Hearts	24. The Heart	Heart
Ace	Wands	Ace of Clubs	25. The Ring	Garden
10	Pentacles	10 of Diamonds	26. The Book	Bird
7	Swords	7 of Spades	27. The Letter	Fish
Ace	Cups	Ace of Hearts	28. The Gentleman	Lion or any Ferocious Beast
Ace	Swords	Ace of Spades	29. The Lady	Green Bush
King	Swords	King of Spades	30. The Lily	Worms
Ace	Pentacles	Ace of Diamonds	31. The Sun	House
8	Cups	8 of Hearts	32. The Moon	Scythe
8	Pentacles	8 of Diamonds	33. The Key	
King	Pentacles	King of Diamonds	34. The Fish	
9	Swords	9 of Spades	35. The Anchor	
6	Wands	6 of Clubs	36. The Cross	

Bibliography

Abraham, Sylvia. *How to Read the Tarot: The Keyword System*. St. Paul, MN: Llewellyn, 2000.

Advertisement section. In *The Monthly Magazine, Or, British Register*, Volume 4, December.

Allen, Jonathan. *Lost Envoy: The Tarot Deck of Austin Osman Spare*. London: Strange Attractor Press, 2016.

Anon. *Meditations on the Tarot*. Longmead, UK: Element Books, 1991.

Auger, Emily E., editor. *Tarot in Culture, Vols. I and II*. Valleyhome Books, 2014.

Ben-Dov, Yoav. *Tarot: The Open Reading*. Charleston, SC: CreateSpace, 2011, 2013.

Calvino, Italo. *The Castle of Crossed Destinies*. London: Harcourt Brace, 1997.

Carey, Tanith. *Never Kiss a Man in a Canoe: Words of Wisdom from the Golden Age of Agony Aunts*. London: Boxtree, 2009.

Carr-Gomm, Philip, and Stephanie Carr-Gomm. *The DruidCraft Tarot*. London: Connections, 2009.

Carroll, Wilma. *The 2-Hour Tarot Tutor: The Fast, Revolutionary Method for Learning to Read Tarot Cards in Two Hours... Without Memorizing Meanings!* London: Piatkus, 2010.

Case, Paul Foster. *The Book of Tokens: Meditations on the Tarot*. London: Builders of the Adytum, 1974.

Clark, Paul A. *Paul Foster Case: His Life and Works*. Covina, CA: Fraternity of Hidden Light, 2013.

Cockin, Katherine. *Edith Craig: Dramatic Lives*. London, UK: Cassell, 1997.

Connolly, Eileen. *Tarot: The Complete Handbook for the Apprentice*. London, UK: Thorsons, 1995.

Crowley, Aleister. *The Book of Thoth*. York Beach, ME: Samuel Weiser, 1985.

Davies, Anne. "The Meaning of Meditation." In *The Lantern*, Vol. 8, No. 4, Summer 2007. Los Angeles: Builders of the Adytum.

De Angeles, Ly. *Tarot Theory and Practice*. Woodbury, MN: Llewellyn, 2007.

Decker, Ronald, and Michael Dummett. *A History of the Occult Tarot: 1870–1970*. London: Gerald Duckworth & Co, 2002.

Decker, Ronald, Michael Dummett, and Thierry Depaulis. *A Wicked Pack of Cards: Origins of the Occult Tarot*. London: Bristol Classical Press, 1996.

Dee, Johnathan, with Sasha Fenton. *Fortune Telling with Playing Cards*. New York: Sterling Publishing, 2004.

Denning, Melita, and Osborne Phillips. *The Llewellyn Practical Guide to the Magick of Tarot*. St. Paul, MN: Llewellyn, 1993.

Doane, Doris Chase. *How to Read Tarot Cards*. New York: Funk & Wagnalls, 1967.

Donaldson, Terry, and Evelyn Donaldson. *Principles of Tarot: The Only Introduction You'll Ever Need*. London: Thorsons, 1996.

Douglas, Alfred. *The Tarot: The Origins, Meaning and Uses of the Cards*. Harmondsworth, UK: Penguin Books, 1981.

Dummett, Michael. *The Game of Tarot from Ferrara to Salt Lake City.* London: Gerald Duckworth & Co, 1980.

Echols, Signe, Robert Muller, and Sandra Thomson. *Spiritual Tarot: Seventy-Eight Paths to Personal Development.* New York: Avon Books, 1996.

Elias, Camelia. *Marseille Tarot: Towards the Art of Reading.* Roskilde, DK: Eyecorner Press, 2015.

Ellershaw, Josephine. *Easy Tarot Reading: The Process Revealed in Ten True Readings.* Woodbury, MN: Llewellyn, 2011.

Enriquez, Enrique. *Tarology.* Roskilde: Eyecorner Press, 2011.

Farley, Helen. *A Cultural History of Tarot: From Entertainment to Esotericism.* London: I. B. Tauris, 2009.

Fenton, Sasha. *Super Tarot: How to Link the Cards to Reveal Your Future.* London: Thorsons, 1994.

Fontana, David. *The Essential Guide to the Tarot: Understanding the Major and Minor Arcana–Using the Tarot to Find Self-Knowledge and Change Your Destiny.* London: Watkins, 2011.

"Fortune-Telling." Washington Bureau Pamphlets. 1927.

Fronteras, Adam. *The Tarot: The Traditional Tarot Reinterpreted for the Modern World.* New York: Stewart, Tabori & Chang, 1996.

Gearheart, Sally, and Susan Rennie. *A Feminist Tarot.* Watertown, MA: Persephone Press, 1977.

Gibson, Christopher. "The Religion of the Stars: The Hermetic Philosophy of C.C. Zain." *Gnosis* magazine, Winter 1996.

Gifford, James. "Left to Themselves: The Subversive Boys Books of Edward Prime-Stevenson (1858–1942)" in *Journal of American & Comparative Cultures,* Vol. 24, issue 3–4, Fall/Winter 2001, 113–116.

Gilchrist, Cherry. *Tarot Triumphs: Using the Marseilles Tarot Trumps for Divination and Inspiration*. Newburyport, MA: Red Wheel/Weiser, 2016.

Godwin, Joscelyn, Christian Chanel, and John P. Deveney, editors. *The Hermetic Brotherhood of Luxor*. York Beach, ME: Samuel Weiser, 1995.

The Golden Dawn Community. *The Golden Dawn Community. Commentaries on the Golden Dawn Flying Rolls*. Dublin, Ireland: Kerubim Press, 2013.

Greer, Mary K. *Tarot for Your Self: A Workbook for Personal Transformation*. Franklin Lakes, NJ: New Page Books, 2002.

Greer, Mary K., Tali Goodwin, and Marcus Katz. *The English Lenormand*. Keswick, UK: Forge Press, 2013.

Grey, Eden. *Mastering the Tarot: Basic Lessons in an Ancient, Mystic Art*. New York: Crown Publishers, 1971.

Guinness, Alec. *Blessings in Disguise*. Pleasantville, NY: Akadine, 2001.

Hall, Evalyne K. *De Jeu des Tarots et Rescherches Sur Les Tarots*. Charleston, SC: CreateSpace, 2016.

Hargreave, Catherine Perry. *A History of Playing Cards and a Bibliography of Cards and Gaming*. New York, NY: Dover Publications, 1966.

Hasbrouck, Muriel Bruce. *Tarot and Astrology: The Pursuit of Destiny*. London: John Gifford, 1949.

Herbin, Evelyne, and Terry Donaldson. *Thorson's Way of Tarot*. London: Thorsons, 2001.

Holy Order of MANS. *Jewels of the Wise*. San Francisco, CA: Epiphany Press, 1979.

Horowitz, Mitch. *Occult America: White House Séances, Ouija Circles, Masons, and the Secret Mystic History of Our Nation*. New York: Bantam, 2009.

Howe, Ellic. *The Magicians of the Golden Dawn: A Documentary History of a Magical Order, 1887–1923*. London: RKP, 1972.

Japikse, Carl. *Exploring the Tarot*. Columbus, OH: Ariel Press, 1989.

Jodorowsky, Alejandro. *The Way of Tarot: The Spiritual Teacher in the Cards*. Rochester, NY: Destiny Books, 2004.

Kaplan, Stuart R. *Tarot Classic*. New York, NY: Grossett & Dunlap, 1972.

Katz, Marcus. *The Magister, vol 0*. Keswick, UK: Forge Press, 2015.

———. *NLP Magick*. Keswick, UK: Forge Press, 2016.

———. "Origins of the Celtic Cross." In *Tarosophist International*, Vol. 2.

———. *Secrets of the Thoth Tarot*. Keswick, UK: Forge Press, 2016.

———. *Tarosophy*. Keswick, UK: Forge Press, 2016.

Katz, Marcus, and Tali Goodwin. *Abiding in the Sanctuary: The Waite-Trinick Tarot: A Christian Mystical Tarot (1917–1923)*. Keswick, UK: Forge Press, 2011.

———. *Learning Lenormand: Traditional Fortune Telling for Modern Life*. Woodbury, MN: Llewellyn, 2013.

———. *Secrets of the Waite-Smith Tarot: The True Story of the World's Most Popular Tarot*. Woodbury, MN: Llewellyn, 2015.

———. *Tarot Face to Face: Using the Cards in Your Everyday Life*. Woodbury, MN: Llewellyn, 2012.

———. *Tarot Flip*. Keswick, UK: Forge Press, 2010.

Kenner, Corinne. *Tarot and Astrology: Enhance Your Readings with the Wisdom of the Zodiac*. Woodbury, MN: Llewellyn, 2011.

Kent, Cicely. *Telling Fortunes by Cards*. London: Herbert Jenkins Limited, n.d.

Knight, Gareth. *Experience of the Inner Worlds.* Cheltenham, UK: Skylight Press, 2010.

Langhamer, Claire. *The English in Love: The Intimate Story of an Emotional Revolution.* Oxford, UK: Oxford University Press, 2013.

Le Normand, Madame Camille. *Fortune-telling by Cards.* New York, NY: Robert M. De Witt, 1872.

Lévi, Eliphas. *The Ritual of Transcendental Magic.* London: Rider & Company, 1995.

———. *Transcendental Magic: Its Doctrine & Ritual.* London: Bracken Books, 1995.

Lionnet, Annie. *The Tarot Directory.* Rochester, UK: Grange Books, 2004.

Louis, Anthony. *Tarot Plain and Simple.* St. Paul, MN: Llewellyn, 2003.

Mann, A. T. *The Elements of the Tarot.* Shaftesbury, UK: Element Books, 1993.

Marson, Linda. *Ticket, Passport and Tarot Cards.* Melbourne, AU: Brolga Publishing, 2005.

Mathers, Samuel Liddell MacGregor. *Tarot.* Brighton, UK: Unicorn Bookshop, n.d.

McIntosh, Christopher. *Eliphas Lévi and the French Occult Revival.* London: Rider & Company, 1975.

Michelsen, Teresa C. *The Complete Tarot Reader: Everything You Need to Know from Start to Finish.* St. Paul, MN: Llewellyn, 2005.

Minetta. *What the Cards Tell.* London: Downey & Co., 1896.

Namron. *The Secrets of the Marseilles Tarot.* London: Namron Books, 1990.

Neville, E. W. *Tarot for Lovers.* Atglen, PA: Schiffer, 1997.

The New Game at Cards Or A Pack of Cards Changed into a Compleat and Perpetual Almanack. In a Dialogue between a Nobleman and His Servant. First Shewing the Use of His Almanack by the Quarters, Months, Weeks and Days of the Year. Secondly, Shewing How He Converts His Cards to a Compleat Monitor or Prayer Book, with Curious Remarks on the Knave. The Whole Adapted to the Entertainment of the Humorous, as Well as to the Satisfaction of the Grave Learned, and Ingenious. The like Never before Published. Stirling: Printed by C. Randall, 1800.

Owen, Alex. *The Place of Enchantment: British Occultism and the Culture of the Modern.* Chicago: University of Chicago Press, 2004.

Ozaniec, Naomi. *Watkins Tarot Handbook.* London: Watkins, 2005.

Papus. *Tarot of the Bohemians.* Hollywood, CA: Wilshire Book Company, 1973.

Peach, Emily. *Discover Tarot: Understanding and Using Tarot Symbolism.* Wellingborough, UK: Aquarian Press, 1990.

———. *Tarot for Tomorrow: An Advanced Handbook of Tarot Prediction.* Wellingborough, UK: Aquarian Press, 1988.

Pennick, Nigel. *Secret Games of the Gods: Ancient Ritual Systems in Board Games.* York Beach, ME: Samuel Weiser, 1997.

Piontek, Tessa. *Tarot for the 21st Century: A Journey Through the Symbolism of the Rider-Waite-Smith Deck.* Ft. Wayne, IN: Dark Moon Press, 2012.

Place, Robert M. *The Tarot: History, Symbolism and Divination.* New York: Tarcher/Penguin, 2005.

Quinn, Paul. *Tarot for Life: Reading the Cards for Everyday Guidance and Growth.* Wheaton, IL: Quest Books, 2009.

Ricklef, James. *Tarot Tells the Tale: Explore Three Card Readings Through Familiar Stories.* St. Paul, MN: Llewellyn, 2003.

Sharman-Burke, Juliet. *The Complete Book of Tarot: The Origins, Meaning & Divinatory Significance of the Cards and How to Use Them in Readings.* London: Pan Books, 1985.

Sharman-Burke, Juliet, and Liz Greene. *The Mythic Tarot: A New Approach to the Tarot Cards.* London, UK: Guild Publishing, 1986.

Sterling, Stephen Walter. *Tarot Awareness: Exploring the Spiritual Path.* St. Paul, MN: Llewellyn, 2000.

Stevenson, E. Irenaeus. *The Square of Sevens.* New York: Harper & Brothers, 1896.

Stuart, Rowena. *Collin's Gem Tarot.* London: Collins, n.d.

Trappe, Ruth E. *Fortune Telling by Playing Cards.* Washington Bureau Bulletin, 1927.

Vargo, Joseph, and Joseph Iorillo. *The Gothic Tarot Compendium.* Strongsville, OH: Monolith Graphics, 2007.

Waite, Arthur E. (writing as "Grand Orient"). *Complete Manual of Occult Divination, Vol. 1.* New Hyde Park, NY: University Books, 1972.

Waite, Arthur Edward. *Shadows in Life and Thought.* London, UK: Selwyn & Blount, 1938.

———. *The Pictorial Key to the Tarot.* London, UK: Rider & Company, 1974.

Westcott, W. W. (trans.). *Sepher Yetzirah.* Lynnwood, WA: Holmes Publishing Group, 1996.

White, Dusty. *The Easiest Way to Learn the Tarot Ever.* North Charleston, SC: Booksurge, 2009.

Art Credit List